Cilantro & Coriander

(Coriandrum sativum)

Herb of the Year™ 2017

International Herb Association

Compiled and edited by Gert Coleman

IHA HERB OF THE YEAR™

Each year the International Herb Association chooses an **Herb of the Year**™ to highlight. The Horticultural Committee evaluates possible choices based on their being outstanding in at least two of the three major categories: culinary, medicinal, and ornamental. Herbal organizations around the world work together with us to educate the public throughout the year.

Herb of the Year™ books are published annually by the

International Herb Association
P.O. Box 5667
Jacksonville, Florida 32247-5667
www.iherb.org

The International Herb Association is a professional trade organization providing education, service, and development for members engaged in all aspects of the herbal industry.

ISBN: 978-1-4951-9801-4

*"Uniting Herb Professionals for Growth
Through Promotion and Education"*

The International Herb Association has some of the most dedicated volunteers who keep the organization afloat, giving their time and talents to ensure that IHA continues to share herbal knowledge and connect those in the profession of herbs. We are deeply indebted to the IHA Board of Directors, the IHA Foundation members, and our webmaster. Thanks for all that you do and for caring enough to move us forward!

Coriander mandala. *Pat Kenny*

ACKNOWLEDGEMENTS

SINCE APRIL, I have been living the cilantro life—growing it, observing it, eating it, brewing it, pinching it, and smelling it. The highly aromatic, exciting, and versatile *Coriandrum sativum* doubles as both an herb (cilantro) and a spice (coriander).

Cilantro & Coriander: Herb of the Year™ 2017 features an assortment of perspectives on this love-it-or-hate-it herb. The herb of the year series continues to grow in depth and diversity with a wealth of articles, photography, illustrations, and poetry. This publication is filled to the brim with facts, stories, and advice about growing, using, marketing, cooking, brewing, and healing with this remarkable herb and spice.

Many thanks to the members and friends of IHA who submitted these wonderful articles, luscious recipes, arresting photographs, and diverting illustrations. We could not have done this without you!

We are privileged to have mentors like **Art Tucker**, **Jim Duke**, and the late **Thomas DeBaggio** in the book; we honor their vast knowledge and how they willingly share it with us. **Chuck Voigt** gives an overview of growing and harvesting cilantro and coriander while **Conrad Richter** cheekily shares his experiences of growing and marketing cilantro and its mimics at his Canadian nursery.

Ken Greene of Hudson Valley Seed Company shares the ups and downs of cilantro trials in upstate New York. Retired nursery owner **Terry Hollembaek**—lovely to have his voice in the book again!—shares the gardening lessons cilantro has taught him.

Jim Long offers practical suggestions on which varieties suit your cilantro and coriander needs. **Jane Taylor** shows how cilantro fits into a children's salsa garden while everyone's favorite gardener **Tina Marie Wilcox** delineates cilantro's growing cycles in a kitchen garden.

Karen O'Brien entwines coriander's colorful history with its (and her) affinity for cordials. **Helen Leach** presents the aromatic cilantro-bed bug association in a provocative, new light. **Stephanie Parello's** paean to cilantro may be the most exuberant of all cilantro-lovers while **Ann Sprayregen** notes the challenges of researching a plant with so many names. **Matthias Reisen** offers practical advice on getting to know an herb, **Pat Kenny** shows us how to research rare plants, and **Davy Dabney** offers the non-culinary benefits of coriander.

Angela Lugo recounts her experiences with both cilantro and culantro in Puerto Rico and New Jersey while **Susan Betz's** photographs finely illustrate her ecological exposition of cilantro's appeal to pollinators. **Diann Nance** uses personal memoir to trace the rise of cilantro as a culinary star and her second article unfolds coriander's significance as Biblical plant and symbol.

From the medicinal perspective, we are delighted to have experts **Dr. James Duke, Daniel Gagnon, Rosemary Gladstar, Carol Little, Dorene Petersen**, and **Marge Powell** charting the many health benefits of fresh cilantro, crushed coriander, and coriander essential oil.

And the recipes—oh, my! The recipes!

Many thanks to regular recipe contributors **Donna Frawley** whose fish tacos with cilantro were the gastronomic hit of the 2016 conference in Maryland, and **Pat Crocker,** a passionate cook who hates cilantro but loves coriander, for highlighting the contradictory attractions of cilantro and coriander. **Susan Belsinger** dances us through the plant's cycle in five acts with delicious recipes while **Skye Suter** combines her love of historical cookery with her love for cilantro.

All the readers, including myself, became instantly hungry reading recipes from **Tamara Huron** and **Rosemary Roman Nolan**. Many thanks to **Marge Powell** for her fragrant olive-cilantro bread recipe, to **Carol Little** for a number of versatile coriander recipes, to **Jim Long** and **Karen O'Brien** for liqueur recipes, and to new contributors **Alicia**

Mann and **Gail** and **Peter Miller** for delicious recipes pairing cilantro with seafood.

Visually, we are grateful for **Pat Kenny's** inspiring illustrations, **Skye Suter's** whimsical illustrations, and **Gail Wood Miller's** evocative sketch. Delightful new illustrators include **Yvonne Sisko, Alicia Mann,** and **Stephanie Parello.**

Special thanks to **Hudson Valley Seed Company** for their permission to use the stirring art packet illustration of cilantro by **Cassie Quakenbush** of Cooperstown, NY. Thanks also to **Susan Belsinger, Susan Betz, Peter Coleman, Pat Crocker, Pat Kenny, Shawn Linehan, Karen O'Brien**, and **Jane Taylor** for their fabulous photographs of all things cilantro and coriander.

Special thanks to my colleagues and friends in the English Department at **Middlesex County College** for stepping up to the coriander challenge—poets **Emanuel di Pasquale, Mat Spano, Shirley Wachtel**, and **Dan Zimmerman**, author **Angela Lugo**, and illustrator **Yvonne Sisko**.

Many thanks to **Diann Nance** and **Skye Suter** for their careful proofreading and gentle support. Taking on this project has been a huge learning curve and I had two pairs of big shoes to fill! Many thanks to **Karen O'Brien**, HOY editor for the past four editions. She has had my back throughout the process, helping me with style, editing, wording, proofreading, and a thousand other important things. Special, enormous thanks goes to **Susan Belsinger,** also past HOY editor, for her generous help with text, organization, placement of photographs and illustrations, cover work, eagle-eyed proofreading, and insightful advice throughout the process.

Deep appreciation to the board members and board of trustees who generously give their time and energy to make the IHA what it is today. Thanks go also to **Diann Nance, Karen O'Brien**, and **Matthias and Andrea Reisen** for their cheerful willingness to store, process, and ship our HOY books; to **Kay Whitlock** for her many years of doing so; to **Marge Powell**, our treasurer extraordinaire, who takes care of orders and our finances; and to webmaster **Jason Ashley** for updating and streamlining the online ordering process.

It's a new and distinct pleasure to work with **Heidi Lowe** and **Marty Jenkins** at Litho Printers.

Thanks also to my husband **Peter Coleman** for his love, patience, help, photographs, and warm sense of humor throughout the process, and of course my children **Lorraine** and **Ian** who have cheerfully eaten and drunk many herbal concoctions!

This one-of-a-kind compilation of science, lore, history, food, medicine, agriculture, artwork, crafts, and poetry is truly a collective work of art from the heart celebrating *Cilantro & Coriander, Herb of the Year™ 2017*!

~Gert Coleman, Editor

Lower cilantro leaves. *Alicia Mann*

Table of Contents

Cilantro seedlings. *Pat Kenny*

BOTANY

CULTIVATION

Coriander flowers. *Susan Belsinger*

Cilantro Around the World

Arthur O. Tucker and Thomas DeBaggio

CORIANDRUM SATIVUM AND the cilantro mimics, though very different in appearance and taxonomy, have a unifying chemical theme—an unusually high proportion of the nose-twisting aldehydes, which are the chemicals produced by the oxidation of alcohols. Aldehydes often smell soapy, which partially explains the reason that many people hate cilantro, but aldehydes also can smell fruity. Thus, aldehydes play a significant role in fragrance and flavors, such as strawberry and peach, and they have imparted a so-called "exulting" quality to many famous perfumes, from *Chanel No. 5* in 1921 to *Nocturnes* in 1981.

The two flavors and aromas most commonly experienced from *Coriandrum sativum,* our "standard" cilantro, are those of the leaves (which we often call *cilantro*) and the ground dried fruits (which is called *coriander* on the grocery spice rack). These flavors differ so immensely that many people are not aware they come from the same plant. And, in fact, the chemical change that occurs during coriander's maturation is unique among herbs. The characteristic aroma of *Coriandrum sativum* leaves is provided by two aldehydes, (E)-2-decenal and decanal. Aldehydes are also the key to the "copycat" aroma of the three primary plants described below: the foliar essential oil of *Eryngium foetidum* derives its scent from the polysyllabic aldehyde 1,4,5-trimethylbensaldehyde + 5-dodecanone + 4-hydroxy-3,5-dimethylacetophenone; that of *Persicaria odorata* is scented of dodecanal and decanal; and that of *Porophyllum ruderale* subsp. *macrocephalum* is dominated by an (E,E)-dodecadienal.

Cilantro and its mimics share a chemistry with the marmorated stinkbug, which has made a rapid appearance in the U.S., starting about 17 years ago. When disturbed, the stinkbugs release two aldehydes, (E)-2-decenal and (E)-2-octenal, the former shared with cilantro.

Beyond the soapy odor and taste of aldehydes, you may have a genetic reason for hating cilantro. Recently, researchers, led by Nicholas Eriksson at *23andMe*, Inc., Mountain View, California, were able to pinpoint genetic variants linked to cilantro hating. In a genetic survey of 30,000 people, they found buried within a cluster of olfactory-receptor genes, a gene called OR6A2, which encodes a receptor that makes people sensitive to aldehydes.

The dramatic difference in flavor and aroma between the leaf and the mature seed of *C. sativum* results from gradual changes in the balance of the two aldehydes and linalool, an alcohol constituent, as the plant matures. These changes accelerate dramatically through the two-to-three-week flowering and fruiting process. The essential oil of the flowers as they begin to open contains 0.34 percent linalool and more than 50 percent aldehydes—nearly the same proportions found in the leaves. The essential oil of the ripe fruits, however, contains at least 60 percent linalool and about 4 percent aldehydes.

Cilantro

Those who don't like the taste of cilantro (*Coriandrum sativum*) are quick to point out that its generic name is derived from the Greek word *koris*, which means "bedbug". But despite its bedbug stink, this herb has achieved worldwide popularity, and its multifaceted character has inspired various names, some with more palatable allusions. In English, the fruits and sometimes the plants in general are called *coriander*, but the foliage is referred to as *cilantro* (a term used also by Latin Americans) or *Chinese parsley*. The French, German, Italian, and Russian names are variations of *coriander*; in Japan it is *koendoro*; the Spanish call it *culantro*; to the Arabs it is *kuzbara*; and the Chinese, for whom it is quite important, have three names for it: *hiu-sui, hsiang-sui,* and *yuan-sui*.

Young coriander leaves are especially popular in Oriental and Mexican cuisines, in which they are added to salads, sauces, and soups. The Vietnamese put a bowl of fresh coriander foliage on the table so each diner may flavor the food individually, often by wrapping it with coriander and a lettuce leaf and consuming it as "finger food". The ripe fruits are an important ingredient in curries and pickling spices, and their essential oil is a commercial flavoring for foods, alcoholic beverages (chiefly gin and some liqueurs), and tobacco.

Although the odor of coriander leaves may be repulsive to some, the taste becomes muted when cooked, and the result is a deep flavor rather than a sharp accent. Because the leaves lose their flavor when dried, they are usually used fresh.

Coriandrum sativum is a member of the carrot family (Apiaceae or Umbelliferae) and is native to southern Europe, Asia Minor, and the Caucasus. A short-lived annual, coriander has two lives. In the first, it resembles a flat-leaved parsley with green segmented leaves on stems rising about 8 inches from a crown. It is in the first stage that the leaves are harvested. Its second life begins about 50 days after germination when another kind of stem soars upward. This stalk, festooned along its 3-foot length with fernlike leaves, will bear the flat-topped clusters of small white, rose, or lavender flowers that produce the spicy-scented egg-shaped or globular fruits. These fruits are often incorrectly called seeds; in fact, each fruit contains two "seeds," or mericarps.

Two types of coriander are cultivated: *Coriandrum sativum* var. *sativum* (*sativum* means "cultivated") and *C. sativum* var. *microcarpum* ("small-fruited"). Fruits of the former measure nearly one quarter inch in diameter whereas those of the latter are only one sixteenth of an inch across. Numerous cultivated varieties offer gardeners subtle variations of these two types.

Coriander grows wild in areas that receive as little as 12 inches and as much as 84 inches of rain annually. Under cultivation, it does best in soil of about pH 6.5, but it will tolerate soil as acid as pH 4.9 and as alkaline as pH 8.2. Most soils will need to be amended with compost, sphagnum peat moss, and manure to achieve the waterholding capacity, good drainage, and fertility necessary to sustain coriander's rapid growth. Clay and sandy soils may need as much as 4 to 6 inches of humus.

You'll read in many herb books that coriander doesn't transplant well. Although bare-root seedlings have little chance of survival, plants grown in 2 1/2 inch pots to harvestable size transplant well to fertile soil. If only a few plants are needed, transplants may be the easiest and quickest method to satisfy a cilantro craving. However, sowing the fruits remains a versatile and traditional method of producing coriander.

The fruits may be sown as soon as the soil can be worked and the danger of heavy frost is past, but maximum germination occurs when day temperatures are about 80° F and nights are in the upper sixties. Sow or broadcast fruits 1-inch deep in garden loam where the plants will receive full sun. When fruits are sown directly in the garden, the germination rate is usually less than 50 percent, and sowing should be dense enough to account for this. Germination occurs in about 25 days. Plants that are grown for fruits should ultimately be spaced 12 inches apart, so groups of 3 to 5 fruits can be sown at that spacing. If plants are grown for foliage, spacing of only a few inches is sufficient, and fruits can be sown one per inch along the row. Allow at least 9 to 12 inches between rows for cultivation.

Germination may be increased above 60 percent, and germination time reduced to about 4 days, by rubbing the fruits until the mericarps separate, then soaking these seeds for three to four days. The water should be changed at least twice each day to remove the coumarins, which are germination-inhibiting chemicals common to umbellifera fruits (parsley is said to go to Hell nine times and back before germination, an allusion to the high concentration of coumarins in its fruits that have to be leached out). Dry the seeds for eight hours, then plant them immediately; seeds treated in this way will not keep well. Because coriander does not compete well with weeds, mulching or manual weeding is important.

Growing for Foliage or Fruit

Leaves may be harvested about a month after germination. They can all be harvested in a bunch: gather the leaves on the outside of the rosette in one hand and cut their stems with shears held in the other. Avoid cutting the new growth that is emerging from the center of the plant. Leaves can be harvested continuously until the central flower stem rises and production of the vegetative leaves ceases. Plants whose foliage is harvested repeatedly may die without continuing to the flowering stage; if they do survive, they will not flower or set seed vigorously.

Where summers are long and hot, coriander is often considered a cool weather crop to be planted in early spring or late summer and fall; low temperatures slow the plant's growth and temper its tendency to flower. Alternatively, you may sow fruits every few weeks during hot weather; just pull the plants up when they reach harvestable size.

To maximize foliage production, gardeners might choose varieties such as 'Leaf' or 'Long Standing' that are slower to flower. These varieties extend foliage production at least two weeks, probably the equivalent of one harvest. But cultural manipulation can further extend the plant's leaf stage, even in the toughest summer heat. Many gardeners wait too long to harvest coriander foliage; transplants are usually harvestable after liquid fertilizer is applied and they are firmed in the soil. Summer heat speeds growth, and plants usually can be harvested fortnightly if fertilizer is applied after each harvest. As many as five or six harvests can be obtained from a single plant this way, three or four times what would normally be expected.

Fruits mature in 90 to 105 days after sowing. When green, they smell like the foliage, but they acquire a spicy aroma and chestnut-like color when dry. If the fruits are allowed to ripen on the plant, they may scatter and be lost during harvest. Therefore, it's best to harvest them when about half have changed from green to gray or when those on the central umbels are ripe. Morning is the best time, as the dew helps keep the fruits from scattering.

Coriander Problems

Coriander is susceptible to fusarium wilt disease and powdery mildew. Fusarium causes plants to collapse suddenly, and the wilting is often mistaken for lack of water. Avoid planting coriander in soil where plants have shown evidence of this disease; if alternative soil is unavailable, grow plants in containers filled with a pasteurized, disease-resistant, or sterile growing medium containing sphagnum peat and perlite or vermiculite. Powdery mildew coats leaves with white matter that resembles powder. The mildew spores reproduce most rapidly at high humidity and in the shade at temperatures between 63º F and 77º F. Increased sunlight and better air circulation are prophylactic, but once present, the spores spread by wind currents and moisture and cannot be completely eliminated without the use of a fungicide. Garden sulfur mixed with water is used by many gardeners to control powdery mildew, but some plants are damaged by sulfur spray, and it can leave residue on the leaves. As with any fungicide, use caution.

Coriander is also susceptible to bacterial leaf spot caused by *Pseudomonas syringae*, an agent of occasional problems on rosemary, nasturtiums, sunflowers, tomatoes, and delphiniums. This disease appears as angular, dark brown lesions on the leaves, and may be transmitted on the surface of the hard coriander fruits. It can be spread on cutting utensils, hands, and clothing, and also by the tarnished plant bug (*Lygus* sp.), a quarter inch-long sucking insect with a yellow, brown, and black body. To reduce the spread of bacterial leaf spot, eliminate overhead watering, plant coriander in a different spot each year, and keep the plants insect free. A natural insecticide called sabadilla (made from the seeds of the Caribbean lily *Schoenocaulon officinale*) effectively controls tarnished plant bugs. Caterpillars and boring grubs occasionally enjoy coriander, too, but these rarely become serious pests.

Three Cilantro "Copycats"

For cilantro fans, *Coriandrum sativum* plants may be only the start of a taste obsession, and perhaps a matching plant collection. At least three other leafy herbs that are less well known in America mimic cilantro's taste and provide new gardening and culinary challenges. Although few recipes that use these herbs are available in English, the herbs may be substituted for coriander foliage in any recipe. All have characteristics that make their cultivation less labor intensive than growing coriander.

Culantro (*Eryngium foetidum*)
Culantro, as Latin Americans commonly call this relative of sea holly, is an unlikely culinary herb at first glance because its lance-shaped green leaves are spiny and forbidding. But the spines on this herb's tender new leaves turn out to be surprisingly soft and easily eaten—and their bed-bug-like aroma is similar to that of coriander leaves.

Culantro is a somewhat tender biennial that is often grown as an annual where temperatures drop below 0° F (zone 7). In its first year, it continues to produce succulent leaves long after summer's heat has chased coriander to seed. It is easily cultivated in moist garden loam (in the wild, it's found in areas that receive 27 to 157 inches of rainfall annually), even in partial shade; its soil preference is more restricted than that of coriander, however (pH 4.3 to 6.8 in the wild). Start this herb from seed sown indoors in late winter, and set transplants outside in well drained, fertile soil after the last spring frost.

Culantro is native to the New World tropics and subtropics but is now widespread throughout tropical Africa and Asia. Stems are 6 to 16 inches long and erect. Leaves are 1 1/2 to 4 3/4 inches long and slightly less than 3/4 inch wide. The egg-shaped flowers are dark green. Like cilantro, this herb is a member of the carrot family.

Slugs have a fanatical predilection for culantro and will bypass almost all their other favorites for it. Four-inch-wide copper flashing formed into an upright barrier around plants or a garden bed will keep the voracious critters away. Slugs will also drown in small bowls of beer (no, they do not prefer non-alcoholic substitutes; they want the real thing).

Papaloquelite (*Porophyllum ruderale* subsp. *macrocephalum*)
This cilantro imitator, a member of the Asteraceae (Compositae) family, is native from Texas to South America. Its generic name, meaning "pored-leaf," refers to the translucent oil glands scattered on the margin and surface of the leaves. The specific epithet *ruderale* means "growing in waste places" and *macrocephalum* means "large-headed." In many Mexican and Texan cafes, branches of papaloquelite are kept in glasses of water, and the fresh leaves are torn off and eaten on beans or with tortillas and garlic, to which they impart a unique cilantro-green pepper-cucumber flavor. Papaloquelite plants may grow 6 feet high and provide plenty of foliage, but the marigold-like flowers and seeds are produced rarely in the shorter growing seasons of the northeastern United States. This annual has broadly egg-shaped leaves a little more than an inch long and about an inch wide with a bluish, waxy sheen. Flower heads carried at the ends of branches consist of 30 or more small purple to olive-green flowers.

While haters of cilantro call this "buzzard's breath", the odor of papaloquelite has not only cilantro in its notes but also cucumber. Almost all the species of *Porophyllum* have a similar odor and are used in Mesoamerica in salsas. If you explore Latin American markets, you might also encounter bunches of the related *pepicha* (*Porophyllum tagetoides*), and recently seeds have become available. Grow and use it in a similar fashion to papaloquelite.

Vietnamese coriander (*Persicaria odorata,* alias *Polygonum odoratum*) Sometimes called rau răm (pronounced "zow zam"), this herb has the odor of cilantro with a hint of lemon. The Vietnamese use this herb to garnish meat dishes, especially fowl, and also serve it with duck eggs. It is one of the flavoring ingredients in a Vietnamese pickled dish, similar to sauerkraut. Rau răm is a tender perennial of the Polygonaceae, or buckwheat family, that resembles the annual European water-pepper (*Persicaria hydropiper*). It may be the same plant sometimes listed as *Polygonum minus* and known as *kesom* in Malaysia, but this identification is difficult to confirm because the plant rarely produces its terminal, pink flowers. This herb requires a rich, moist soil in semi-shade, although full sun is desirable if abundant moisture is provided. Plants grown indoors respond vigorously to fluorescent lights placed 6 to 8 inches above the topmost leaves. Container grown plants should not be allowed to dry and wilt because leaf damage will occur. Rau răm bears branching, sometimes trailing stems that are smooth and often reddish. Leaves are narrowly lance-shaped to somewhat egg-shaped and marked with red lines. Fungus is the chief hazard in the cultivation of this herb: watch for lower leaves that begin to brown and dry. Fungus problems are lessened by keeping plants free of decayed foliage and pinching stems frequently to encourage branching.

If you enjoy cilantro...

Cilantro is a kind of garden paradox. It has an uncommon odor and is named after a bedbug, yet it shares a bit of chemistry with some of the century's most popular perfumes. Its culinary popularity is internationally confirmed—it tames spicy foods and enlivens boring dishes the world over—yet many people cannot abide its distinctive odor and flavor. It is an herb that underscores the old dictum: there's no accounting for taste.

Arthur O. Tucker, Emeritus Professor at Delaware State University, has spent more than 50 years using, researching, and writing about herbs in popular and scientific media.

Thomas DeBaggio, the founder of DeBaggio's Herb Farm and Nursery, now located in Chantilly, Virginia and run by his son, Francesco, worked as both a professional herb grower and journalist.

Cilantro in the garden. *Susan Belsinger*

Coriander and dill seeds drying in the garden. *Susan Belsinger*

Cilantro: Lesson 1

Terry Hollembaek

I DON'T REMEMBER where or how the book came into our possession, but it had been around for a while before I picked it up to read. And almost every iota of what I knew, or had been taught about agriculture in general and gardening specifically, fell under immediate question. Masanobu Fukuoka's poorly (charmingly so) translated book *The One Straw Revolution* wasn't just a different perspective, it was a rejection of most of the ideas and methods "traditional" American gardeners and farmers considered gospel. Since his writings seem to have helped spawn permaculture and Korean National Farming, I'd say he was right, at least to some extent when he called it a revolution.

My first opportunity to test out one of his insights was with cilantro/coriander. We were already growing 4-inch potted herbs at our nursery when we finally got a real herb garden going. We didn't sell every last pot of cilantro that year, so I planted ten or twelve 4-inch pots of cilantro directly into the garden. Each pot had 5 to 8 cilantro seedlings and looked perfect, ready for sale. They bolted so fast I couldn't believe it, quit producing foliage, produced a sickly, skinny flower stalk and a few seeds, and were ready for turning under in a few short weeks.

The next year we were able to get into our garden fairly early and I direct seeded a patch of cilantro. Big difference! Nice plants that lasted well into the hot season, with good seed production. That summer I read "The Book," so instead of trying to gather all the coriander seeds, I left some right on the plant. Mr. Fukuoka had realized that the best time to plant seeds is when they choose to fall or float away on their own. My coriander seeds fell off just before Christmas and lay in the hay mulch I used throughout the long Wisconsin winter. They sprouted in early spring and produced the most gorgeous cilantro I had ever grown. They were taller, leafier, slower to flower, and produced a stunning crop of seed. They were mouth-droppingly better in every respect.

I began planting a lot of seeds in the fall or left them to fall on their own. I soon found that dill, lovage, poppies, fennel, and several other herbs loved to be fall-planted. They seemed to germinate just as well and produced more robust, hunkier (my favorite nurseryman word) plants that were slower to go to seed, yielded more leaves and stems, and a profusion of seed that were fat-looking, very viable, and tasty.

By the time I retired, I had tested out many of Masanobu Fukuoka's ideas and progressed to some of the elaborations on his original ideas by Master Chou of Korea and other experimenters throughout the world. The proof to me that these insights were valid, however, was a cluster of cilantro plants in my garden: bigger, leafier, seedier, hunkier than any I'd ever grown, and tasty. Salsa, anyone?

Terry Hollembaek: Alaskan farm kid. A freshman teacher illuminated the world. Completed high school in the Marine Corps. Vietnam. Eclectic college career. Varied work life. Major plant freak. Love self-learning. Love Nancy. Love music. Love life. Love history. Love kids. Love herbs in my life. Love writing. Love poetry. Love dressing in historic costumes and talking to people. Built Wisconsin home and nursery. Retired to Hawaii. Still growing plants and gardening. Appreciating a soft climate and learning what and how to grow in a rainforest; and always important, meeting young plant people with new ideas. Feel very, very rich.

Coriander, the Seed
of the Cilantro Plant

Jim Long

In India, the word *coriander* designates the leafy plant we know in the United States as *cilantro*. We know coriander as the seed of the cilantro plant but the flavors of the two are quite different.

Coriander has a long and admirable history of medicinal uses—for upset stomach, digestion problems, diarrhea, gas, and loss of appetite. In ancient times the seed was ground and used for preserving meats to prevent spoilage. It has historically been used to treat high cholesterol, mouth ulcers, and skin inflammation. There is some evidence that coriander may possibly lower blood sugar but no reliable evidence exists to support that claim.

The flavor of the seed is mild, sweetish, and warm, with undertones of citrus. It is one of the prominent flavors in curry powders and in the Indian spice mixture known as *garam masala*. Pickling spice mixes found in the grocery store contain a varying amount of coriander seed, along with mustard seed, celery seed, allspice, and red pepper flakes.

In America we generally use coriander *raw*, meaning with no other preparation. However in Arabia, India, North Africa, and Morocco, the seed is always roasted or dry-fried first. This process of dry-frying the whole seed before grinding releases and intensifies the flavors. Often combined with garlic, crushed red pepper, cumin (also roasted first), and toasted sesame seeds, the blend is used on pork, fish, sausages, and other dishes. Coriander is one of the seasonings in falafel.

When growing cilantro for the seed, choose a variety known to be quick-bolting and prone to going to seed. Varieties that are good, rapid seed producers include 'Calypso' (*Coriandrum sativum* 'Calypso'), 'Jantar' (*C. sativum* 'Jantar'), and 'Leisure' (*C. sativum* 'Leisure'). Of course all varieties of cilantro produce seed; some just do so earlier and faster than others.

Coriander/Cilantro Root

When I traveled to Thailand some years back for cooking classes, we used coriander root in our cooking. The coriander/cilantro we bought at the local market had larger roots than cilantro I've grown in my own garden. What we found there in the markets were cilantro plants, leaves still attached to the roots, the roots being slightly larger than the size of a pencil. Since there are many varieties of cilantro, it appears a variety with slightly larger roots is cultivated there.

The flavor of the root isn't as strong as cilantro leaves and gives a delicate flavor and pleasant texture to curry pastes. Cilantro root is used to bring together stronger flavors such as hot chiles, garlic, and galangal for a very pleasing effect. In Thailand I learned it was common to go to the outdoor produce markets every day for cooking supplies, but if the root isn't readily available, it can be easily frozen and will keep for about two months.

A traditional Thai marinade can be used on grilled chicken pieces, as well as on chicken or pork, cut into strips and strung on bamboo skewers, called *satay*, then slowly grilled. The paste/marinade is simply garlic, white peppercorns, and cilantro root, ground in a mortar and pestle until it has the texture of a paste. If you don't use a mortar and pestle, a food processor would work fairly well but the texture will be more chopped and less paste-like.

To use cilantro root this way, wash and dry the roots, then chop them into small pieces. Add an equal amount of both white peppercorns and peeled garlic together in the mortar. Grind the mixture with the pestle, scraping from the sides back to the center until you have a thick paste. Spread that on the chicken or pork strips for the satay and place inside a zip-lock plastic bag. Refrigerate for a few hours or even overnight.

An hour before you start the grill, put the bamboo skewers in a pan of water and let soak. When the grill is low to medium hot, string the marinated satay meat onto the skewers and begin grilling. Leave the grill on

Coriander roots. *Susan Belsinger*

medium heat to slightly char the strips rapidly, then turn down the heat to low. Turn the skewers about once a minute, allowing the satay to cook slowly on all sides, about 6 or 7 minutes, then remove the satay to plates. Serve with Thai peanut dipping sauce.

Coriander/Cilantro Varieties

There are a sizable number of cilantro varieties. Some are so-called varieties named by the seed company or nursery that grows them. Others are distinctive in their differences, flavors, or growing conditions. Below is a listing of some of the more prominent ones, with sources when available. You may note some varieties are considered a biennial while others are listed as annual. In tropical climates they are considered to be biennials, completing their life cycle in two years. Because the plants are only partially hardy and can only tolerate a light frost and cold weather will kill them completely, we grow them all as annuals in much of the United States.

'Asian' (*C. sativum* 'Asian') is considered a somewhat hardy plant, meaning it will survive near-freezing temperatures.

'**Big Leaf**' (*C. sativum* 'Big Leaf') and '**Large Leaf**' (*C. sativum* 'Large Leaf'). As the name suggests it has larger than average leaves. 'Big Leaf' is probably the same variety as 'Large Leaf' and similar names, just different seed sellers attaching their own name. 'Large Leaf' is available from Pinetree Garden Seeds at superseeds.com.

'**Calypso**' (*C. sativum* 'Calypso') is typically 3 weeks slower to bolt than similar varieties. Good leaf production and withstands hot weather. Also known as 'Jantar' cilantro. Available from Johnny's Selected Seeds at johnnyseeds.com.

'**Caribe**' (*C. sativum* 'Caribe') is a variety developed to be more bolt-resistant and withstand summer heat better than most other varieties. Has larger leaves than typical varieties. Biennial. Available from High Mowing Organic Seeds at highmowingseeds.com.

'**Costa Rican**' (*C. sativum* 'Costa Rican'), while sometimes listed as a variety, is simply any cilantro grown for culinary use in Costa Rica.

'**Chinese Parsley**' (*C. sativum* 'Chinese Parsley') is a biennial, growing about 2 1/2 feet tall. Available from Kitazawa Seed at kitazawaseed.com.

'**Oaxaca**' (*C. sativum* 'Oaxaca') is considered a biennial. It isn't a distinct variety, simply any cilantro grown in that region of Mexico. Mexican cilantro is sometimes confused with a similarly flavored plant, known as Culantro or Saw-Leaf cilantro (*Eryngium foetidum*). Culantro can be more difficult to grow in the United States outside of Florida. It is common in Thailand, Vietnam, and Mexico and has distinctive long, narrow leaves.

'**Confetti**' (*C. sativum* 'Confetti') has feathery, dill-like foliage and is grown for its milder, sweeter flavor. This one is an annual and, if planted in late summer, often withstands light frost. Available from Territorial Seed Co. at territorialseed.com.

'**Cut and Come Again**' (*C. sativum* 'Cut and Come Again') is a biennial, although once long days and summer heat hits, it will diminish quickly. Like its name suggests, it holds up well to repeated harvesting. Available from Jung Seed at jungseed.com.

'**Delfino**' (*C. sativum* 'Delfino') is another variety with fern-like, feathery leaves that resemble carrot or dill leaves. This was an All American Selections (AAS) winner in 2006. The flavor is a combination of cilantro and parsley with a hint of citrus undertone. This is a biennial, often living a second year in warmer climates, provided the white flowers and flower stalks are kept cut back. This variety is excellent for coriander seed production. One of its attributes is you can begin harvesting leaves in just 5 weeks after planting. Available from 2BSeeds at 2bseeds.com.

'**Fine Leaved**' (*C. sativum* 'Fine Leaved') is likely a localized name for 'Delfino'.

'**Ghanat**' (*C. sativum* 'Ghanat') is an open pollinated variety with a strong cilantro flavor. Available from Sand Hill Heirloom Seeds & Poultry at sandhillpreservation.com.

'**Indian Summer**' (*C. sativum* 'Indian Summer') is another biennial and prefers part sun to part shade. No sources known in the U.S. currently.

'**Jantar**' (*C. sativum* 'Jantar'), biennial, does best in part to nearly full sunlight. This variety is short lived and especially prone to bolting, so repeated sowing of the seeds is essential to have a continuous crop. It does not transplant well. Excellent for seed production of coriander; heat resistant. (See also 'Calypso', above, as they appear to be the same variety.) Available from Park Seed at parkseed.com/calypso.

'**Leisure**' (*C. sativum* 'Leisure'), an heirloom variety that bolts somewhat slower than some of the newer varieties. The leaves are large and fragrant and an added bonus is that the leaves can continue to be used when the plant is flowering. Annual. Available from Kitazawa Seed at kitazawaseed.com.

'**Lemon**' (*C. sativum* 'Lemon') is another biennial although grown as an annual in most places. The flavor is a combination of cilantro and lemony-citrus and quite nice to cook with, and is especially good for seed production. Very difficult to find seed in the U.S.

'**Long Lasting**' (*C. sativum* 'Long-Lasting') stands up well to summer heat and produces nice, large leaves with excellent flavor. The name appears to be a regional listing and is likely the same plant as 'Long Standing' and 'Slow Bolt'.

'Marino' (*C. sativum* 'Marino') grows as an annual. Excellent leaf production, mild flavor, resists bolting. Available from Restoration Seeds at restorationseeds.com and Territorial Seed at territorialseed.com.

'Moroccan' (*C. sativum* 'Moroccan') originates in Morocco and North Africa and has larger seed, very aromatic. Available from Gourmet Seed at gourmetseed.com.

'Pokey Joe' (*C. sativum* 'Pokey Joe') is said to be one of the best flavored cilantros from extensive trials held in the Willamette Valley in Oregon. Slow bolting, prolific, award-winning flavor. Available from Nichols Garden Nursery at nicholsgardennursery.com.

'Rani' (*C. sativum* 'Rani') is fairly slow to bolt, has a mild flavor, and tolerates the heat of summer better than some varieties. Best grown for seed production rather than the leaves, which tend to be small. Available from Sustainable Seeds at sustainableseedco.com.

'Santo' (*C. sativum* 'Santo') is a biennial grown as an annual. The leaves have a robust flavor with flat, toothed leaves and is common in Mexican cooking. This one is considered the best for field production, is slow to bolt, with excellent flavor on an upright plant. Available from High Mowing Seeds at highmowingseeds.com and Johnny's Selected Seeds at johnnyseeds.com.

'Slow Bolt' (*C. sativum* 'Slowbolt'). You'll find this listed by several names including 'Slow Bolt', 'Slowbolt', and 'Slobolt'. As its name suggests, it is slow to bolt into flowering and grows a bit taller than other varieties. Available from Baker Creek Seed at rareseeds.com.

'Surprise' (*C. sativum* 'Surprise') is grown as an annual with delicate, fernlike foliage with good cilantro flavor. While it bolts into flowering as quickly as standard varieties, the leaves can be continuously harvested. Seed is not widely available.

'**Tang Improved**' (*C. sativum* 'Tang Improved') is an annual, native to India and Southern Asia. It is fast growing, bushy, and can be harvested repeatedly. Listed also as 'Chinese parsley', Yan Sui 'Tang' or 'Improved', the seed is difficult to find in the U.S.

'**Xiang Cai**' (*C. sativum* 'Xiang Cai'), biennial, also known as 'Chinese parsley'. Available from Kitazawa Seed at kitazawaseed.com.

Cultivation

When growing cilantro, loosen the soil, smooth it, then plant cilantro/coriander seeds about 1/4 inch deep with spacing between plants about 5 inches. Plant in early spring as cilantro does best in cool weather. Seeding directly in the soil is preferred as cilantro does not transplant well from pots.

An alternative method for growing cilantro in zones 6 and 7 is to loosen the soil in early winter and scatter the seed and lightly tamp the soil. The plants will emerge in early spring as the weather warms.

Jim Long is a professional gardener and author of more than two dozen books on herbs, gardening, and historical subjects. His books and herb products, including his best-selling formula, Herbal Nail Fungus Soak™, are available at herb shops, health foods stores, and from his website LongCreekHerbs.com.

Cilantro Seed Packet. *Hudson Valley Seed Company*

Cilantro's Seedy Side

Ken Greene

PART OF THE reason seed savers love cilantro *(Coriandrum sativum)* is the same reason some gardeners find it difficult to manage—it goes to seed quickly!

Cilantro is actually one of the easiest herbs for seed saving. Just plant the seeds densely in rows and, in a few short weeks, harvest every other plant for fresh young cilantro leaves. Then, in another week or so, harvest every third and fourth plant for eating. After that, let the rest bolt, grow tall and bushy, and go to seed—which they are more than happy to do. The seeds will form in clusters and are ready when they are brown and dry but still attached to the plant. These seeds can then be used in the kitchen for coriander spice. Put a few in an envelope and you have everything you need to plant the next spring.

But what about gardeners who want to harvest more of the herb when its leaves are still green and tasty? Cilantro has a habit of bolting at the first hint of heat. Other than succession sowing in spring and fall or freezing cilantro cubes to use in summer, there's not much to do to keep your kitchen stocked with fresh bright tasty cilantro. Or is there?

Here at the Hudson Valley Seed Company we love cilantro but can't grow it during our hot and humid summers. For the most part, the cilantro choices for gardeners are extremely limited—usually you see just one or two again and again. We started to wonder if there were more varieties out there. It turns out there's more diversity in cilantro varieties than what you see in seed catalogs.

We reached out to the U.S. National Plant Germplasm System (NPGS) which is a collaborative effort safeguarding the genetic diversity of agriculturally important plants. Through their extensive database of seed collections from all over the world, we rounded up nineteen varieties that originated from places that are hot. We hope that these regional cultivars will be less prone to bolt when our temperatures start to rise.

To find out, we'll be growing them side by side in our 2017 variety trial gardens. We'll be monitoring them not only for their ability to produce greens longer than the typical varieties, but also for taste, their texture and leaf size, their productivity, and the character of their coriander spice.

If we find a great new variety, we'll grow it out for seed harvests and add it to our organic seed catalog the following season.

Our organic seed farm and trial gardens are open to the public a few times per year. If you'd like to visit our farm or grow with our seeds, visit hudsonvalleyseed.com and sign up for our Seeder's Digest gardening newsletter.

Stay seedy!

Ken Greene started the Valley Educational Seed Saving Exchange and Library (VESSEL) in 2004 while working as a librarian at the Gardiner Public Library in Gardiner, New York. Having developed a strong interest in preserving heirloom seed varieties, he decided to add them to the library catalog so that patrons could "check them out," grow them in their home gardens, and then "return" saved seed at the end of the season. The program was a small but successful endeavor—one of the first of its kind in the country. After four years of running the program at the library, Ken and his partner Doug decided to turn the library into a mission-driven, homestead-based small business—which it still is today as the Hudson Valley Seed Company. He is a tireless advocate for seed sovereignty and the important role of art in celebrating our agricultural and horticultural heritage. hudsonvalleyseed.com/blog/

Cilantro, Mimics, and Memes

Conrad Richter

"Ew! Smells like soap!"

That was the response from gardeners back in the 1960s and 1970s when offered a sample of fresh coriander to try. Noses turned up, they quickly moved on to the geraniums, petunias, and tomatoes on display in the greenhouses at Richters. In those days, herbs amounted to three things: mint, parsley, and an illegal herb that some hippies smoked. Everything else was a spice on the spice rack, brought in from faraway places, and that's where coriander was situated in the gastronomic landscape—as a spice for baking, pickling, sausages, and seasonings.

The people who grew coriander those days wanted it only for seeds, not the leaf. Life was good since the seeds we got from Europe were of the type that produced a nice crop of seeds and not much leaf. Coriander was simply coriander; there were no named varieties available at the time. It was just *Coriandrum sativum* to the botanists.

As herbs began to take off in popularity in the late 1980s, coriander suddenly became a schizophrenic conundrum for growers. People were waking up to the culinary virtues of fresh coriander leaf, or *cilantro*, as it became known in the popular lexicon. The plant was now two different herbs, leaf and seed, each with different personalities and different uses in the kitchen. Meanwhile we started to see nice large bunches of imported fresh cilantro showing up in the local food markets. They had long stems and beautiful dark green leaves about the same size as Italian parsley. Local growers couldn't compete with the imported stuff, and were asking why their coriander zoomed straight to flower before they could get a decent harvest of leaves.

What was wrong? Was it the way they were growing it? Were they seeding too late or too early? Were field conditions too hot or were the plants getting too much sun? In those days we could not find much reliable production information, and most of what was available was focused on growing coriander seeds for the spice market.

One of our customers, a commercial fresh herb grower, heard a rumour that some Chinese farmers were growing a different type of coriander that didn't bolt or go to flower so quickly. The seeds were smaller than usual, he said. We began to look around at ethnic food stores and it was true that there were different corianders with varying seed sizes. So we decided to try some of these. In a quick and dirty trial in our greenhouses, we planted pots with large seeds, small seeds, and seeds in between. Some seeds came from South Asian food markets in Toronto. Some came from Egypt and Turkey, while others came from American sources. But all of the plants bolted just like our standard no-name variety from Europe. We were stumped.

Unknown to us at the time, German researchers were looking at hundreds of coriander strains collected around the world. Their work showed that certain varietal features are strongly correlated with whether or not a variety will be slow to bolt. The more leaves the variety has at the base of the stems, the more likely it will be a slow-bolting type. And varieties with many basal leaves also correlate with smaller seed size, so that small-seeded varieties are less likely to bolt compared to the large-seeded varieties. So the rumour of Chinese farmers growing a small-seeded, slow-bolting variety could well have been true.

But as our little greenhouse trial showed, there are exceptions, because all of the small-seeded varieties we tested bolted quickly, just like the large seeded ones. Looking back, we cannot rule out the possibility that high summer heat during our trial may have pushed even slow-bolting varieties to bolt early. We know from research that environmental factors, particularly high heat, can trigger premature flowering and seed set.

By the 1990s, commercial slow bolting varieties started to hit the market in North America, varieties such as 'Long Standing', 'Slo-Bolt', 'Santo', and 'Leisure'. Our own field trial of these varieties, along with 16 landraces from Europe, Central Asia, North Africa and the Far East, revealed that 'Santo' and 'Leisure' performed best in our test plots. So, it seemed, life was good again. We now had both types of coriander, the original spice type that produced lots of seeds, and the cilantro type that produced lots of leaves.

As interest in herbs grew, people wanted to grow their own on their kitchen windowsills to harvest year round. Indoor growing works reasonably well for easier herbs like basil and mint—herbs that regrow after cutting—but cilantro is not one of them. Like other tap-rooted members of the parsley family, the Apiaceae, cilantro does not respond well to human grazing, and the only way to produce a continuous supply of fresh leaves indoors is to reseed repeatedly to replace cut-back plants as they are discarded. That proposition was simply too taxing for would be kitchen growers, and many dropped the idea of indoor herbs altogether. Like a demanding diva, cilantro ruined the show for everybody.

From all the questions we were getting, it was already clear to us by the 1980s that finding a cilantro that thrives indoors and tolerates repeated haircuts would be a *really big* deal.

Introducing Rau Răm

"It's not the same!" she exclaimed. "You can't use it like coriander!"

My friend Yen and I were visiting a local green grocer in Toronto's bustling Chinatown on Spadina Avenue. Yen, at the time, owned a Vietnamese delicatessen in the area that served eat-on-the-go food Vietnamese style to shoppers looking for a quick bite. I told her that we had added the Vietnamese herb called *rau răm* to the next Richters catalog and we called it *Vietnamese coriander*. She insisted that the taste was all different. She said that no Vietnamese would ever use rau răm in place of cilantro.

Traditionally, rau răm is used in very specific ways, for *hột vịt lộn* made with fertilized duck eggs and for various raw salads collectively called *gỏi*. It is not used for much else according to Vietnamese people I have talked to. From Yen's reaction, it was pretty clear that my appreciation of fine coriander was about as nuanced as a prohibitionist's appreciation of fine wine.

"Well, maybe it is not exactly the same," I said, plaintively, "but it's close enough, at least for North Americans, isn't it?" She would have none of that, and gave it to me in no uncertain terms, "No! No! No!" But even as she delivered that stern evaluation, it came with a barely concealed giggle that she and her assistant, who had joined us from Yen's store, shared at my expense.

This was a giant bucket of cold water on my idea. We already had a nice crop of plants growing in the greenhouses. It was super easy to grow, tolerant of repeated cutting, and definitely had strong aroma and flavour. How could this not be the perfect mimic of cilantro, I thought. Disconsolate, and searching for something—anything—to grab on to, I meekly asked, "Why the giggles? What was so funny?"

With a mirthful smile and tone, she said rau răm suppresses sexual desire in men. I don't remember the exact words she used, but oriental modesty would have demanded some sort of indirect way of being very direct. It might have taken me more than a few seconds to digest this surprising turn, but I am sure that the way she put it was almost as if rau răm was a woman's secret joke on men, shared among the sisterhood to be used when needed. Or maybe I was just set off-balance enough in that moment to think the worst.

We went ahead with our plan to introduce this Vietnamese coriander to gardeners in 1985. Then known botanically as *Polygonum odoratum* (and now as *Persicaria odorata*), it became a bestseller as people wanted it for both outdoors and indoors. The aroma and flavour *were* different but not different enough, and soon the herb took a place in the pantheon of must-have herbs. And it is still selling strong more than 30 years later. I suppose that if there were any remorse about doing a disservice to my fellow menfolk by launching a covert male anaphrodisiac on the unsuspecting, I can persuade myself that, in the battle to control men's sexual urges, men soon had Viagra to help. That's the thought that I take comfort in anyway.

But this idea that rau răm suppresses male sexual desire stuck like a burr on my back. What if there is something to it? I have long touted the power of traditional knowledge and how we cannot glibly dismiss it. I believe that knowledge handed down from generation to generation usually has a nub of truth behind it—enough to justify the effort to learn and master the knowledge and pass it on to the next generation—even if science has not yet provided a rational basis.

On the possible libido-altering effects of rau răm, the literature is not very forthcoming. Wikipedia has something about Buddhist monks growing and using the herb to control their urges, but when I checked the source cited to back up that claim, the cited online article no longer mentioned anything about monks. Wikipedia also offers the aphorism "Rau răm, giá sống", which supposedly works as a juxtaposition of the libido-suppressing rau răm next to libido-boosting bean sprouts giá sống. I asked Vietnamese friends if they knew this saying but none did. In the scientific literature, all references to libido effects seem to point back to a book published in Saigon in 1954 by a French botanist, Paul Alfred Pételot. From what I can tell, this was the first scientifically documented link between Buddhist monks and rau răm.

In the popular Vietnamese literature one can find articles that mention the use of rau răm by Dominican monks, not Buddhist monks. If true, this use could go back as far as the 1600s when the first missionaries arrived in Vietnam. If I could read Vietnamese, I would like to dig deeper to find out how far back modern Vietnamese accounts of this story can be traced and whether they predate the information in Pételot's book.

Oddly enough, for all of its association with preventing sex, rau răm is a symbol of wanton male love in Vietnamese culture, and there is an aphorism about it:

> Rau răm, difficult to grow in hard soil, easy to uproot,
> No matter how much in love, he will be someone else's husband.

What this is saying is that men, symbolized by rau răm, are difficult to keep in hard conditions and are quick to leave. So whether or not they are in love or how much love is showered on them, they can leave for another woman. The two lines in Vietnamese have a sing-song cadence, and according to a Vietnamese friend, the saying has been shared among women as a warning about the nature of men. In Vietnamese poetry, women are portrayed as flowers, symbols of beauty and fragility, while the rampant rau răm with its nondescript flowers is an apt symbol of men. Since men can be despicable, I have to wonder if there is another aphorism somewhere that tells women to add rau răm to a man's dinner to keep him in line.

So what about that soap smell? Is coriander really that bad? John Gerard, the 16th century English herbalist and botanist, certainly thought so. In his famous compendium, *The Herball, or, Generall historie of plantes*, he called coriander "a very stinking herbe, smelling like the stinking worme called in Latine *Cimex*." While it is not clear what this "stinking worme" was since *Cimex* today refers to bed bugs and they don't have a larvae stage, his scathing assessment clearly did little to recommend fresh leaves for English kitchens. Meanwhile, the seeds fared better, for he also wrote that the "pleasant and well savouring seed is warme, and very convenient to sundry purposes."

Gerard's "stinking herb" meme is not too different from how many people describe the fresh leaves of coriander today. Those who dislike cilan-

Cilantro leaf. *Pat Kenny*

tro compare it to "dish soap", "paint", "stink bugs", "mouldy carpet", "dirt", "rancid body odour" or worse. There's even a website devoted to disparaging cilantro, ihatecilantro.com, where thousands of members commiserate about their encounters with cilantro and share ways to fight back. Meanwhile, at least one cilantro lover is fighting back at the haters in an expletive-filled blog with recipes and tips on irritating the haters. I must admit that I never imagined herbs could become so divisive, or political even. One cilantro hater tweeted, "I wish Donald Trump chose to hate cilantro instead of Muslims and Mexicans." Well, now we know this is serious!

Scientists have been looking at why people have such sharp opinions on cilantro. It is not just a droll fascination with a silly debate; it is actually trying to get to the core of an important part of the puzzle of how we perceive odour and flavour. Most people know that tastebuds in our mouth help us to discern tastes such as sweet, salty, savory and bitter. These tastebuds are loaded with receptors that bind specific chemicals found in our foods. When, say, a sugar molecule nears a sweet receptor, it binds to the receptor, setting off a signal that gets sent to the brain indicating that something sweet is in the mouth. In a similar fashion, there are receptors in the nose that bind to specific chemicals we breathe in, and those receptors also send signals to the brain. It so happens that there are receptors that are known to bind to key molecules in cilantro. That's how we use our sense of smell and sense of taste to detect cilantro.

Research has shown that there is an important genetic component that affects how we perceive cilantro. Lilli Mauer, a graduate student at the University of Toronto, looked at how people of six different ethnic backgrounds perceive cilantro, and discovered that Caucasians and East Asians disliked cilantro significantly more than South Asians and other groups surveyed. And although the sample size was small, she found that the ethnic group that most liked cilantro was Hispanics. It so happens that humans are endowed with taste and smell receptors that come in different models and these function slightly differently, and which model we have is controlled genetically.

What Mauer was able to show was that the presence of one or another model correlated strongly with the frequency at which people liked or disliked cilantro. Her work showed for the first time that perception of cilantro is strongly affected by our genes. But, she points out, our genetic differences do not explain completely our reactions to cilantro because other factors appear to play a role as well. She gave the example that in cultures accustomed to using a lot of cilantro, the intensity of the signal to the brain could be altered over time, even in individuals who have the genes to dislike cilantro.

Close on the heels of Mauer's work, a study was published by the American personal genomics company, *23andme*, in which the genome data of over 14,000 customers was compared to customer perception of and preference for cilantro. Customers wanting to know about their genetics can send in a sample of their saliva and the company will analyze their DNA. Customers answer a lot of detailed questions, including whether cilantro tastes like soap and whether they like the taste. In the study the results were broken down by sex and by ethnic group. Compared to men, women were significantly more likely to find cilantro to be soapy and more likely to dislike it. Among seven ethnic groups looked at, Ashkenazi Jews, followed closely by South and North Europeans, were most likely to find the taste to be soapy, at a frequency of about 1 in 7 or 1 in 8. African-Americans, Latinos, and East Asians were less likely to find it soapy, about 1 in 11 or 1 in 12, and South Asians were the least likely, at a rate of only 1 in 26.

The study found that those who found cilantro to be soapy had sections of DNA that were closely linked to a specific receptor called OR6A2. This receptor is known to bind to fatty aldehydes, a group of compounds commonly found in cilantro and in soap. These compounds are volatile meaning that they can easily escape to the air at room temperature and enter the nose. A handful of these fatty aldehydes are important components of the essential oil from cilantro leaves, often accounting for more than 40% of the oil[1], and are often described as "waxy" or "soapy" as well as "citrusy", 'floral', "meaty" or "herbal". With this connection to

---

1 It should be pointed out that there is evidence that steam distillation methods used to extract essential oils from plants can alter component chemicals and do not necessarily give you oils that accurately reflect the natural composition in the fresh leaves. There are recent indications that this does happen with coriander leaf oil. Trying to draw conclusions based on comparing essential oils is a hazardous practice and any conclusions based on them should be taken with a grain of salt. Still, the overall importance of the fatty aldehydes in coriander and its mimics is well established.

OR6A2, we now have a genetic smoking gun, and a target for further investigation.

About the same time the *23andme* study was published, there was another study that looked at identical and fraternal twins and how they reacted to cilantro. The study was important because it looked at the role of genetics in a more precise way. Identical twins share 100% of their DNA while fraternal twins share only 50%. It stands to reason that identical twins should be more likely to agree on their perceptions of cilantro than fraternal twins. Indeed, the results showed exactly that.

The picture emerging is getting clearer. We are learning how our genetics affect our perceptions, not just of cilantro, but of everything we experience. Poor John Gerard, the 16th century English herbalist, didn't know it at the time but he must have been the one out of eight Englishmen condemned by his genes to perceive cilantro as soap. If the ihatecilantro.com website had existed in his time, no doubt he would have joined it and added his "stinking worme" pronouncement to the website's long list of disparaging comments about the taste submitted by members.

With all this talk about oils and aldehydes and such, you might ask how Vietnamese coriander and true coriander stack up against each other. If Vietnamese coriander, or rau răm, is a good mimic of true coriander, then does it have any of the fatty aldehydes found in cilantro? In fact it does. It has decanal and dodecanal, two important cilantro aldehydes, and at much higher concentrations, with these two making up more than half of the leaf oil. Dodecanal in particular can rise up to 60%, a level never seen in true cilantro oil. Dodecanal is described as having a soapy, waxy, citrusy, and floral scent. So the soap element is definitely more pronounced. This could be part of the reason why Vietnamese cooks do not consider rau răm to be a true substitute for true cilantro. However, for the rest of us with a less refined appreciation of fine coriander, the high decanal content may be a compensating factor. This aldehyde, known for its "sweet", "waxy", "orange peel" and "floral" notes, has the kind of organoleptic profile that the flavour industry actually likes and uses in food products. But, of course, for Vietnamese cooks, there is that unsexy libido-repressing meme about rau răm that seems to get in the way...

The Vietnamese have the Chinese to thank for bringing another coriander mimic to Vietnam, a plant called *culantro*. It has many regional and local names, none of which seemed to take hold in the English literature, so at Richters we decided to use *Mexican coriander*. Botanists know it as *Eryngium foetidum*. Its origin is believed to be a pan-Atlantic region encompassing tropical Africa, tropical America, and especially the Caribbean Islands. The Chinese are believed to have introduced it to Southeast Asia in the 1880s as a substitute for fresh coriander. Adopted like a native son in Vietnam, the herb was christened *ngò gai* and is commonly offered alongside true coriander in markets.

Although it belongs to the same botanical family (the Apiaceae) as true coriander, it is a very different beast in many ways. In the tropics the biennial is found growing in shaded wet areas near cultivated fields. Sometimes known as *thorny coriander* or *spiny coriander*, it can actually be quite prickly, with small yellow spines forming at the leaf margins. Under the hot sun and long days of summer, it tends to bolt, producing flowers that are even more prickly than the leaves. Yet despite its sharp differences in morphology, its scent and flavour are similar to true coriander, only more intense. Its essential oil is very high in those aromatic fatty aldehydes that we have been discussing, and among them, (E)-2-dodecenal is by far the most important. As much as two thirds of the extracted leaf oil consists of this one aldehyde.

This fatty aldehyde has a really low odour detection threshold value, which means that our noses can detect it better than most other aldehydes. So the combination of this aldehyde's high concentration and low odour detection value helps to explain culantro's incredibly strong aroma. This is just my own speculation, but I think the relative absence of other aldehydes in the mix makes its odour "cleaner" than true coriander. Perhaps it is this intense, clean aroma that induced the Chinese to bring this plant to Southeast Asia. There had to be something amazing about it; otherwise why would they bother when they already had cilantro?

Okay, after all this beating around the bush, I am sure you are wondering where I stand on the cilantro lover-hater divide. Without a doubt, I am with the lovers. But not too much rau răm, please.

References

Eriksson, N., Wu, S., Do, C. B., Kiefer, A.K., Tung, J.Y., Mountain, J.L., Hinds, D.A. and U. Francke. 2012. A genetic variant near olfactory receptor genes influences cilantro preference. *Flavour* 1:22. Retrieved from http://www.flavourjournal.com/content/pdf/2044-7248-1-22.pdf.

Knaapila A., Hwang, L.D., Lysenko, A., Duke, F. F., Fesi, B., Khoshnevisan, A., James, R. S., Wysocki, C. J., Rhyu, M., Tordoff, M. G., Bachmanov, A. A., Mura, E., Nagai, H., and D. R. Reed. 2012. Genetic analysis of chemosensory traits in human twins. *Chem. Senses* 37: 869.

Mauer, L. and A. El-Sohemy. 2012. Prevalence of cilantro (*Coriandrum sativum*) disliking among different ethnocultural groups. *Flavour* 1:8. Retrieved from http://www.flavourjournal.com/content/pdf/2044-7248-1-8.pdf.

Mauer, L. 2011. Genetic determinants of cilantro preference (Master's thesis). Retrieved from https://tspace.library.utoronto.ca/bitstream/1807/31335/1/Mauer_Lilli_K_201108_Msc_Thesis.pdf.

Pételot, P. A.1954. Les plantes médicinales du Cambodge, du Laos et du Vietnam. III. Archives des recherches agronomiques au Cambodge, au Laos et au Viêtnam, ne 22: 23.

Conrad Richter is president of Richters Herbs, a business specializing in herb seeds, plants and dried herbs. He has been involved with Richters since its inception in 1967 when he was still a child, helping in the greenhouses and in the fields after school and on weekends. His interest in herbs took flight when he helped his father prepare the first Richters herb catalogue in 1970. He has worked on every Richters catalogue since. He has a primary responsibility for research and development. Through his efforts many herbs have been introduced to gardeners in North America for the first time. Conrad is responsible for the introduction of famous Richters varieties such as Orange Spice™ Thyme and Profusion® Chives. Conrad has a Master of Science degree in botany from the University of Toronto. He is a long time member of the International Herb Association and a former member of the boards of the IHA and the IHA Foundation.

The Foundation's Otto Richter Memorial Lecture, delivered by a respected herb professional at the IHA's annual conference, is named in honour of Conrad's father who was an early board member of the Herb Growers and Marketers Association, the organization that later became the IHA.

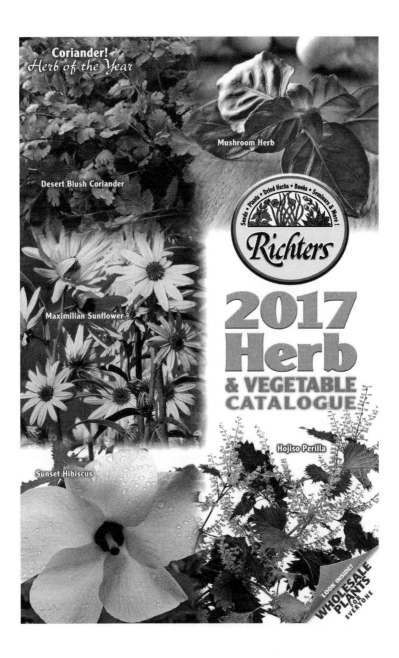

Coriander!
Herb of the Year

Mushroom Herb

Desert Blush Coriander

Richters
Seeds • Plants • Dried Herbs • Books • Seminars & More !

2017
Herb
& VEGETABLE
CATALOGUE

Maximilian Sunflower

Hojiso Perilla

Sunset Hibiscus

LOOK INSIDE!
WHOLESALE
PLANTS
FOR
EVERYONE

Cilantro and Coriander Varieties

as Listed in Richter's 2016 Catalog

Conrad Richter

CORIANDER VARIETIES

Spice Coriander *Coriandrum sativum*
(Culantro; Thorny coriander; Ngo gai) Native to Central America, but now cultivated throughout Southeast Asia and Latin America. Favoured where the true coriander (*Coriandrum sativum*) does not do well because it can stand hot, steamy weather. Leaves are tough, but if sliced and then chopped they are quite tasty. Unlike other corianders, this variety dries well, retaining good colour and flavour, and it can stand some cooking—properties that may become significant to the dried spice market.

Uses: Culinary/Medicinal/Industrial
Duration: Annual
When to Sow: Spring/Late Summer/Early Fall
Ease of Germination: Easy

Mexican Coriander *Eryngium foetidum*
Variety grown for its seeds. Seeds add fresh, spicy flavour to soups and stews. Main ingredient in chili sauces, curries and exotic dishes.

Uses: Culinary/Medicinal
Duration: Perennial (hardy in zones 8-11)
When to Sow: Spring/Anytime
Ease of Germination: Moderate

Vietnamese Coriander *Persicaria odorata*

(Rau răm) Tired of growing coriander from seed several times a year? This is your answer; this remarkable herb from Vietnam has excellent flavour. Grow this perennial indoors in good light.

Uses: Culinary/Medicinal/Industrial
Duration: Perennial (hardy in zones 11+)

THE HERB: CILANTRO VARIETIES

Cilantro *Coriandrum sativum*

(Chinese parsley) The piquant flavour of fresh coriander leaves, so essential in authentic Chinese and Latin American cuisines, is very popular.

Uses: Culinary/Medicinal/Industrial

Marino Cilantro *Coriandrum sativum 'Marino'*

Uses: Culinary/Medicinal/Industrial
Duration: Annual
When to Sow: Spring/Late Summer/Early Fall
Ease of Germination: Easy

Longstanding Cilantro *Coriandrum sativum 'Longstanding'*

(Chinese parsley) The piquant flavour of fresh coriander leaves, so essential in authentic Chinese and Latin American cuisines, has become very popular in recent years. 'Longstanding' is the strain commonly grown in North America for fresh leaves. Slow bolting.

Uses: Culinary/Medicinal/Industrial
Duration: Annual
When to Sow: Spring/Late Summer/Early Fall
Ease of Germination: Easy

Pot Cilantro *Coriandrum sativum '99057'*
(Chinese parsley) First true cilantro developed for potted plant production. Sow direct in pots.

Uses: Culinary/Medicinal
Duration: Annual
When to Sow: Spring
Ease of Germination: Easy

Cilantro Stoneware Marker
Virtually unbreakable, weather-resistant stoneware marker to enhance the natural beauty of your garden. Each marker comes with a rustproof 10" stake (not shown).

richters.com

Cilantro marker in DeBaggio's garden. *Karen O'Brien*

Coriander in Madeline Hill's Pharmacy Garden. *Susan Betz*

Cilantro Leaf and Coriander Seed Yarb Tales

Tina Marie Wilcox

CILANTRO LEAF AND coriander seed are produced by the cool season annual *Coriandrum sativum*. During June, in the Kitchen Garden at the Ozark Folk Center, there are large stands of it in shades of gold and brown, just ripening its seed. To the uneducated eye, it looks like the garden is in need of weeding, but, in fact, a very important process is coming to fruition.

Cilantro, like lettuce and spinach, is a cool season crop. When hot weather sets in, these annuals bolt—they stop growing large, tender leaves—becoming a bit pungent and less aromatic. The plants bolt upward towards the sun, producing fine foliage on waist-high stalks, then burst into delicate, white, lacy, flat-topped blooms. Pollinators and beneficial predators visit the blossoms for sweet nectar; every breeze shakes the unmistakable scent of cilantro into the garden. When pollination is complete, the flowers form clusters of plump green seeds. Both flowers and green seeds are edible with the inimitable flavor of the cilantro leaf and hints of citrus. Use green cilantro seeds the same way that you would use the leaves, only mash or chop the seeds before putting them in salsa, beans, or sauce.

Botanically speaking, the pods are non-fleshy fruits correctly called schizocarps. There are two mericarps in each schizocarp. Each mericarp contains a seed. The schizocarps are the spice known as coriander. The seeds take their time to cure and ripen. When the schizocarps are brittle, dry, and have turned tan, they are ready for harvest.

On a dry, sunny day, cut the flower stalks into a paper bag or clean 5-gallon plastic bucket. The fruits can then be rubbed off the stems. Pick out insects and foreign material before storing the seeds at room temperature in a closed, labeled container. Be sure to include the date and all pertinent information on the label. The coriander seeds can be used in the kitchen, ground, and added to everything from beans and grains to salsas, breads, muffins, and cakes. The flavor is enhanced by lightly toasting the seeds in an iron skillet before crushing and adding them to dishes.

Those of us who are eating fresh tomatoes and chiles from the garden want cilantro leaves during the heat of the summer. This can be accomplished by sowing cilantro in the shade of tomato plants every two to four weeks. When the young plants appear, quickly cut and use them as they will want to bolt right away. Repeated plantings will provide enough tasty leaves for fresh use and canning. Plant a large patch of the seeds in August to have cilantro for the chile harvest and through most of the winter and as a seed crop next summer. If I don't see you in the future—I'll see you in the pasture!

Tina Marie Wilcox has been the head gardener and herbalist at the Ozark Folk Center State Park's Heritage Herb Garden in Mountain View, Arkansas since 1984. She coordinates annual herb events and facilitates the production of herb seeds and plants for the park. She writes a weekly herb and garden column entitled "Yarb Tales" published by the *Stone County Leader* and www.ozarkfolkcenter.com. She co-authored the reference book *the creative herbal home* with Susan Belsinger

Double the Pleasure

Two Herbs in One

Charles Voigt

THERE ARE TWO main species within this genus, *Coriandrum sativum* and *Coriandrum tordylium*, but the one most commonly grown is *Coriandrum sativum*. This is a unique species in that, in its vegetative stage, the leaves are harvested fresh as an herb known as *cilantro* or *Chinese parsley* while its mature dry fruits are the spice known as *coriander*. From one plant, there are two very different and distinct products. While coriander has a long history of use in the United States, the growth in usage of cilantro over the last thirty years has been phenomenal. Somewhere in that time frame, salsa passed ketchup as the number one condiment in the country.

History

The genus name for coriander comes from the Greek *koriannon*, the root of which is *koris* or bedbug. Gerard described it as "a very stinking herb" and many associate its smell or taste with that of a bedbug. It is one of the most ancient herbs in use today with accounts of cultivation by the ancient Egyptians as long ago as 2,000 or 3,000 B.C.E. It has been found in funeral offerings in tombs from this time period, including that of King Tutankhamen.

Hippocrates used it about 500 B.C.E. By the time the plant reached China, around 200 B.C.E., it had acquired a reputation for bestowing immortality, and Chinese herbalists developed several compounds with that end in mind. Others thought it aroused passion, and it was referred to as an aphrodisiac in *One Thousand and One Nights*. There is some evidence that coriander seeds can have a somewhat narcotic effect if ingested in excessive amounts. It was a component of Roman vinegar, used to preserve meats, and ground coriander was used to flavor Roman wines. It is still used in the making of such liqueurs as Chartreuse and Benedictine.

It was known in the British Isles in the 15th century, although it probably arrived there much earlier with the Romans. Coriander was first brought to the American Colonies in the 17th century. *Coriandrum sativum* is native to southern Europe, Northern Africa, Asia Minor, and the Caucasus, but has now been distributed all around the world. As an indicator of just how widespread it has become, both the Zuni of the American Southwest and natives in Peru have adopted it as a preferred flavoring.

Botany

Coriander is a somewhat tender annual plant which does not survive heavy frost. In the vegetative stage, the foliage is a bright green color, smooth in appearance, and borne in a basal rosette. The leaves are compound, pinnate, round and lobed at the base, then becoming more finely divided as the stem elongates toward flowering.

Reaction to the flavor and fragrance of the leaves varies among individuals. A small portion of the population is genetically predisposed to find the scent of cilantro disgusting, soapy, or rotten. On the other hand, those who find it pleasant say it has a refreshing, lemony or lime-like flavor. Populations from areas where the leaves are used widely in local cuisine tend to have a lower percentage of people who are genetically predisposed to hate it.

C. sativum is in the Apiaceae plant family, formerly known as Umbelliferae, because their flowers are borne in umbels, flat-topped or rounded flower clusters, in which the individual flower stalks arise from about the same point of attachment, like the ribs in an upside-down umbrella.

The vegetative rosette may grow 6 to 12 inches high, and in flower, the plant can reach 2 to 3 feet in height. The flower stalk is lightly grooved, bearing a flattish cluster of white to pale pink flowers, which are followed by spherical, ribbed fruits, which are less than 1/4- inch diameter. These eventually mature and dry to a tan color. Immature fruits smell and taste like the foliage, but with a resinous, citrus finish. When dry, this scent turns into a flowery, citrus spice aroma, very different from the foliage.

Uses

Coriander is regarded as being pretty mild, although taking an infusion of coriander seeds or chewing them may soothe an upset stomach or aid digestion. Coriander can be useful as a tea for its positive effects on the digestive tract and appetite stimulation as well as relieving nausea, diarrhea, flatulence, and indigestion. It may enhance circulation and relieve fluid retention. Poultices of crushed seeds have been recommended for relieving the pain of rheumatism. *The U.S. Dispensatory* has described it as a rather "feeble aromatic and carminative." Modern pharmacy tends to use it mainly as a flavoring to mask the taste of other compounds in medicines.

As a culinary herb, the flavor and fragrance of the leaves are very bold, a sage-like flavor paired with a tangy citrus zing, which blends especially well with chile peppers. Cooking mellows the sharpness of the taste, making it deeper yet muted. In Peru and Egypt, the leaves are a staple of soups and broths. Cuisines as diverse as Southeast Asian, Chinese, Mexican, East Indian, South American, Spanish, Central American, and Central African all utilize its unique flavor. The root is also edible and very popular in Thai cooking where it is minced and added to salads and relishes.

Whole or ground coriander fruits add zest to marinades, salad dressings, cheese, eggs, chili sauce, pasta salads, and curries. Ripe fruits are used in pickling spices, and sometimes sugar-coated, called coriander comfits. Dyed, sugar-coated fruits have also been used as multicolored cake sprinkles. The Zuni of the American Southwest mix the powdered seeds with ground chile as a condiment with meat. Coriander seed essential oil is a commercial flavoring for foods, alcoholic beverages, and tobacco. Flowers have a light flavor of the foliage and can be used as an edible garnish.

Culture

Coriander seeds should be planted in near-neutral pH, moderately rich, light, well-drained soil, in full sun to partial shade, in spring when the chance of frost is nearly over. Excess nitrogen fertilizer may dull the flavor. Although plants will endure a light frost, anything more will kill them. Plants have a taproot, and so are difficult to transplant unless started and grown in pots or cell packs. Fall planting can be done late enough in the summer, so day length will not cause bolting to seed.

Seeds may be slow to germinate, especially with unbroken fruits, and should be planted 1/2- to 1-inch deep in furrows at least 5 to 10 inches apart. Soaking fruits broken in half for 3 to 4 days before planting may enhance germination. Plants should be thinned to no closer than 4 inches apart. Succession plantings may be sown every 2 to 3 weeks from mid-spring, but should cease before the onset of hot weather. A few plants may be grown in a pot, which can be protected from frost, and thus sown earlier. Plants grown for production of coriander fruits can be made at the same time, but are allowed to grow, flower, and produce seeds without interference.

Coriander seedlings are poor competitors, so early season weed control is essential. A soil-cooling organic mulch may be helpful once plants are large enough not to be overwhelmed by it. Otherwise, timely hoeing and hand weeding will be needed.

High humidity is bad for the plants, particularly in the early vegetative stage. Hot temperatures and lengthening days will initiate flowering in the plants. Some cultivars have been selected to stay in the vegetative leafy condition for extended harvest of the leaves, including 'Leaf,' 'Long-Standing,' 'Slo-Bolt,' 'Calypso,' and 'Santo.' Although these resist bolting a little, the extended harvest may only last one to two extra weeks.

Planting cilantro where it will be shaded by a taller crop as days lengthen and get warmer, or covering with shade cloth, may also help to slow the bolting process. The soil should be kept evenly moist during coriander's growth. Fruits that shatter before harvest may re-sow themselves for a fall harvest. These plants will survive light frost, and the season can be lengthened even further with the protection of a spun-bonded floating row cover over fall-maturing cilantro.

Harvesting and Storing

Cilantro is harvested by cutting off the petioles of the leaves around the outside of the rosette near the crown of the plant. The center of the rosette will then continue to grow and produce more leaves. Cut leaves to be stored for later use should be rinsed, excess moisture shaken off, and the moist but not wet bundle placed in a zip-lock plastic bag, then stored in a refrigerator at 50° F for 1 to 2 weeks. Drying is not recommended, since dried leaves lose their flavor. Fresh leaves may be frozen, either whole or ground to a paste. Flavor may not be as sharp as fresh, but will be better than doing without.

Coriander fruits should be harvested as they turn from green to tan. Left on the plant for too long after maturity, they will shatter and fall to the ground. Individual umbels may be harvested as this color change is observed, or whole plants may be cut and placed in paper bags to finish drying when a number of the central umbels have turned to tan in color. It just depends on how many plants need to be harvested, and how much time is available for the operation. As drying progresses, the aroma becomes very spicy and pleasant, making the chore of cutting mature heads more palatable than leaf harvest. When fully dry, seeds can be shaken or rubbed free from the umbels. Chaff can be winnowed in the breeze or with a low-speed fan. Some sources advocate using a vacuum cleaner to pull out the small bits of leaves and leave behind the heavier fruits. Once cleaned and thoroughly dry, store fruits in jars, away from sunlight. They should easily last until next year's crop.

The year 2017 will be a celebration of the genus *Coriandrum*, imbued with the flavors of cilantro, coriander, and possibly one of the other plants that mimic the flavor of cilantro. There should be plenty of room for learning new ways to use this ancient plant, beloved by Egyptians, Romans, Hebrews, Chinese, Middle Easterners, Spanish, and a host of others.

Chuck Voigt, recently retired academic professional at the University of Illinois College of Agriculture, specializes in culture and management of vegetable and herb crops. He first spoke at an IHGMA (now the IHA) conference in Minneapolis in 1991. He has been associated with the IHA ever since, serving as chair of Horticulture and Program committees and a member of the IHA Foundation (IHAF). He received the IHA Service Award in 2001, the IHA Professional Award in 2010, and the Otto Richter Award in 2012.

Pollinator on cilantro flower. *Susan Betz*

Coriander: Honoring the Past, Planting the Future

Susan Betz

The herb becomes the teacher.
Men stray after false goals
When the herb he treads
Knows much, much more.

~Henry Vaughan

CULTIVATING FRIENDSHIPS AND cultivating plants are similar in many respects; sometimes there is an instant connection with a plant or person and other times more careful effort is required to establish a growing relationship.

A dear friend of mine and I have traded seeds for years, and one year she passed along a small packet of coriander in exchange for marigold seed. Due to the strong odor of the fresh foliage, I had never been very fond of coriander. But, remembering Henry David Thoreau's words, "Though I do not believe that a plant will spring up where no seed has been, I have great faith in a seed. Convince me you have a seed there, and I am prepared to expect wonders," I planted the seeds and told myself to look at the plant from a new and different perspective.

I was surprised to learn that coriander (*Coriandrum sativum*) signifies "hidden merit" and "Your closeness is welcome" in the language of flowers. Native to southern Europe and the Mediterranean, coriander is known by similar-sounding terms the world over, testifying to the plant's long association with humankind and extensive range, from central and southern Europe, Asia, and India to parts of North and South America.

Cilantro is the Spanish word used for the plant's strongly scented bright-green foliage while *coriander* in America refers to the dried seeds or fruits rather than the fresh leaves.

A Plant with a Past

One of the most documented culinary and medicinal herbs, coriander is known to have been cultivated in Egyptian gardens thousands of years before the birth of Christ. The Chinese used the herb as far back as the Han Dynasty in 207 B.C. and believed that the seeds bestowed eternal life upon those who consumed them. Greek and Roman physicians, including Hippocrates, made medicines from them. Coriander, a highly regarded culinary spice, traveled to Britain with the Romans where it was cultivated in monastery gardens during the Middle Ages.

The legendary book of Arabian fairy tales *One Thousand and One Nights* mentions coriander both as an aphrodisiac and, along with fennel, as an ingredient in an incense used to summon the devil. That being said, in *The Rodale Herb Book: How to Use, Grow and Buy Nature's Miracle Plants*, gardeners are cautioned not to place the two herbs together in the garden because coriander is reputed to hinder the seed formation of fennel (Rodale 416).

Historically, John Josselyn's seventeenth-century list of New England colonial garden plants includes coriander. In France, coriander seed was a prime ingredient of the famous Parisian Eau de Carmes which was consumed as a pleasing cordial and used as cologne to freshen the body and spirit. Quite a versatile plant!

Description and Culture

The coriander plant belongs to the Apiaceae or Parsley family. Chervil, cumin, dill, anise, caraway, and fennel are a few other well-known family members. Coriander is a quickly maturing herbaceous annual growing to three feet tall with a long taproot and slender, finely grooved stems. The plant's first, lower, roundish lobed leaves resemble Italian parsley, but later on, the new, upper foliage becomes fernlike and more jaggedly cut. Tiny white or lilac-tinged flowers grow in small, loose 1½-inch umbels neatly arranged in symmetrical clusters. The larger, outer florets open first, followed by the smaller, compact inner florets. The fruits are light brown, round globose seeds, about one quarter-inch long occurring in clusters. Depending on weather conditions, it may only take about two months for the plant to mature fully.

Field-grown coriander does not transplant well and grows best from seed sown directly into a sunny garden location. Old time gardeners relied on the bloom sequence of common plants growing in their local regions to let them know when it was safe to sow seeds and set plants in the garden. When the apple and cherry trees bloom in Michigan, it is a good time to plant coriander seed. When my friend Katja notices her tomatoes start to bloom, she plants extra coriander seed to harvest fresh cilantro for use in her salsa when her tomatoes ripen in late summer.

Experts on companion planting believe that planting coriander near anise will benefit the formation of anise seeds. Coriander and caraway are sometimes planted in the same row to help with weed control. Caraway is a biennial whose first year growth does not interfere with the coriander seedlings; the next year caraway has the row to itself. Sow seeds at two to three week intervals for a continued harvest. It is important to thin the seedlings to about six inches apart and keep them well weeded and watered until they are firmly established. Coriander readily self-sows so allow at least one plant to make seed in an area that will not be disturbed early in the spring.

Coriander is two herbs in one, and its varied uses are based on different parts of the plant. Coriander seed takes roughly ninety days to mature. You can use the fresh leaves for seasoning early on in salsas, salads, and dips. Harvest the seeds when light tan in color before they begin to fall off. The crushed seeds are excellent in baked dishes using molasses, apples, cherries, or other fruits. Whole seeds are an ingredient in pickling spice mixtures and used to flavor gin and other liqueurs. Coarsely ground coriander adds a bergamot-like fragrance to potpourri.

Planting the Future

Herb gardeners often tend to start with plants and their herbal uses when planning a garden. Their usefulness in fulfilling a landscape function is often discovered after growing the plant for some other reason.

Humans are not the only ones who like coriander. Pollinators do too, especially bees.

Protecting wildlife, particularly pollinators, has become a worldwide priority. Private citizens and advocacy organizations are planting trees, herbs, and wildflowers to re-create habitat for pollinators. The role of the suburban landscape and home garden has become crucial to the future health and well-being of our planet. We can all make a difference one garden or one plant at a time bridging the gap between nature and our cultivated landscapes. Easygoing and companionable, coriander has a long history of use in and out of the garden. Coriander is particularly attractive to our less conspicuous pollinators: bees, wasps, and flies.

Coriander in garden. *Susan Betz*

In his monograph *Coriandrum sativum* L.: *Promoting the Conservation and Use of Underutilized and Neglected Crops,* research scientist Axel Diederichsen, Ph.D. verifies this: "A further benefit of coriander derives from the reproductive biology of this plant. Coriander produces a considerable quantity of nectar and thereby attracts many different insects for pollination, an external effect which is of both ecological and economic value" (22).

According to the North American Pollination Protection website, 80 percent of all plants depend on pollinators. Pollinators, which are mainly insects, are indispensable partners for an estimated one out of every three mouthfuls of the food, herbs, condiments, and beverages we consume. They are essential for growing the plant fibers used in our clothing and many of the medicines that keep us healthy (Hanson 25). Pollinators are vital members of the delicate web that supports biological diversity in natural ecosystems that contribute to our quality of life. Coriander is one of those plants.

Bees, both managed honeybees and native bees, are primary pollinators in most areas of North America, with over 4,000 species of native bees. Bumblebees, leaf cutters, orchard mason bees, carpenter, sweat, and digger bees are just a few that were living in America long before the arrival of the honeybee. Native bee populations are declining due to lack of foraging plants, suitable nesting sites, and the use of pesticides.

Native bees and other pollinators need forage plants with overlapping bloom times as they need pollen and nectar sources from early spring until late fall. Depending on location and weather, coriander sometimes begins blooming in Michigan in late-April and continues with successive plantings through October. Native bees and other pollinators come in many sizes, and they also require flowers of various shapes, sizes, and colors to forage on.

The flowers of the coriander plant attract many different pollinator and insect visitors. The plant is classified by ecologists as an insectary plant, that is, a flowering plant used to attract insect predators to feed on garden pests. Organic gardeners often interplant coriander in vegetable beds intentionally allowing it to bolt to attract beneficial insects. Adult parasitoid wasps depend on the nectar sources in the form of tiny flowers on plants such as coriander. Syrphid flies, often mistaken for bees, are predatory insects as larvae, primarily feeding on aphids before maturing into important pollinators as adults.

Bees are not the only form of wildlife attracted to coriander; so are fish. For catching fish in large quantities, mix thoroughly equal parts of the following herb seeds: lovage, fennel, cumin, coriander, and anise. Steep seven teaspoons of mixture in a cup of water on the back of the stove for one hour, then strain. When cold, put a few drops on any bait (Meyer 51).

Time honored garden lore confirms "Happy is he that has the power to gather wisdom from a flower." Each spring, I look forward with anticipation for the coriander plants to pop up in my garden. And when I first spot them, I think to myself, what a wonderful world!

Web Resources

The GreenBridges™ Initiative, The Herb Society of America— herbsociety.org
A program for gardeners interested in native herb conservation and discovering ways to incorporate native herbs into their yards and neighborhoods. Invasive plants, ecosystem function, and reputable sources for native herbs are among the key concepts covered in program materials.

Ecosystem services fact sheets—
esa.org/ecoservices/comm/body.comm.fact.ecos.html
Fact sheets developed for public dissemination on the general topic of ecosystem services, and one for each service covered in the Tool Kits. The fact sheets can be downloaded and distributed at local gardening events.

Ask Nature—asknature.org
Biomimicry is an approach to innovation that seeks sustainable solutions to human challenges by emulating nature's time-tested patterns and strategies. Their goal is to create products, processes, and policies—new ways of living—that are well-adapted to life on earth over the long haul.

Pollinator Partnership/North American Pollinator Protection Campaign—pollinator.org
Information for gardeners, educators, and resource managers to encourage the health of resident and migratory pollinator animals. Extensive planting references and resources.

Bug Guide—bugguide.net
An online resource devoted to insect, spiders and their kin, with identification help and information for the United States and Canada.

Ecological Landscape Alliance—ecolandscaping.org/wp-content/
uploads/2011/05/Discover-Ecological-Landscaping-Brochure.pdf
Discover ecological landscaping [2005 Brochure].

Olympia Beekeepers Association— friendsofthehoneybee.com
Bee-Friendly with Winnie-the Pooh. The Olympia Beekeeper Association
worked with Egmont Publishing to create this 2015 special bee-friendly
guide (pdf) inspired by Winnie the Pooh and friends. Filled with fun
upbeat educational materials.

Habitat Network —yardmap.org
Developed by Cornell Lab and powered by YardMap, Habitat Network
is a citizen science project designed to help you work together with your
neighbors to create nature-friendly regional landscapes. One of the best
citizen science projects in the United States. Extensive ecoregion planting references and resources.

References

Clarkson Rosetta E. *Magic Gardens: A Modern Chronicle of Herbs and Savory Seeds.* Macmillan, 1942.

Darke, Rick and Tallamy W. Douglas. *The Living Landscape: Designing for Beauty and Biodiversity in the Home Garden.* Timber Press, 2014.

Diederichsen, Axel. *Coriander (Coriandrum sativum L.).* Promoting the conservation and use of underutilized and neglected crops. *Institute of Plant Genetics and Plant Research,* Gatersleben/ International Plant Genetics Institute, Rome. 1996. 22.

Gibbs, Jay, Ashley Bennett, Rufus Isaacs and Joy Landis. *Bees of the Great Lakes Region and Wildflowers to Support Them.* Michigan State University Extension Bulletin. E3282. 2015.

Hanson, Michael. Michigan Pollinators. *The Michigan Landscape Magazine.* August, 2009. 25.

Hyiton, William H. *The Rodale Herb Book: How to Use, Grow and Buy Nature's Miracle Plants.* Rodale Press, 1974. 416.

Meyer, Joseph E. *The Herb Doctor & Medicine Man: A Collection of Valuable Medicinal Formulae & Guide to the Manufacture of Botanical Medicines.* Indiana Botanical Garden, 1922. 51.

North American Pollination Protection. Accessed 9/30/2016. http://www.nrcs. usda.gov/wps/portal/nrcs/main/national/plantsanimals/pollinate/.

Tucker, Arthur O. and Thomas DeBaggio. *The Encyclopedia of Herbs: A Comprehensive Illustrated Reference to Herbs of Flavor and Fragrance.* Timber Press, 2009.

Pollinator on cilantro flower. *Susan Betz*

Susan Betz is an author, teacher, lecturer, and conservationist specializing in herbs and native plants. A charter member and past president of the Michigan Herb Associates, she has been actively involved in promoting gardening with herbs for the past 30 years. Susan is a member of the International Herb Association, Garden Writers Association, and the Ecological Landscape Alliance. A life-member of The Herb Society of America, Susan serves on HSA's Native Herb Conservation Committee and Green Bridges™, the Society's sustainable garden initiative. Author of the book *Magical Moons & Seasonal Circles: Stop-Look-Listen Stepping into the Circles of the Seasons*, she lives and gardens in Jonesville, Michigan.

Ode to Coriander

Dan Zimmerman

its leaves an herb, its seeds a spice,

it straddles Europe & Asia.

its name from Greek *koriannon*,

apparently non-Indo-European.

it welcomes the touch of morning sun,

but left untamed, it'll bolt

like a colt. do not repot: let it stay put.

it abhors peregrinations.

for 7,000 years & more,

it's shunned fennel, bitterly.

do the Chinese call it Chinese parsley?

clump into salsa for savor.

Daniel Zimmerman, a former reporter in Vermont and professor of English at Middlesex County College in New Jersey since 1979, edited NJCEA's *College English Notes* for five years, and has served as an editor of *Middlesex: A Literary Journal* since 2008. His books of poetry include *Perspective* (1974), *See All the People* (1976), *At That* (1978), *blue horitals* (1997), *ISOTOPES* (2001), and *Post-Avant* (2002).

Coriander mandala #2. *Pat Kenny*

LORE
HISTORY
MISCELLANY

Cilantro for sale, Rennes, France farmers' market. *Peter Coleman*

The Lore and Allure of
Coriandum sativum

Gert Coleman

CRUSH IT, BRUISE it, steep it, or keep it whole—coriander has been used for millennia to boost libido, ease digestive woes, and add flavor to breads and beverages. Love potion, fertility charm, medicinal aid, fragrant herb, or legendary culinary spice—there is much that is alluring about coriander.

Historically, the aromatic seed has been so highly prized that ancient Egyptians included it in funeral offerings and Chinese believed it promoted longevity and conferred immortality. The Romans boiled its leaves with other greens and barley to make porridge. Europeans have long added coriander essential oil to fragrance potpourri, soaps, lotions, and perfumes, and coriander was one of the first plants colonists brought to the New World.

With two kinds of leaves, white-to-lavender flowers, and tannish, round seeds, *Coriandum sativum* is versatile enough to be included in healing gardens, kitchen gardens, children's gardens, beverage gardens, Biblical gardens, pollinator gardens, and scented gardens. Sales of its leaves, known as *cilantro* in the United States, have soared over the last three decades, particularly with the rise in popularity of Mexican and Thai cuisines. Cilantro is a major ingredient in most salsas; corn chips and dips come in cilantro-lime flavors; and at least three fresh-ingredient Tex-Mex chains, Moe's, Baja Fresh, and Qdoba, offer freshly chopped cilantro leaves for their burritos and tacos.

Coriander leaf's distinctive scent led ancient and medieval cultures to surmise that such a strong smelling plant must possess curative and magical powers. Assigned to the planet Mars, under the element of fire, coriander is associated with love, healing, and health. Coriander seeds and leaves contain many chemical constituents—from linalool to flavonoids to aldehydes; when ingested or used topically, these substances can bring about changes in the body. Whether we call that magical thinking or scientific objectivity, flavorful coriander has served cultures globally as a culinary star, aphrodisiac, scent, medicine, and preservative.

Fresh coriander leaves can stimulate and increase appetite. To ninety percent of the population, cilantro's nearly indescribable scent with its sagey, citrusy undertones is invigorating and enticing, while the other ten percent (so vocal you'd think it was more!) is genetically averse to its scent. With the exception of such mimics as *rau răm (Persicaria odorata), culantro (Eryngium foetidum), papaloquelite (Porophylum ruderale),* and some rare peperomias, no other plant smells—or excites—quite like cilantro.

The Bible tells us that manna tasted like coriander. Roman soldiers under Julius Caesar used the ground seed to preserve and flavor food on expeditions; Algerians still preserve food with coriander, salt, and pepper. Traditionally added to preserve meats, crushed coriander seed contains substances that can kill bacteria, insect larvae, and fungi. Medicinally, ground coriander can be sprinkled into cleaned minor wounds and abrasions to reduce or prevent infections (Castleman 138). Chewing coriander seeds after eating garlic can reduce the scent on the breath and ease digestion.

As far back as the Han Dynasty, the Chinese consumed coriander seed to enhance libido. In *One Thousand and One Nights,* the story-within-a-story that Scheherazade crafted to entertain and enthrall her sultan husband, a love potion containing coriander helps a couple childless for forty years to conceive at long last.

Centuries later, Europeans infused crushed coriander in wine as an aphrodisiac. According to some traditions, to bring a budding romance to a head, the newly enamored could steep coriander seeds and dried marjoram together in wine and serve warmed. If marriage were the aim, for three months one could wear an amulet or carry a sachet filled with coriander seeds and yarrow. To strengthen the charm, chant when cutting the yarrow:

I cut thee, Yarrow,

So that Love may grow.

Secretly, women during the Middle Ages might secure a string of coriander seeds to their inner thighs as a talisman to promote fertility, preferably during a waxing moon. The number of seeds varied from 11 to 30, based on availability, menstrual rhythms, superstition, or age. According to an old adage, coriander can bring on good outcomes: "If pregnant women eat coriander, their child will be ingenious" (Cunningham 25).

Coriander in the language of flowers means *hidden worth*. In poetry and romance, herbs and flowers offer a versatile yet subtle form of communication to express love, congratulations, commiseration, and other sentiments appropriate to social situations and religious ceremonies (Reppert 104). The 16th century poem "To Mistress Margaret Hussey" by John Skelton opens with flower and animal imagery to praise the woman he loves:

> *Merry Margaret*
> *As midsummer flower*
> *Gentle as falcon*
> *Or hawk of the tower.*

A few lines later, he rhymes "Coriander" and "Sweet pomander" as evidence of her evocative scent and his romantic feelings.

Since folks lived much closer to nature in earlier times, observing coriander plants mature from leaf to flower, pollinated by bees and many other insects, then turn into rounded fruits, green to brown, might have suggested fertility and pregnancy to the ancients. In addition, coriander's ability to produce numerous viable seeds would reinforce its aphrodisiacal aspect.

Does coriander really help in the bedroom? According to Ayurvedic medicine, consuming coriander promotes mental clarity, improves mood and memory, and relieves lethargy and anxiety (McIntyre 351). Coriander can also reduce stress, a major libido-depressant, making it an effective aphrodisiacal aid. If lovemaking is thwarted by tension in the home, folklore suggests tying a bunch of fresh coriander leaves with a red ribbon to hang in the kitchen to restore harmony and balance (Telesco 98).

While the seed is traditionally used in digestive teas, its fresh, citrusy flavor can also be used to mask bitter, unpleasant medicines. As such, coriander has a special affinity with liquor and is an integral ingredient in cordials like Benedictine and Chartreuse. The ancient Egyptians believed that adding coriander to wine increased its intoxicating effects. The Victorians celebrated life-changing events by steeping crushed coriander seeds with a sprig of basil in red wine, served in special goblets to mark new beginnings (98). For those who want to avoid alcohol, bruise or crush coriander seeds and steep in honey for a sweet aphrodisiacal treat.

Whether combined with sugar or steeped in honey, coriander has long appealed to our sweet tooth and is commonly added to cookies, cakes, breads, and candies. In C. Clement Moore's "A Visit from Saint Nicholas," children dream of coriander on the night before Christmas:

'Twas the night before Christmas, when all through the house
Not a creature was stirring, not even a mouse;
The stockings were hung by the chimney with care,
In hopes that St. Nicholas soon would be there;
The children were nestled all snug in their beds,
While visions of sugar-plums danced in their heads[.]

Not the sugared fruits of my imagination, sugar plums were actually small, brightly colored, oval or spherical crunchy confections of sugar-coated seeds, most often coriander, caraway, or cardamom. Those candies were once known as *comfits, dragees,* and *sugar plums.* Difficult to make because the sugar coating had to be built up a layer at a time, these candies were an expensive and popular holiday treat in 1823 when the poem first appeared.

The term *sugar plum* later came to mean anything sweet and desirable, an expanded meaning Tchaikovsky used to great effect in "The Dance of the Sugar Plum Fairy" in his Nutcracker Ballet where holiday candy is heavily featured. By the late nineteenth century, such candies became cheaper and more universally available with the mechanized improvements of the Industrial Revolution. Today's equivalent, the round, hard Jawbreakers® had coriander seeds encased in their centers through the late twentieth century.

Coriander, a Level One herb generally recognized as safe (GRAS) in all of its forms, can, in extremely high doses, have a slightly narcotic or sedating effect, which accounts for one of its sillier names, *dizzycorn*. That would entail eating a great many sugar plums!

But, then, many foods with coriander—in all of its forms—go down easily.

May coriander dance in your gardens!

References

Benn Hurley, Judith. *The Good Herb: recipes and remedies from nature.* William Morrow & Co., 1995.

Buchanan, Rita. *The Shaker Herb and Garden Book.* Houghton Mifflin, 1996.

Castleman, Michael. *The Healing Herbs.* Rodale Press, 1991. 138-140.

Cunningham, Scott. *Magical Herbalism.* Llewellyn, 1995.

Kawash, Samira. "Sugar Plums: They're Not What You Think They Are." *The Atlantic.* December 2010. http://www.theatlantic. com/health/archive/2010/12/sugar-plums-theyre-not-what-you-think-they-are/68385/ Accessed 10/10/16.

Keville, Kathi. *Herbs: An Illustrated Encyclopedia.* Barnes & Noble, 1997. 72.

Laws, Bill. *Fifty Plants that Changed the Course of History.* Firefly, 2013. 51.

McIntyre, Anne. *The Ayurveda Bible: The definitive guide to Ayurvedic healing.* Godsfield/Octopus Publ., 2012.

Meunscher, Walter Conrad Leopold. *Garden Spice and Wild Pot-Herbs.* Cornell UP, 1955. 57.

Poetry Foundation, The. "To Mistress Margaret Hussey" by John Skelton. https:// www.poetryfoundation.org/poems-and-poets/poems/detail/50011. Accessed 6/23/16.

Reppert, Bertha. *Herbs for Weddings & Other Celebrations.* Storey Books, 1994.

Herbs of the Zodiac. The Rosemary House, 1984.

Rodale's Illustrated Encyclopedia of Herbs. Rodale Press, 1987.

Rupp, Rebecca. "What Are Sugar Plums Anyway?" *The Plate. National Geographic.* http://theplate.nationalgeographic. com/2014/12/23/visions-of-sugarplums/. Accessed 10/10/16.

Swenson, Allan A. *Plants of the Bible and How to Grow Them.* Citadel Press, 1995.

Telesco, Patricia. *The Victorian Grimoire: Enchantment, Romance, Magic.* Llewellyn, 1998.

Coriander products and mid-summer flowers. *Peter Coleman*

Passionate about herbs, Gert Coleman is a recently retired Associate Professor of English at Middlesex County College in New Jersey. Co-editor of the IHA newsletter, she frequently writes about the legends, lore, and poetry of herbs. Past president of the Staten Island Herb Society, Gert helps to maintain the Colonial Herb Garden at Conference House Park, lectures on various aspects of herbs, leads nature walks, and teaches workshops on nature writing. She has a BA from SUNY Geneseo, an MS from CUNY Richmond, and an MA from CUNY College of Staten Island.

To The Mistress
Margaret Hussey

John Skelton (1460?–1529)

I first heard this poem in a graduate poetry class. My professor, an expert on Renaissance literature, actually did a little dance when he read the line about coriander to romantically evoke the narrator's admiration for the lady's beauty and character. In my memory, he repeated the line "Coriander" but upon reading it again, I see that "coriander" (originally spelled "coliander") instead rhymes with "sweet pomander". The imagery is aromatic as well as romantic. ~GC

Merry Margaret

As midsummer flower,

Gentle as falcon

Or hawk of the tower:

With solace and gladness,

Much mirth and no madness,

All good and no badness;

So joyously,

So maidenly,

So womanly

Her demeaning

In every thing,

Far, far passing

That I can indite,

Or suffice to write

Of Merry Margaret

As midsummer flower,

Gentle as falcon

Or hawk of the tower.

As patient and still

And as full of good will

As fair Isaphill,

Coriander,

Sweet pomander,

Good Cassander;

Steadfast of thought,

Well made, well wrought,

Far may be sought,

Ere that ye can find

So courteous, so kind

As merry Margaret,

This midsummer flower,

Gentle as falcon

Or hawk of the tower.

A Sniff or a Snort—
Coriander Suits

Karen O'Brien

CORIANDER IS NOT something that necessarily comes to mind when one thinks of either fragrance or spirits. However, coriander has a rich history and a legacy of being an integral component in both scented products and alcohols, going back to ancient times.

Distillation of Essential Oils

Historically, those who created flavored brandies, liqueurs, and other alcoholic drinks were often involved in perfumes, as well. With a distillation unit, or still, precious oils were extracted that could be used either in flavoring alcohol or perfumes. In fact, many types of alcohol-based drinks could and indeed were used as both a libation and as a way to perfume one's body. Queen of Hungary water—created by a monk for Queen Isabel (or Elizabeth, depending on the account) circa 1370—was fashioned to be both imbibed and applied to her person, with positive results. The legend surrounding this "toilet water" includes directions to apply liberally to the body and to drink a specific amount each day, in order to keep the complexion young and flawless. It certainly seemed to work for the queen, as she was proposed to by the archduke of Lithuania when he was 25 and she was 73, if you can believe the stories. Another early perfume, Carmelite water, or *eau de Carmes*, was fashioned in 1379 by the nuns of Abbaye Saint Just. It consisted of coriander, angelica, lemon balm, cloves, and nutmeg. Sounds good enough to drink!

Several later writers enlarged and commented on earlier writings on distillation for both perfumes and alcohols. Giovanni Battista della Porta's *Magia Naturalis* (1537–1615) contains instruction in the chapter "Eleventh Book of Natural Magic" for distillation of perfumes and how to make "sweet water" by infusion, or as he refers to them, "perfumed liquors." Another treatise, *Chimie du goût et de l'odorat,* or *The Chemistry of Taste and Smell,* by Larbalestier Petit in 1774 also referred to scented waters and liqueurs to drink, aligning the two senses as was common at the time. Today, perfumes are now made with denatured alcohol, rendering them unfit for consumption.

Perfumes were not just used as a scent for the body, but frequently were used medicinally or to ward off pests, germs, or even evil spirits. The Chinese have a saying, "Every perfume is a medicine," and many essential oils do, in fact, act as antiseptics and antibacterials that are useful for microbial threats. In the latter part of the nineteenth century, it was found that workers in the perfumeries at Grasse, France, had a lower rate of cholera and tuberculosis than those not working with these essential oils.

Perfumes and Scenting

The first perfumes, though, were incense, and the word *perfume* comes from *per* (through) and *fumum* (smoke). In ancient Egypt, as offerings to the gods, when embalming the dead, and even in private homes, incense was prevalent in everyday life, and believed to be the key to a healthy and prosperous life. Incense served the dual purpose of attracting good influences while repelling maleficent spirits. The burning of incense—made of various herbs and spices—was essential to creating a harmonious home, while anointing oneself with fragrant oils or taking a scented bath also became an essential requirement in many cultures.

As sanitation was not always available, covering oneself with scent made life more bearable. It was fashionable in Egypt to adorn one's head with large wax cones impregnated with essential oils. As the heat of the day melted the wax, one's body would become saturated with the scent. King Hammurabi of Babylon decreed that everyone must bathe in scented waters or oils and coriander was one of the herbs grown in the famous Hanging Gardens. During the Krishna festival in India, perfumes are splashed on revelers to wash away the sins and impurities of the past year. Even today, in Latin American countries during Mardi Gras, partygoers delight in using *chisquetis* or perfume sprayers with abandon, filling the air with fragrance and fun.

The habit of using perfumes or essential oils daily, especially those containing coriander oil, is a wise move for one's health and well-being. Coriander oil contains twenty chemicals with antibacterial action that control body odor, and smells nice, to boot.

Egyptians with wax incense cones. *Karen O'Brien*

Coriander Through the Ages

The oldest archaeological find of coriander remains occurred in Nahal Hemar cave in Israel (7600–6000 B.C.). Coriander was mentioned in the *Ebers Papyrus* of 1550 B.C. and was well known to ancient Egyptians, the seeds being found in Tutankhamen's tomb. It was cultivated in Greece in the second century B.C.; tablets from Pylos indicate it was grown for its use in perfumes. Considered a key ingredient in love potions, it is also referred to in the story of Ala-al-Din Abu-al, better known as *One Thousand and One Nights*. Coriander was thought to be particularly effective as a love philter if picked in the last quarter of the moon. The Sanskrit author Someshvana (circa 1130) describes the daily bath of the king as being fragrant with sesame oil scented with jasmine, coriander, cardamom, holy basil, and saffron. In medieval England, a mixture containing coriander was used to conjure an army of demons, and remains of coriander seed were found in a Bronze Age settlement in Kent. George Wilson, apothecary to James II (1685–88), used it in his Honey Water as an aftershave. One of the earliest spices to be brought to the New World, coriander was grown in Massachusetts as early as 1670. It is clear that coriander has a long and valued presence around the world.

Coriander perfume. *Karen O'Brien*

The Allure of Coriander

Coriander oil is a pleasing blend of spicy, sweet, and woody scents. It is digestive, good for aching muscles, combats exhaustion and mental fatigue, and it stimulates circulation (hence its efficacy as an aphrodisiac). The ripened fruit, from which the oil is extracted, smells like orange, anise, and cumin. The oil is dominated by linalool (citrus), thymol (thyme), and geranyl acetate (geranium). Courterier, a perfume house of note, introduced a perfume in 1973 called *Coriandre*, which is still available today. The oil blends well with other scents such as clary sage, jasmine, and lilac. In the language of flowers, coriander means "hidden worth," which seems appropriate as it is almost never used solely but to great effect with other spices or scents.

Let's Drink to Coriander

Coriander is an ingredient in almost all gins, and in absinthe, aquavit, and pastis, most likely due to its complex flavors, especially the anise/licorice notes. Coriander fruit, or seed, undergoes a chemical change as it dries, changing the flavor dramatically. Many people do not like the taste of the coriander plant's leaves or flowers, also known as cilantro, claiming it tastes like soap. The word coriander comes from "koros" meaning "bug" and alludes to the smell of the leaves which some say smell like bedbugs. However, once the fruit is dry, there is no bug-like aroma, rather a clean, fresh taste that is very desirable in liqueurs and other spirits.

A spiced wine known as *Hippocras* was a popular drink of antiquity. First mentioned in writing in the 1300s, it was often included in receipt or other books and is a fermented drink dating back to much earlier times. The *manicum Hippocraticum*—or sleeve of Hippocrates—is a conical bag used to strain particles from the liquid and is attributed to the fifth century Greek physician Hippocrates. Edward Spencer described in 1898 how this drink was prepared:

Hippocras: Take of cardamine, carpolbalsamum of each half an ounce, coriander seeds prepared, nutmegs, ginger of each two ounces, cloves two drachms; bruise and infuse these two days in two gallons of the richest sweet cider, often stirring together, then add thereto of milk three pints, strain all through an hippocras bag, and sweeten with a pound of sugar candy.

I'll take my coriander in a gin martini, thank you!

Rose and coriander liqueur. *Susan Belsinger*

As I like both coriander and cilantro, I thought I would try making a liqueur using both. The result was a mild, pleasingly spicy and citrusy drink.

YIELDS 7 CUPS

3 cups 190-proof vodka
3 cups water
1/2 cup coriander seeds, whole
One large bunch fresh cilantro
Zest from two limes
1 cup water
1 cup sugar

In a 2-quart glass or other non-reactive container with a tight lid, mix the vodka and 3 cups of water. Add the coriander seeds, bunch of cilantro, and lime zest. Cover and place in a cool, dry place.

Shake every once in a while. Let infuse for a month. Strain the liquid through a fine mesh sieve or coffee filter into another container. In a small saucepan, heat the 1 cup of water and 1 cup of sugar until dissolved.

Let cool to room temperature, then add to the vodka mix. Let sit for another month to age. Enjoy!

This recipe is adapted from one of my favorite liqueur books **Folk Wines, Cordials & Brandies** *by M.A. Jagendorf. It is a lovely pink color because of the dark pink rose petals. Remember to use unsprayed, fresh, and fragrant petals.*

YIELDS 2 TO 3 QUARTS

2 quarts fresh rose petals
2 quarts water
1/2 to 1 pound sugar
1 to 2 quarts brandy or vodka
1 ounce broken cinnamon stick or chips
1 ounce coriander seeds

Take 1 quart of rose petals and put them in a gallon glass jar or a crock. Pour over them a little more than 1 quart lukewarm water. Cover and let stand for 24 hours. Strain into an enamel or glass vessel, squeezing every drop out of the rose petals.

Pick another quart of scented rose petals and put those into the rose water. Let stand for 48 hours, then strain, squeezing the petals dry. You can repeat this a few times, as long as you have enough roses, until the liquid is strongly rose-scented.

Now add half to 1 pound sugar (depending on how sweet you like it), and 1 to 2 quarts of any brandy, vodka, or alcohol (depending on how strong you want it), 1 ounce broken stick cinnamon, and 1 ounce coriander. Cover well and let stand for three to four weeks. Then strain and bottle.

References

Duke, James A. *Herbs of the Bible: 200 Years of Plant Medicine*. Interweave Press, 1999.

Gallowglass.org/jadwiga/herbs/hungarywater.html. Accessed July 2, 2016.

Grieve, Maud. *A Modern Herbal: Vol 1*. Harcourt, Brace & Co, 1931.

Hawkins, Kathryn and Gail Duff. *A Dash of Spice*. Chartwell Books, 1997.

Hayes, Elizabeth S. *Spices and Herbs Around the World*. Doubleday & Co, 1961.

Historicfood.com/HippocrasRecipes.htm. Accessed July 2, 2016.

Jagendorf, M.A. *Folk Wines, Cordials, & Brandies*. Vanguard Press, 1963.

Johnson, Paula. *The Language of Herbs and Their Companions*. The Herb Patch, 1988.

Leyel, Mrs. C.F. *Herbal Delights*. Grammercy Publishing Co., 1986.

Manniche, Lise. *An Egyptian Herbal*. The American University Press, 2006.

Morris, Edwin T. *Fragrance: The Story of Perfume from Cleopatra to Chanel*. Charles Scribner's Sons, 1984.

Norman, Jill. *The Complete Book of Spices*. Viking Studio, 1990.

Porta, John Baptisia. *Natural Magick (Magiae natrualis)*. Accessed July 2, 2016. http://www.faculty.umb.edu/gary_zabel/Courses/Phil%20281b/Philosophy%20of%20Magic/Natural_Magic/jportat2.html.

Sayre, James Kedzie. *Ancient Herbs and Modern Herbs: A Comprehensive Reference Guide to Medicinal Herbs, Human Ailments and Possible Herbal Remedies*. Bottlebrush Press, 2001.

Stewart, Amy. *The Drunken Botanist*. Algonquin Books, 2013.

Verril, A. Hyatt. *Perfumes and Spices*. L.C. Page & Co, 1945.

Karen O'Brien runs her herbal business "The Green Woman's Garden" in the central Massachusetts town of Mendon. She grows herbs, heirloom vegetables, and ornamental flowers, runs workshops on various herbal adventures, and occasionally participates at farmers' markets and fairs. She has gardened for more than thirty years and is certified as a Master Gardener. She is the Botany and Horticulture Chair of The Herb Society of America, has served as Chairman of the New England Unit of HSA, is Secretary of the International Herb Association, is a member of Garden Writers, and has edited four IHA Herb of the Year™ books: *Capsicum 2016, Savory 2015, Artemisia 2014,* and *Elder 2013.*

Coriander Haiku

Mat Spano

MY DAUGHTER AND I planted and harvested coriander—the lingering scent on my fingers took me back to many previous memories of enjoying this wonderful plant with loved ones. You might even say that I followed the scent through the labyrinth of memory to some wonderful times. Imagine my surprise when I discovered that coriander may be etymologically linked to Ariadne (Minos' daughter whose spool of thread—also called a "clue"—allowed Theseus to find his way out of the labyrinth to his beloved and to safety)! I tried to capture all of this in the haiku.

coriander scent
lingers on my fingertips
Ariadne's clue

Mathew V. Spano has published poetry, short stories, and essays in various literary journals and anthologies over the last twenty years, the best of which appears in his recent book *Hellgrammite* (BLAST Press, 2016). He teaches English Composition and Mythology in Literature at Middlesex County College in Edison, New Jersey, where he also serves as Freshman Composition Coordinator. He earned his Ph.D. in Comparative Literature from Rutgers University, his dissertation focusing on the work of Nobel laureate Hermann Hesse. An avid fly-fisherman, he lives with his family in central New Jersey.

Cilantro leaves. *Pat Kenny*

When Did Cilantro First Tease Our Taste Buds?

Diann Nance

You MAY BE surprised that, growing up in Texas in the 1950s, I was not familiar with cilantro since now it's synonymous with Tex-Mex food. Because coriander (the seed) was prevalent in Mexico, everyone assumes that the taste for Mexican food would have been responsible for the leaves (cilantro) wending their way north to the United States. However, I don't remember cilantro being used much in Tex-Mex restaurants. Coriander was an important spice, even in Texas. Cucumbers could not be pickles without coriander, and you can't make delicious spiced peaches without coriander. Cilantro, or *Chinese parsley,* as it was called when I first encountered it, was a rarity. Cilantro would have been difficult to grow since it doesn't tolerate the summer heat.

Recently I've wondered how cilantro made its way to the United States. I believe it's not coincidental that cilantro rose in popularity in the late 60s and 70s as Americans were returning from stays in Asia during the Vietnam War. It wouldn't be the first time in history that war caused foods and herbs from one part of the world to move to another. The Crusades created a demand in Europe for herbs and spices from the Orient.

I got my first real introduction to cilantro while living in Taiwan from 1965 to 1966. I had gone to Taiwan for a year to teach high school students who were dependents of military advisory personnel taking part in the Vietnam conflict. Yes, the United States was involved in Vietnam as early as 1965. That year was filled with many culinary firsts for me. After a briefing in San Francisco, I was winging my way east and experienced my first exotic fruits, papaya and mango, when we had a layover in

Hawaii. Even though papayas and mangos are very common in grocery stores now, I still savor that first velvety, sweet bite of mango.

In Taipei, Taiwan, I gathered with other teachers. There, we were treated to Peking Duck, another exotic culinary experience. The duck came to the table whole, and the first savory slice was crispy skin with a sliver of meat which we wrapped around a scallion for an appetizer. The entrée was slices of the dark meat served with sticky rice and vegetables. In Asia, desserts were rare; instead the meal ended with thin, highly-seasoned soup, possibly made from the bones of the entrée.

Another teacher and I chose to take the train down-island to our assigned schools. Seeing the villages and the landscape gave us a perspective on our new home. Although the tea service did not involve food, it was a magical experience. How one person in the narrow aisle of a moving train could manage a huge kettle of boiling water while picking up a glass, removing the lid, retrieving a small paper bag of tea from his apron pocket, opening the tea bag, putting loose tea in the glass, pouring hot water into the glass, putting the lid back on the glass, and returning it to the cup holder without spilling a drop or burning anyone never ceased to amaze me, even after seeing this event several times.

Every day was an adventure, especially shopping in the local markets and getting used to the food. Four of us lived right in the middle of Tainan, Taiwan, sharing a Japanese house left over from the Japanese occupation. Although we had access to the commissary on the military base, when it was my turn to manage the kitchen, I liked to go with Ashu, our house-girl, to get a few things at the local market—mostly fruits and vegetables, sometimes fresh fish or a duck. But we never mastered Peking Duck. It was Ashu's first job, and she was just learning to cook, so we learned some lessons together. The one I remember vividly is that Chinese peppers can be extremely hot. The only Asian experience I had had in Texas was eating in Mandarin Chinese restaurants; I had no knowledge then of Szechwan Chinese or Korean cuisine, which can be quite hot. I just wanted to spice up some cauliflower with a little chile. Wearing no gloves, I chopped my little chile, put it in the cauliflower, then wiped my upper lip with my hand. My face was on fire for two days. Texas chili had never been that hot.

The staple food was noodles. Our house was located in a lane off the main thoroughfare. The people who lived in the house at the corner made noodles to sell twice a week. They would hang the eight-foot long noodles outside to dry over a rack similar to a clothes drying rack. I'm sure cooking dispelled any gifts left by the flies that attended the drying. We were often warned about eating the local fare, but our digestive systems quickly adjusted to it.

I often got up early to see the farmers bringing produce in from the country. I was fascinated by the ones balancing half a pork carcass on a bicycle. I never saw one fall. Locals sat outside on their haunches around their hibachis keeping warm and eating breakfast of sticky rice and broth. The first time I went to a market for rice in Tainan, I was confounded to see at least a dozen different kinds of rice. Before my visit to the market, I didn't know there were so many kinds of rice.

One of the special eating places we discovered was a Mongolian barbecue restaurant located in a lean-to attached to a residence. The cafe did not keep regular hours, but it was within a few blocks of our house, so we easily found out when it was open. An enormous tub held tender thinly-sliced meat (probably pork) heavily seasoned with garlic; another tub held Chinese parsley; and there was a basket of pocket bread. We filled our pocket bread with a generous helping of meat, which was not really Mongolian nor was it barbecued; it was more like stir-fried. A generous portion of cilantro topped off this treat which became one of my favorite culinary memories. The strong flavor of cilantro was a perfect complement for the highly-seasoned meat. As Mongolian barbecue became popular and migrated to the West, a variety of vegetables was added, but cilantro remained an essential ingredient of the dish and spread as the popularity of the dish carried it to America. Last weekend, my grandson, who just started college, came to visit, and asked if I had ever tasted Mongolian barbecue. He had discovered a Mongolian barbecue restaurant in Martin, Tennessee.

Upon my return to Texas in 1966, one of my sisters and her husband were growing their first crop of cilantro. I had traveled around the world, and it was like a little piece of my journey had preceded me back home. They were growing it to put in salsa, another recent addition to Texas cuisine. In a few years cilantro seemed to be everywhere.

At the 2016 IHA Conference Tina Marie Wilcox asked the attendees if they had had cilantro when they were young. Only a few responded positively. There's an assumption that cilantro came from Mexico long ago where coriander had been grown and used for many years. However, my theory is that it came more directly from Asia, and that the desire for cilantro traveled with Americans having developed a taste for it while serving in the Far East during the Vietnam War.

Diann Nance, born and raised on a farm in north central Texas, is presently living and growing herbs among the beautiful rolling hills of Tennessee. After a forty-year teaching career which included time spent in Texas, Taiwan, Germany, and finally Tennessee, she realized a long held dream of starting a plant-growing business. Diann's Greenhouse specializes in herbs, propagating over 150 varieties of culinary, medicinal, and aromatic plants.

Diann's interest in herbs and their uses in our daily life can be attributed to her mother who loved plants and sharing her knowledge. Diann continues this tradition by growing plants, conducting workshops, and demonstrating the uses of herbs. Diann is a Master Gardener, an active member of the Beachaven Garden Club, the Herb Society of America, and the International Herb Association, and a curious learner about all plants and nature in general. Diann currently serves as president of the International Herb Association, which chooses the Herb of the Year™ and publishes the Herb of the Year™ series.

You may like Diann's Greenhouse on Facebook. Diann's contact information and quarterly newsletter can be found at diann'sgreenhouse.com.

The Rest of the Story
Other Uses for Coriander

Davy Dabney

When most people hear the word *cilantro* or *coriander*, they think of seasoning for food. However, it is only relatively recently that *Coriandrum sativum* has come into such favor in so many places in the world. Most people would be surprised to learn that cilantro (the leaves) and coriander (the seed) have played many roles over the centuries in the Middle East, Asia, and Central America. Native to Morocco, Asia, and the Mediterranean, coriander was brought to England by the Romans. There are two species of cilantro, but only one, *C. sativum*, is used extensively.

This 12- to 24-inches tall annual now grows in North and South America, Europe, China, India and the Mediterranean area. Small roots produce finely cut leaves and, during mid-to-late-summer, white to reddish flowers bloom on compound umbels, resulting in round, light brown seeds. The green seeds emit a rather unpleasant odor—to some people—until they ripen and produce a spicy aroma. The longer the seeds dry, the better they smell. To retain the best fragrance, store whole dried seeds in a closed glass container in a cool, dark place. Formerly thought to have aphrodisiac effects, coriander is now effectively used as an antispasmodic, appetite-stimulant, digestive, and flavoring to improve the taste of medicines.

Ancient civilizations used plants along with rituals and other charms to enhance lifestyle and cure ailments. As long ago as 1000 BC, Egyptians fed coriander, garlic, mint, grains, and seeds to the slaves who worked on the pyramids to give them energy to work longer hours. Coriander was referred to as "the herb of happiness" when used to flavor wine. Cleopatra used coriander in cosmetics and for fragrance. The Romans made it into sweet lozenges to settle stomachs after their enormous banquets.

Widely known as a digestive, a cure for flatulence, a meat preservative, and a wound healer, coriander has been mentioned in the Bible, in *One Thousand and One Nights,* and many other stories. According to legend, witches used it in love and other potions. Found in ancient tombs, coriander is one of the oldest herbs known and one of the ingredients in formulas used in the preservation of bodies. In India it has been used in Ayurvedic remedies. During the mid-1800s and later, crushed coriander was used in medicinal bitters. More recent studies have discovered many other useful attributes for both cilantro and coriander. It is listed by the FDA as GRAS (generally recognized as safe).

Now that aromatherapy has joined the medical community as a useful protocol, studies have shown that the oil made from coriander seed may be effective in several areas. For example it may be used to lessen symptoms of ADD and ADHD. An ingredient in coriander oil may prevent a bad enzyme (AChE) from attacking the part of the brain that causes memory loss. Studies are now underway to discover if the oil can be of help in controlling diabetes, and of course it is still effective as a stomach soother and aid for colic, as a flavoring for liqueurs, tobaccos, and as an ingredient in men's grooming aids.

Chemical analysis of cilantro oil shows the largest amounts of the following: linalool, decanal, trans-2 decanal, a-piene, y-terpinene, plus much smaller amounts of several others. Chemical analysis of coriander seed oil showed it contains linalool, a-pinene, y-terpinene, geraniol acetate, camphor, plus smaller amounts of 11 other oils.

One cup of whole seed weighs 2.94 ounces. One cup of ground seed weighs 3.57 ounces. It takes about 67 pounds of whole seed to make 16 ounces of coriander oil. The oil extracted from both cilantro and coriander by steam distillation varies from almost clear to a very pale yellow. Experts recommend using it sparingly as it is a soporific in larger amounts.

The only way you can know for sure that any essential oil you buy is pure is by proper testing. Many oils are diluted or blended with cheaper oils and are therefore not of any use for aromatherapy. When you know what makes up the essential oils you are using, it is easier to make blends that work together. It can also help you to choose substitutes with the same effects, in case your original choice isn't available. Seeds of the 'Jantar' variety of cilantro originally grown in Ukraine are richest in essential oils. Seeds from plants grown in England and Russia usually provide the most oil.

Due to the relatively small use of many medicinal plants when compared to the large support for improving plants for fodder and cereal grains, support from private and government sources is vital to the continuing improvement of herbs such as cilantro, chamomile, marjoram and hyssop. For species with multiple uses, new cultivars are necessary.

There are many uses for cilantro and coriander beyond the culinary.

Insect Repellent for Plants

Chop enough cilantro leaves, stems, and flower heads into small pieces to make a cupful. Heat 1 quart of water in a 2-or 3-quart pan until tiny bubbles start to form. Turn off heat and add chopped herb. Stir and cover. Let steep overnight. Strain into a large bowl and press the herbs against the strainer to extract as much liquid as possible. Discard herbs in compost pile. Add 1 teaspoon unscented liquid soap and stir to blend. (The soap will help the liquid to adhere to the leaves). Pour into a spray bottle and shake.

To repel chewing insects, be sure to spray both the top and bottom of the leaves. Repeat as often as necessary. Safe to use on food crops.

Carpet Freshener

Chop 2/3 cup each of fresh mint, thyme, and lemon balm with 1/3 cup ground coriander seed. Put in blender with 1 cup baking soda. Blend and sprinkle over carpet. Leave overnight and vacuum the next day.

Muscle Massage

Into an 8 ounce bottle, pour 1/2 cup witch hazel, 3 drops lemon essential oil, and 2 drops coriander essential oil. Shake well. Rub on legs after exercise, especially if you can't take a shower right away.

Cilantro flower. *Alicia Mann*

Achy Joints Poultice

To make a poultice for rheumatic joints, crush 1/2 cup coriander seed with 1/3 cup black mustard seed, adding just enough water to make a paste. Spread paste on a piece of flannel a little larger than the area you wish to cover. Place over achy joint with soft side against skin. Use gauze to bind gently but not tightly and leave in place for up to 30 minutes. For those with sensitive skin, substitute 1/2 cup crushed comfrey leaves for the mustard.

Home-Style Potpourri

To create the base, or fixative, add 6 drops coriander essential oil, 5 drops orange essential oil, and 1/2 teaspoon of pure vanilla extract to 1/2 cup chopped dried moss, or oak moss. Put in glass container and shake till oil is distributed. Store for two or more days. Meanwhile, have ready some dried herbs and flowers, such as pink or white clover, dried violet leaves, sage leaves, and any other pretty flowers you have collected and dried. Blend them together with the fixative and put in a pretty container. This is a great project for children. Their ideas may surprise you.

Through the centuries trial and error have played a large role in discovering uses for plants, but modern methods have made it much easier and quicker to bring new and natural remedies into being. As people are demanding more natural products, let us hope that those engaged in doing scientific studies will continue to find new ways for plants to play a vital role in human and animal health.

Remember to always take time to try new ideas. That's how discoveries are made!

References

Bailey, Liberty Hyde. *Hortus Third*. Macmillan, 1976.

Duke, James A. *Handbook of Medicinal Herbs*. CRC Press, 1986.

Foster, Steven and James A. Duke. *Eastern/Central Medicinal Herbs*. Houghton Mifflin, 1989.

Grieve, Maude *A Modern Herbal*. Dover Publications, 1982.

Tyler, Varro E. *Pharmacognosy*, 9 ed. Lea & Febiger, 1988.

Valnet, Jean. *The Practice of Aromatherapy*. C.W. Daniel Co., 1982.

Verlet, N. and G. Leclercq. "Production and Breeding of Medicinal and Aromatic Plants in the European Union." *Symposium Proceedings in Trade*. C.W. Daniel Co, 1998. 121-123.

Davy Dabney, a founding member of the IHA (originally known as IHGMA, the International Herb Growers and Marketers Association), has been a business owner, an instructor, and mentor in the world of herbs and plants. She is a Life Member of The Herb Society of America, member of the Kentucky Herb Business Association, and owner of Dabney Herbs. With the help of the Wednesday Weeders, she has planted and tended a superior herb garden at Farmington Historic Home in Kentucky. In 2003 she became Superintendent of the Plant and Flower Department of the Kentucky State Fair. During the 10-day fair, her department takes in and displays over 3000 entries including plants and arrangements. Recently, due to the loss of a 100-year old maple tree, Davy has been redesigning her garden from shade to a low maintenance, sun-filled space. She loves learning about exciting new plants, consulting and writing, and occasionally sitting on her deck with friends, enjoying the beauty of nature, and letting someone else do the weeding!

Green coriander seeds. *Karen O'Brien*

Meeting the Stranger
Called "Coriander"

Matthias Reisen

THERE IT IS, that plant in the garden that we don't know. Maybe we planted the seed, or somehow it might have just showed up because we need it.

How do you introduce yourself to a plant, enter into its world when you don't know it, don't care about it, and have no desire to meet it? How can that be?

One thing we have to remember both in the plant and human world is that everything has an essence to add to the recipe of life, as we are all connected.

How can we start that interface, that connection, that communication with coriander (*Coriandrum sativum*)?

Reading this book will start your journey learning. Then go to the web and read, read, read, and get hundreds of different ideas and confused concepts.

Go take a couple of cooking classes explaining the many different ways to use coriander. Your food and beverages will be enhanced by the good taste that is added by coriander. You missed a whole series of such cooking classes if you weren't at the 2016 IHA Conference in Maryland.

Find out how it grows in your area, the best time to seed, and whether you should do multiple plantings to ensure a continuous supply of this delicious herb. Then plant some coriander (also known as cilantro) seeds and every few days visit your garden to see what is happening.

If you don't want to get your hands dirty (shame on you!), go to your local plant nursery and purchase a few plants and put them on your windowsill and watch them grow.

Sit down with the plant and have a conversation. Write down what it said with your non-dominant hand and journey with its content. What is it saying to you?

Invite the plant into your dream time to leave a footprint you can follow into your awake time. If that's not clear enough to you, devise a method of communication in the dream time that you can work with. For example, write its name on the blackboard or bring it up on a computer screen.

Draw, paint, or illustrate the plant and experience the feeling. I like to sit down and write a poem about what feelings and emotions flow through the plant to help with my healing process.

Matthias Reisen has been a community herbalist for over 25 years. He co-founded Healing Spirits Herb Farm and Education Center with his wife Andrea in 1991. Healing Spirits Herb Farm is located in western New York and produces high-quality, certified organic medicinal herbs both fresh and dry for shipment throughout the United States and some foreign countries. Together they have created their own line of products under the Healing Spirits label and also produce Rosemary Gladstar's line of quality products on the farm. He is a former Peace Corp volunteer in the Philippines and has consulted overseas in Belarus, Nepal, Jamaica, Colombia, and the Dominican Republic regarding medicinal and aromatic plants. Together he and Andrea have raised five children; there are three generations now living on the farm.

Matthias has been involved with many different aspects of working with the land and receives his greatest pleasure from teaching people about the land and plants. Matthias has a B.Sc. in Agronomy and has completed the one year course in Biodynamic Agriculture at the Pfeiffer Center. Matthias is also past president of the International Herb Association. healingspiritsherbfarm.com

In Praise of
the Coriander Seed

Emanuel di Pasquale

within the coriander seed

where blackness feeds

lives the cosmic brightness

of genesis

the full smile of God

where Mother Nature lives

it opens

and connects with the divinity of earth

rain-driven

heat leavened

Emanuel di Pasquale is currently Poet Laureate of Long Branch, New Jersey. He is an editor, a poet, and a translator. His latest translation was Dante's *La Vita Nuova*. His latest two books are *The Ocean's Will* (Guernica) and *Self-Portrait* (The New York Quarterly Press). He teaches English at Middlesex County College in Edison, New Jersey.

Coriander seeds. *Susan Belsinger*

Coriander:
Manna from Heaven

Diann Nance

THERE IS EVIDENCE of coriander (*Coriandrum sativum*) being cultivated in ancient Egypt, and passages from the Bible clearly show that the Jews were familiar with it and its uses. The references in Exodus and Numbers show that coriander was considered a life-sustaining source of food. Whether the allusion was literal, metaphorical, or spiritual does not alter the fact that these references illustrate the historical importance of coriander.

When Moses rescued the Israelites and led them out of Egypt, they wandered in the desert; many of them were unhappy with the hardships they endured. They grumbled to Moses, "Why did we ever leave Egypt?" (Numbers 11:20). "Would that we had died at the Lord's hand in the land of Egypt…You had to lead us into this desert to make the whole community die of famine!" (Exodus 16:3). They even romanticized their time of enslavement. "Oh, how well off we were in Egypt!" (Numbers 11:18). "In Egypt we sat by our fleshpots and ate our fill of bread" (Exodus 16:3). It's not likely that as slaves in Egypt they were treated to much meat or even to all the bread they wanted to eat.

God heard their complaining and promised Moses that he would feed them, "I will now rain down bread from heaven" (Exodus 16:4). "And in the morning [you shall have] your fill of bread" (Exodus 16:12).

"At night when the dew fell upon the camp, the manna also fell" (Numbers 11:9). "In the morning a dew lay all about the camp, and when the dew evaporated, there on the surface of the desert were fine flakes like hoar-frost on the ground. On seeing it, the Israelites asked one another, 'What is this?' for they did not know what it was, but Moses told them, 'This is the bread which the Lord has given you to eat'" (Exodus 16:13–15).

"When they had gone about and gathered it up, the people would grind it between millstones or pound it in a mortar, then cook it in a pot and make it into loaves, which tasted like cakes made with oil" (Numbers 16: 8). "Morning after morning they gathered it till each had enough to eat; but when the sun grew hot, the manna melted away" (Exodus 16: 21).

"The Israelites called this food manna. It was like coriander seed, but white, and it tasted like wafers made with honey" (Exodus 16: 31). This is confirmed in Numbers 11:7: "Manna was like coriander seed."

"The Israelites ate this manna for forty years, until they came to settled land; they ate manna until they reached the borders of Canaan" (Exodus 16:3).

Coriander seems a strange source of nutrition to depend on for forty years. But apparently coriander has been a staple in some cultures for hundreds, even thousands, of years. According to Pennsylvania State Extension Service, coriander originated in southern Europe and reached other areas centuries ago. It was even included in the Hanging Gardens of Babylon. Several ancient documents, including Sanskrit texts, Egyptian papyrus records, as well as the Bible, all mention coriander. The Chinese believed it imparted immortality. Maybe the Israelites thought so also.

Carolyn Adams Roth, who edits the blog *godasgardener.com* states that the origin of coriander is "most likely the Eastern Mediterranean or Asia Minor. In ancient times coriander plants grew wild in Egypt and Israel. Coriander has been used to enhance the taste of food for more than 5000 years. Today, in the Middle East coriander seeds are used to flavor bread."

Theologians and historians have speculated for years as to just what manna was. It's not likely that I could solve the mystery; however, whether manna was coriander or something else isn't as important as the fact that Moses and the Israelites were familiar enough with and thought highly enough of coriander to give it a place of significance not enjoyed by many herbs.

Diann's bio appears on page 82.

Cilantro/Coriander—Love It!

Stephanie L. Parello

No MATTER HOW you look at it, I'm on the "love it" side of this champion herb. I can't even decide which part I like best. And despite experience, cilantro (*Coriandrum sativum*) never ceases to surprise me in food—its bright flavor catches me off-guard even when I know it's in there—it lifts my palate and alters my perspective.

Then there's the plant itself. Its delicate greenery is visually fancier than plain ol' parsley (well, at least the flat-leaf kind) especially as the stem grows taller and the upper leaves transform into fine, ferny, feathery elegance.

Every part of the coriander plant is edible. The long taproot so indicative of its Apiaceae family (along with Queen Anne's Lace and carrots) makes cilantro difficult to transplant once it gets going, so sow in situ. And remember to eat the roots at the end of the season—they have even more intense flavor than the leaves!

The beautiful, tiny, white flowers deserve admiration for their variable petals that point away from the slight pink details in the compound center—and can be added as a pretty garnish for a hint of what's in store.

For continual bounty, sow cilantro every 2 to 3 weeks as it grows quite quickly—from seed to seedling to leafy harvest to bolting flowers, and then to those seeds.

Those lovely, lovely seeds! As much as I love the leaves for their bright refreshing zing, when the flowers give way to ripened seeds, I can't help but pluck a few from my front herb box as I head out into the world. With the delightful crunch of their woody shell, those little gems awaken my senses and put pep in my step.

Now, while I love it, some people (about 10%) adamantly swear cilantro smells and tastes like soap. Turns out, they're not lying. Our DNA includes about 400 olfactory (smell) receptor genes. And since smell impacts taste by 80%, it makes sense that if you have a gene that causes you to be hyper-aware of certain smells—in the case of cilantro, specific aldehydes that are also involved in the production of soap—there's a good chance you may think cilantro is soapy.

Genes are funny things, though. Just because you have a particular gene or gene variation, doesn't necessarily mean it gets turned on (or off)—this is the realm of meta-genetics (which has nothing to do with metaphysics). There's great potential for more study about which genes might be involved in the great cilantro-disgust some people experience.

Other cilantro-haters claim that cilantro smells musty, like bedbugs. Personally, I've never smelled a bedbug, but apparently they can emit distress pheromones that stink. And some say they smell like…coriander leaves.

Still, I'd like to forget the bedbug theory of how coriander got its name. In the world of language in general, and etymology (word origin) in particular, the paths between words of one language to another, or between an ancient form of a language and more modern versions, often twist and turn in strange and interesting ways—but sometimes they're amazingly straight.

As herbalists we know we must always return to the botanical name to be sure we're talking about what we're really talking about—that is, common names sometimes stretch far from the scientific family or genus we mean. In the same way, the claim that the name *coriander* derives from the Greek word *koris* for bedbug is a stretch that goes too far. I believe that closer inspection of history, archeology, and linguistic anthropology reveals that the name coriander really originates from two very similar words that name the same herb, in ancient Dioskurides (~2000 years old) and Mycenaean (±16,000 years old) Greek words—*korion* and *koriadna*, respectively. So, the word coriander to name this plant has quite a long history, indeed! References to a linguistic association to *koris* have only been around only a couple hundred years.

This would be a rather lengthy dissertation if I were to belabor all the details—to the point you'd fall asleep. Interestingly enough, I subsequently discovered a scholar who shares my opinion, and has done the historical work on this. New Zealand anthropologist Helen Leach wrote an article in 2001 for a journal called *Gastronomica* in which she traces coriander's etymology as well as its ins-and-outs of fashion throughout history. Her article is well worth a read if you can get your hands on it. Her insight reassures my suspicion that this whole bedbug claim is an unfortunate case of bitter bias against cilantro, which, being a good story, has been unwittingly propagated as the final word.

And speaking of bitter, what of coriander being used as one of the bitter herbs for Passover? I don't find it bitter at all. Is this another case of genetics allowing me to enjoy this herb more than other people?

All that said, I remain firmly on the "love it" side of this herb, so perhaps it is I who is attempting to redeem the distinguished name of cilantro and coriander.

Cilantro flowers. *Stephanie Parello*

References

Callaway, Ewen. "Soapy taste of coriander linked to genetic variants: Dislike of herb traced to genes encoding odour and taste receptors." *Nature.* 12 September 2012. http://www.nature.com/news/soapy-taste-of-coriander-linked-to-genetic-variants-1.11398. Accessed June 30, 2016.

Eriksson, Nicholas; Wu, Shirley; Do, Chuong B; Kiefer, Amy K; Yung, Joyce Y.; Mountain, Joanna L.; Hinds, David A.; Francke, Uta. "A genetic variant near olfactory receptor genes influences cilantro preference." *Flavour Journal.* Biomedical Central, 29 November 2012. https://flavourjournal.biomedcentral.com/articles/10.1186/2044-7248-1-22. Accessed June 30, 2016.

Gernot Katzer's Spice Pages - Coriander. (*Coriandrum sativum* bot L.). http://gernot-katzers-spice-pages.com/engl/Cori_sat.html. Accessed 30 June 2016.

Green, Hank. "Why Does Cilantro Taste Like Soap?" *SciShow.* 16 June 2015. https://www.youtube.com/watch?v=6ymoPRWxZl8. Accessed June 30, 2016.

Leach, Helen. "Rehabilitating the 'Stinking Herbe:' A Case Study of Culinary Prejudice."

Gastronomica: The Journal of Food and Culture. 1.2 (2001): 10-15. JSTOR.org. http://www.jstor.org/stable/10.1525/gfc.2001.1.2.10. Accessed June 30, 2016.

Ledbetter, Carly. "Science Explains Why Cilantro Tastes Like Soap For Certain People." *Huffington Post.* 24 June 2015. http://www.huffingtonpost.com/2015/06/24/why-does-cilantro-taste-bad-like-soap_n_7653808.html. Accessed June 30, 2016.

Oxford English Dictionary. http://www.oed.com. Accessed June 30, 2016.

Palaeolexicon: Word study tool for ancient languages (The Linear B word ko-ri-ja-da-na). http://www.palaeolexicon.com/ShowWord.aspx?Id=16788. Accessed June 30, 2016.

Vallance, Richard. "Coriander in Linear B. How does it measure up? Big time!" *Minoan Linear A, Linear B, Knossos & Mycenae Blog.* 1 March 2015. https://linearbknossosmycenae.wordpress.com/2015/03/01/coriander-in-linear-b-how-does-it-measure-up-big-time-click-to-enlarge/. Accessed June 30, 2016.

Wikipedia. https://en.wikipedia.org/wiki/Coriander. Accessed June 30, 2016.

Stephanie L. Parello is an ever-evolving polymath, and she delighted in meandering through the eclectic research path that lead to this article. She is on the board of the Staten Island Herb Society.

Coriander in the Cook's Herb Garden

Helen M. Leach

"I KNOW OF no other herb that is quite so provocative," said Elisabeth Lambert Ortiz, the author of authoritative books on both Mexican and Japanese cooking. She was referring to *Coriandrum sativum's* capacity to divide the world into coriander users and abusers. Mexicans, Peruvians, Indians, Afghans, Egyptians, Moroccans, and Portuguese rank among the passionate users of both the aromatic dried seed heads (technically fruits) and the young green leaves. The Thai even consume the root, grinding it into a paste with garlic for their distinctive green and red curries.

Many other cultures use the dried fruits as a spice, but regard the green leaves as inedible. The latter opinion is often expressed in strongly abusive language. John Gerard (1597) referred to "the venomous quality of the leaves" calling it a "stinking herbe." Olivier de Serres (1605) perversely included it in his flower garden because its leaves, rubbed between hands, enhanced the good scents of the other flowers. John Evelyn (1699) did not consider it a suitable salad herb because it is "offensive to the Head." Twentieth century writers have described it as "intensely foetid", "objectionable", "disagreeable", "nauseating," and "nasty." The same writers usually prop up this opinion by pointing out that the word "coriander" comes from *koris*, the classical Greek term for a bedbug, and the plant was so named because it smells like bedbugs.

Should we accept this derivation? A more likely origin is from the term *ko-ri-ja-da-no*, found in lists of spices from Late Bronze Age (1415–1100 BC) Aegean texts written in Linear B, before the Greek language developed. When the supposed connection with bedbugs was thought up in the 16th or 17th century, Linear B had not yet been discovered, let alone deciphered. Nor is any association of the plant with bedbugs evident in classical Greek or Latin literature. Perhaps it is a case of spurious etymology dreamed up by a coriander-hater?

Does fresh coriander really smell of bedbugs? In his 1977 book *Herbs, Spices and Flavourings*, Tom Stobart wrote: "Most readers will not have experienced the joys of bedbugs, but if they have travelled rough in the East, they may be in a position to judge. There is really little similarity." A Thai colleague has confirmed this opinion. The distinctive smell emanates from aliphatic aldehydes in the oil canals of the leaves and on the outside of the green, unripe fruit. As the fruit ripens to a chestnut colour, these canals flatten and the strong-smelling oil evaporates, leaving just the aromatic spicy oil that fills the oil canals in the centre of the fruit.

Coriander has a long history as a food plant in the eastern Mediterranean and Middle East. The wild form (as yet unidentified) was probably a native of Greece and Asia Minor. As an annual plant growing in rather open oak forest and scrubland, it was adapted to germination at the onset of winter rains and growth through the cooler months, followed by rapid flower and seed development during the short spring before summer drought set in. Most of the varieties grown today retain this propensity to bolt. Three subspecies have been identified: subsp. *sativum* selected to produce large seeds, subsp. *microcarpum* with enhanced leaf production, and subsp. *indicum* grown for its fruit and distinctive oil signature.

The earliest archaeological evidence for coriander fruits comes from a cave in Israel, possibly before 7000 BC. Whether or not this finding is confirmed by further discoveries, we know that by 2000 BC, coriander was grown in Baluchistan (SW Pakistan), and by 1500 BC, it was used in considerable quantities throughout the Middle East and eastern Mediterranean. Its name was inscribed in cuneiform script on clay tablets found at the Old Babylonian cities of Mari and Karana about 1815 BC, along with black and white varieties of cumin, fenugreek, and saffron. Large quantities were listed in the Mari records, raising the possibility that the leaves were used as well as the fruits.

Documents from Late Bronze Age sites around the Aegean also list coriander along with spices such as cumin and fennel. The coriander at the palace of Knossos on Crete was described as coming from Cyprus, from where coriander seed has been identified in the 13th-century BC site of

Apliki. The earliest record for coriander in Egypt is from 1550 BC. By the time that half a litre of coriander seeds was placed with other burial goods in Tutankhamun's tomb in 1327 BC, coriander had become the dominant flavouring spice that today characterises the cooking traditions of North Africa and other Arab nations. Since these culinary cultures also use fresh coriander leaves, it is highly likely that these too were eaten by the young Tutankhamun, Agamemnon, or King Midas.

The Mycenaeans pressed coriander oil for perfumed unguents, and by the time of classical Greece and Rome, there was a long list of medicinal uses. The famous Roman cookbook of Apicius called for coriander in 18% of the recipes, according to recent research. In many cases the context suggests that it was the fruit; however, Margaret Visser has recently argued that the Romans made a type of coriander pesto with the green leaves.

This broad range of uses continued into the Middle Ages, though quantities may have declined. Barbara Santich calls mediaeval cooking the original Mediterranean cuisine, inheritor of a time-honoured tradition of spicy dishes flavoured with the dominant spices coriander and cumin. One mediaeval specialty was the comfit, in which sugar-coated seeds of fennel, caraway, anise, and coriander were offered at the conclusion of a meal to aid digestion. The same seeds were often employed to flavour wines and preserves. These usages persisted in England through to the end of the 16th century. Then the plant disappears from the gardening manuals. Only its dried fruits were retained, mentioned in recipe books as optional ingredients for seed cakes, "Shrewsberie" cakes, "cracknel" biscuits, and spiced wine. By the late 17th century, coriander was grown in the drier counties of England primarily for fruits to flavour "strong waters" such as gin as well as gripe mixtures. In Eastern Europe, coriander oil was pressed for use in perfumes, liqueurs, medicines, and eventually for industrially prepared foods. Varieties were developed with a significantly higher oil content.

Only one European culinary tradition continued to use fresh coriander leaves through to the 20th century. In Portuguese cuisine, according to Margaret Visser, the plant is "all but indispensable." Curiously, the Spanish do not use fresh coriander, which makes the plant's popularity in parts of Central and South America hard to explain. While there is no mystery about its use in Brazil, which was influenced primarily by the Portuguese,

Coriander's cycle. *Alicia Mann*

the success of *cilantro*, as coriander is known in Spanish-colonised Mexico and Peru, raises more questions. Elisabeth Lambert Ortiz speculated that, when Columbus reached America, Arab influences on Spanish cooking may still have been important. This view was supported by Elizabeth David's discovery of 16th-century potage recipes calling for green coriander in a Catalan cookbook. Alternatively, the plant may have reached Mexico and Peru via the Manila galleons, trading between the Philippines and the New World across the Pacific. Philippinos remain heavy users of green coriander. In fact, apart from Japan, most cooks in Asia were familiar with fresh coriander long before Columbus.

The Indian subcontinent was using coriander by at least 2000 BC, with writers of Sanskrit texts calling it by names borrowed from earlier Asiatic languages. The same names occur in Malay and Indonesian, indicating the early spread of the plant through Southeast Asia. By about 100 BC, it had reached China early in the Han dynasty. Its green leaves became the most common garnish in soups, while the dried fruits contributed to the spicy dishes of Szechuan.

The last two centuries have seen coriander return to European cuisines after several centuries of neglect. First, British colonial experiences in India led to the introduction of curry powder to British kitchens from the late 18th century on, and this blend of spices can contain up to 40% ground coriander. The second wave of influence involved migrants to Britain, France, and Germany from coriander-loving countries such as India, Pakistan, Algeria, Turkey, and the West Indies. Their desire for fresh coriander led to a sharp increase in local production. At the same time, European cuisines opened themselves to cosmopolitan influences. The critical step in the rehabilitation of coriander was the renaming of fresh coriander greens as Chinese parsley, Indian parsley, Arab parsley, even Afghan parsley, a process that occurred in German and French as well as English. Undoubtedly the change of name drove out the taint of bedbugs!

Helen M. Leach's article was originally published as the "Historical Box on Coriander" in **The Cook's Herb Garden Revisited** *by Mary Browne, Helen Leach, and Nancy Tichborne. Craig Potton Publishing, 2010. 70–71.*

References

David, E. "Concerning Coriander." *Petits Propos Culinaires* 2 (1979). 68-69.

de Serres, O. *Le Théâtre d'Agriculture et Mesnages des Champs*, Editions Slatkine, Geneva, 1991 [1605 ed.]. 570. Trans. HML.

Evelyn, J. *Acetari: A Discourse of Sallets*. Prospect Books, 1982 [1699].73,76.

Gerard, John. *The Herball or General Historie of Plants*. Theatrum Orbis Terrarum, 1974 [1597 ed.]. 860.

Leach, Helen, 2001. "Rehabilitating the 'Stinking Herbe'": A Case Study of Culinary Prejudice. *Gastronomica* 1(2): 10–15. http://www.jstor.org/stable/10.1525/gfc.2001.1.2.10.

Ortiz, E.L. "Coriander." *Petits Propos Culinaires* 1 (1979). 18.

Santich, B. *The Original Mediterranean Cuisine: Medieval Recipes for Today*. Wakefield Press, 1995. 31.

Stobart, T. *Herbs, Spices and Flavourings*. Penguin, 1977. 90.

Visser, M. "Moretum: Ancient Roman Pesto" in H. Walker (ed.) *Spicing up the Palate. Studies of Flavourings—Ancient and Modern*. Proceedings of the Oxford Symposium on Food and Cookery 1992, Prospect Books, 1992. 268.

Helen Leach is an Emeritus Professor of Anthropology at the University of Otago and a Fellow of the Royal Society of New Zealand. She has a special interest in the anthropology of domestic life, including cooking and gardening. Her doctoral research in the 1970s was on the prehistoric gardens of Palliser Bay. In 1980 to 1981, she held a Rhodes Visiting Fellowship in Oxford and researched the history of the gardening techniques introduced to New Zealand by European colonists. The resulting book *1,000 Years of Gardening in New Zealand* (1984) was followed by a critical study of myths and fashions in garden history entitled *Cultivating Myths* (2000). With her sisters Mary Browne and Nancy Tichborne, she has co-authored ten books on growing and cooking vegetables and herbs and on bread making. Her most recent book is *Kitchens, a history of the New Zealand kitchen in the 20th century*. She was awarded the Royal New Zealand Institute of Horticulture's Medal for contributions in Garden History in 2008.

CULINARY
COOKING
BAKING
INFUSING

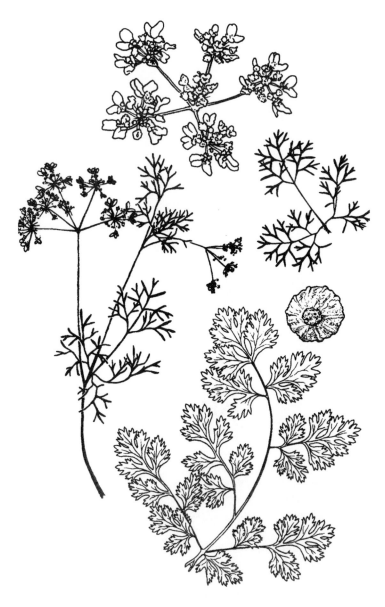

The five "acts" of coriander. *Pat Kenny*

Cooking with
Coriander and Cilantro:
A Feast in Five Acts

Susan Belsinger

HAVING SOME BACKGROUND in dance, I like to think of coriander as the herb that performs one of my favorite garden ballets. Coriander's seasonal performance consists of five "acts", each a different phase of development in its brief life and each with its unique characteristics of appearance and flavor.

Act 1, the first stage of growth, reveals bright green tender leaves. These are supplemented in Act 2 by more feathery, fernlike foliage. The first leaves are flat and broad, the second thin, lacy, and delicate, somewhat like dill weed. The flavor of the broad leaf is strong, pungent, and a bit oily (some say soapy); it contains elements of grass, humus, and orange. The lacy leaf (which I call coriander weed) is more delicate. Though it contains the same grassy and orange elements and is also slightly oily, its more pronounced perfume makes it seem slightly sweeter.

Act 3—flowering—follows quickly. Borne in umbels, the small white flowers cover the tops of the feathery leaves. They are fairly fragile after being cut so their fresh-cut stems should be put in water just like any cut flower to avoid wilting. The flowers' flavor is less intense than that of the leaves, though it does have some of the grassy, oily pungency. It is stronger of citrus and has a mild, sweet aroma. Use the flowers wherever you want just a hint of flavor or a lovely garnish.

Acts 4 and 5 feature the seeds. (Technically, they're fruits because each contains two seeds, known as a *schizocarp*; however, for simplicity, I'll call them seeds.) The tiny green seeds replace the blooms, swelling to form globes about 1/8 inch in diameter. When crushed or bitten, the unripe seeds release a burst of intense flavor, strong of citrus with slight suggestions of nuttiness and anise, yet very green-tasting, oily, and perfumey (and, yes, they do occasionally bring stink bugs to mind). The seeds are harvested when ripe—not in the green stage—just after when they start to turn yellow to tan, and they dry to a pale brown. If allowed to dry in the garden, they may fall before the final curtain call. I often leave a few seed heads to become next year's performers. The pleasant flavor of the dried seed is more fragile, a combination of lemon, orange and anise, with a bare hint of cumin; it loses most of the peculiar oiliness that characterizes the other stages.

Coriander is one of my favorite herbs because of its diversity of form and flavor. This plant that offers the cook such variety, that serves as both herb and spice, is grown throughout the world and is known by many names. Called *cilantro* in Spanish-speaking countries, it is often referred to as *Chinese parsley* in Europe and Asia, and the leaves are used in cooking from Japan and Thailand to Russia and South America. The seeds are favored in India, Iran, and the Middle East for making curries and *garam masalas*, and in Europe and the United States for pickling and baking. In Thai and some other cuisines, the root is pounded in a mortar, often with garlic, for marinades and sauces.

The following dishes were created with the five stages of coriander in mind; each part of the plant is represented.

Herb Sauce with Roasted Chiles

This recipe is sufficient for about 1 1/2 pounds of pasta. I came up with the idea while doing a chile pepper calendar with a recipe for each month. Italian pesto is probably my favorite sauce. Cilantro and chiles go well together and are staples in my kitchen. This sauce evolved from the herbs and chiles from one of my harvests. Pounded cilantro root could be added to this sauce. Though I like it best on homemade fettuccine or cheese ravioli, it is also good with grilled fish and cooked vegetables, such as grilled tomatoes and eggplant or steamed or boiled summer squash and potatoes. Choose your favorite green chiles, and add a few extra, or add a serrano or jalapeño pepper for a spicier sauce.

MAKES ABOUT 2 CUPS

1 cup packed cilantro leaves
2/3 cup packed basil leaves
1/3 cup packed Italian parsley leaves
1 cup pecans, lightly toasted
3 large cloves garlic
1 large poblano and 1 large Anaheim chile, roasted, peeled, and seeded
3/4 cup freshly grated Parmesan cheese
1/4 cup olive oil

Place the cilantro, basil, parsley, pecans, garlic, and chiles in a food processor bowl. Pulse until the ingredients are coarsely chopped. Add the cheese. Start the processor and pour in the olive oil in a steady stream until it has been incorporated. The sauce should be fairly thick, like pesto. If necessary, add a little more cheese to thicken or olive oil to thin. Serve immediately. If refrigerated, bring to room temperature or heat gently before serving.

This vegetable stir fry is fast and easy. Onions and scallions may be used in place of the leeks, and the quantities of the various vegetables may be varied as well. (Don't use more than the first 2 inches of the green, leafy part of the leek; it tends to be tough and stringy.)

Depending upon the maturity of my coriander plants, I often pull the plant and use a handful of roots, washed and chopped in the stir fry; this is optional (be sure to sample them for toughness—they should be crunchy though not tough). The perfumey flavor of the feathery coriander weed brightens and complements the flavor of both the eggplants and the chilies. Adjust the amount of chili paste or chiles to taste. Serve this dish with brown or white rice and cold beer.

SERVES 4

3 tablespoons peanut or vegetable oil
1 large or two medium leeks, rinsed well and cut into 1/4-inch slices
1 large eggplant, peeled and cut into 1/2-inch dice
1 small red or green bell pepper, seeded and cut into strips about 1/4-inch to 1-inch
2 or 3 large cloves garlic, minced
1/4 pound mushrooms, brushed clean and sliced thinly
Handful of coriander root, washed and coarsely chopped, optional
3 teaspoons red chili paste or 4 to 6 fresh hot chiles, minced
3 tablespoons water
1 1/2 tablespoons miso (yellow bean paste)
4 tablespoons tamari soy sauce
1 1/2 tablespoons rice wine vinegar
1 1/2 teaspoons organic sugar
Salt
3 tablespoons coarsely chopped coriander weed
Fresh coriander weed or flowers for garnish

Heat the oil in a large sauté pan or wok over medium heat and sauté the leeks for a minute. Add the eggplant and cook for 3 minutes, stirring well. Add the bell pepper and garlic and stir for a few minutes more. Add the mushrooms and the coriander root if you have it, stir, and sauté for about 2 minutes. Cover the pan, reduce heat to medium low, and let cook for a few minutes.

Meanwhile, combine the red chili paste or chiles with the hot water and stir with a fork until the paste is dissolved. Stir in the miso and mix until dissolved. Add 3 tablespoons tamari, vinegar, and sugar and stir to combine. Add this sauce to the pan and toss well to distribute evenly. Cover for a minute or two, then add the coriander weed, stir, and cover for 1 minute more. Taste and add salt, soy sauce, or vinegar if necessary. Spoon over rice, garnish, and serve.

Salsa with Coriander Flowers

This salsa goes well with chips as an appetizer, and it's wonderful as a condiment with any of your favorite Southwestern-style dishes. The roasted capsicums lend a lovely, rich, smoky taste to this salsa. If you don't have some tomatilloes, you can use tomatoes; sometimes I even add a green tomato. Like your salsa really hot? Use a couple more jalapeños or try other chile pepper cultivars.

MAKES ABOUT 5 CUPS

1/2 pound tomatillos, roasted and husked
3 large ripe tomatoes (about 1 1/2 pounds), cored and cut into eighths
4 Anaheim or New Mexico chiles, roasted, seeded, and peeled
1 medium red bell pepper, roasted, seeded, peeled, and cut into eighths
3 jalapeño peppers (fresh or pickled), halved and seeded
1 medium onion, cut into eighths
2 cloves garlic
About 1/2 teaspoon salt
About 1/4 cup fresh coriander flowers

Combine all ingredients except the flowers in a food processor and pulse until they are coarsely pureed. The salsa should not be totally smooth; little pieces of vegetables should be noticeable.

Refrigerate for 30 minutes. Serve at cool room temperature and garnish with coriander flowers.

Toasted and ground coriander seeds are a staple in my kitchen. I usually pre-pare this spice and keep it on hand for all sorts of delicious dishes. One of my favorite and most often used spice blends is easily prepared by toasting equal amounts of coriander and cumin seeds together, then grinding them to use in beans and Southwestern recipes.

I toast and grind about 1/2 ounce of seed at a time; I recommend that you prepare only as much as you'll use within two weeks.

To toast the seeds, place them in a small skillet over the lowest possible heat for just a minute or two, shaking the pan once or twice. They are done when you can just start to smell a coriander aroma. Don't brown them, or they will taste over-toasted and bitter.

Remove the seeds from the heat and grind them with a spice grinder or mortar and pestle. Store the ground spice away from light and heat in a jar with a tight-fitting lid. The toasted seeds can be stored whole and ground as needed.

Toasting coriander seeds. *Susan Belsinger*

This salad is not for the timid! The combination of citrus, allium, and corian-der in various forms titillates the taste buds with every bite. I like this dressing, prepared with the optional zest, served with earthy spring vegetables: fresh steamed beets, new potatoes, and even asparagus.

SERVES 4 TO 6

1 head Boston or red leaf lettuce
1 cup fresh coriander leaves
2 or 3 medium to large oranges or 4 to 5 clementines
1 small red onion, sliced into thin rings
1/2 cup freshly squeezed orange juice
1/2 cup olive oil
1 garlic clove
1/2 teaspoon coriander seed, toasted and finely ground
1 teaspoon orange zest, optional
Salt and freshly ground pepper
About 1 tablespoon vanilla bean vinegar or balsamic vinegar, optional
Fresh coriander flowers for garnish

Wash and pick over the lettuce, then tear it into large bite-sized pieces. Rinse the coriander leaves, then spin or pat them dry with the lettuce. Peel the oranges and cut them in half lengthwise. Seed them if necessary, then cut them crosswise into 3/8-inch slices. Soak the onion rings in a bowl of cold (which removes some of their pungency, mellows out their flavor and removes some of the aftertaste) water for 10 to 15 minutes. If using clementines, use the whole small segments.

Combine the orange juice and olive oil in a bowl or measuring cup. Put the garlic through a press into the dressing and add the ground coriander, zest, salt, and pepper. Blend well with a fork and taste for seasoning; add vinegar if desired.

Drain the onions and squeeze or pat them dry. Arrange the lettuce and coriander leaves on a platter or salad plates. Place the oranges decoratively on top and scatter the onion rings over them. Cover the salad with coriander flowers and drizzle about half the dressing over it. Serve the salad immediately and pass the remaining dressing.

Green Coriander Seed Raita

Raitas are relishes made with yogurt and are usually served with Indian food. Several raitas may accompany a meal as their different flavors are designed to accent certain dishes and cool down fiery ones. This simple raita is a wonderful accompaniment to spicy curries or dishes containing lots of hot chiles. It also goes well with grilled fish or fowl.

For a sweeter raita (which goes particularly well with chicken), I sometimes delete the garlic and cucumber and substitute a large ripe peach, finely chopped, or about a cup of finely chopped pineapple, papaya, or mango. Sometimes I add a few leaves of chopped spearmint which is cooling and works well with the flavor of the coriander seed as well as both the cucumber and fruits. Although the flavor is not as intense, if you don't have green coriander seed, you can use about 2 teaspoons dried seed, toasted and ground, and a few tablespoons of chopped fresh cilantro.

MAKES ABOUT 2 CUPS

1 cup yogurt
1 cucumber peeled, seeded, and grated
2 tablespoons green coriander seeds
1 clove garlic, crushed
Pinch of cayenne pepper
Salt and freshly ground pepper to taste

Combine the yogurt and cucumber in a bowl. Crush the coriander seeds in a mortar to release their essence, but do not mash them to a paste; there should be little pieces to bite into. Add them to the yogurt mixture along with the garlic and cayenne, and season lightly with salt and pepper.

Refrigerate for at least 30 minutes to let the flavors meld, and remove from the refrigerator about 15 minutes before serving and taste for seasoning.

Serve at cool room temperature.

This European-style dessert is full of flavor and interestingly delicious. It is only about 1- to 1 1/2-inches tall and a bit more dry and dense than cakelike. Prunes are my preference, and they should be moist and sticky; if they are dry and leathery, soak them in warm water (rum or brandy is also lovely) for 20 to 30 minutes and drain them well. Dried apricots, treated in the same way, can be substituted.

SERVES 8

3/4 cup organic sugar
1 1/4 cups unbleached flour
1/2 teaspoon sea salt
1 teaspoon baking powder
1 tablespoon and 2 teaspoons coriander seed, toasted and ground
Zest of 1 lemon or tangerine
1/2 cup cold, unsalted butter cut into 8 pieces
2 extra-large eggs
1 teaspoon pure vanilla extract
1 cup sliced pitted prunes, cut into strips
2 teaspoons confectioners' sugar

Lightly grease and flour a 9- or 9-1/2-inch tart or springform pan with a removable bottom. Preheat the oven to 350° F.

In a bowl (or food processor), combine the sugar, flour, salt, baking powder, 1 tablespoon ground coriander seed, and citrus zest and blend well. Add the butter and cut it (or pulse) until the mixture is a coarse meal. Add the eggs and vanilla and stir (or process) until the dough just comes together.

Transfer the batter to the prepared pan, spreading it evenly with a spatula. Arrange the prune slivers decoratively on the batter, pressing them lightly. Bake the torte in the center of the oven for 25 to 30 minutes, until golden brown on top, or a cake tester comes out clean. Cool on a baking rack while still in the pan.

Mix the remaining ground coriander with the confectioners' sugar. After the torte has cooled for 10 minutes, sift the spiced sugar over the top of the cake. Let cool, remove the tart ring, and serve at room temperature. This torte is lovely served with a cup of tea, or with fresh fruit for dessert.

Coriander seeds in mortar and pestle. *Susan Belsinger*

Susan Belsinger originally wrote this article for the *Herb Companion*; it appeared in the 1992 April/May issue. She has changed and updated a few of the recipes only slightly since the recipes are tried and true. As with all herbs, she looks forward from when she sows the seed, strikes the root cutting, or transplants a plant to the end result—the harvest. She celebrates coriander's garden stage production at least three or four times in a growing season, with successive plantings so she has it from spring to late fall.

Compensating for Misocoriandriopathy

Pat Crocker

*No normally functioning human being
would ever in a lifetime consider cilantro edible.*

–from the home page *www.ihatecilantro.com*

ARE YOU LIKE me, someone who abhors the smell and taste of cilantro? When you eat at Thai or other Asian restaurants, do you ask that cilantro not be added to your plate? Do you cringe if a tiny piece of it accidentally finds its way anywhere near your fork or—horrors!—into your food? If so, you are a true *misocoriandrist*.

In fact, you are not alone, and you can't actually alter the fact that you hate cilantro because it all comes down to your genes, specifically, to genetic variants in your olfactory receptors. A genetics firm based in Mountain View, California, identified one olfactory-receptor gene in a study of 14,604 individuals that makes some people sensitive to the aldehyde chemicals that cause cilantro to smell, well, like soap, or doll hair, or something much worse. It seems that those who love the fragrance and taste of cilantro (and there are a lot more who love cilantro than those who hate it) simply do not have the nose for those specific aldehydes. And since they can't detect the offending constituents, they can't smell or taste their offending properties.

Loving Coriander Seeds

It's not something one ever grows out of. No amount of exposure to the fresh cilantro leaf will ever win me over. Believe me, I've tried. I've grown *Coriandrum sativum*, hoping that perhaps the freshest of sprigs, lovingly added to summer salsa, would spark a tender spot in my bosom. Not a chance. *Nada.*

And yet, there is a ray of hope in my cilantro-hating world. I found that when my neglected cilantro plant bolted and quickly went to seed, those small, tan-colored orbs were a gift that offered an orange-spiked floral taste to recipes. Hooray! Now I had a key component for spice blends, including curry and *garam masala*; I could add their pleasantly sweet and spicy flavour boost to pickles, sausages, vegetable dishes, stew, and chili recipes. In fact, I have found that coriander seed combines well with other sweet spices for baked goods or fruit compotes.

The fruit develops as green berries, which mature to small, round if Moroccan coriander (*C. sativum* var. *microcarpum*), or oblong if Indian coriander (*C. sativum* var. *sativum*), tan-coloured fruits, called seeds. These are dried and ground and used as a spice in, among others, Middle Eastern, Indian, and Thai spice blends. I use a small cast iron mortar and pestle to grind coriander seeds.

Cilantro Mimics

As it does in all plants, the chemical makeup of the essential oil is what gives cilantro its characteristic flavour and fragrance. The oils in *C. sativum* are comprised of the following constituents that give it the characteristic flavour and taste we either love or hate: monoterpene hydrocarbons, oxides, carbonyls, esters, and alcohols; sesquiterpenes and phenols; aliphatic hydrocarbons, alcohols and aldehydes. So it is not a surprise that if other plants, even if they are not in the same genus, share many of the same constituents, they will taste like *C. sativum*.

It may come as somewhat of a shock that stink bugs, those beetle-like pests that, when provoked, secrete a foul smell (and taste, if eaten) are comprised of concentrated aldehydes. The same people that dislike the fragrance of cilantro have compared this stink bug smell to that of *C. sativum*. Mexican stink bugs, called *jumiles*, are celebrated in a festival dedicated to their honour and they are gathered and eaten cooked or raw in tacos, burritos, and quesadillas or ground and used to season salsas.

What follows is a list of some cilantro mimic plants that may be found in Asian markets or farmers' markets in large, urban centers where there is a strong Asian community. Because their chemical make-up is similar to that of cilantro, we cilantro haters are not likely to delight in using them.

Chameleon (*Houttuynia cordata*). The Chinese plant, available at Asian markets and some urban farmers' markets, has been shown to be rich in myrcene, 2-undecanone, limonene, and decanoyl acetaldehyde. Native to Japan, Korea, southern China, and Southeast Asia, it grows well in moist to wet soil and can be quite invasive. Use it as a leaf herb—the variegated green and white with red-tinged leaves are stunning—in salads, dips and sauces and to garnish dishes.

Culantro (*Eryngium foetidum*). Perhaps the closest in chemical make-up to *C. sativum*, culantro shares Z-4-decenal (pungent, citronellol, and fruity fragrance), E-2-dodecenal (pungent, spicy, coriander leaf), dodecenal (pungent, spicy, citrus), beta-ionone (rose/violet) and Eugenol (medicinal, clove-like). Related to sea holly (*eryngium maritimum*), culantro grows in rosettes of sharply toothed oblong leaves, which are edible and tender when young. Use it in recipes as you would fresh green cilantro—guacamole, salsa verde, dips, soup, stew. Unlike cilantro, culantro retains flavour when dried and when added to dishes about halfway during cooking.

Papalo aka Papaloquelite (*Porophyllum ruderale* var. *macrocephalum*). A Mexican and South American native with fragrance and taste similar to *C. sativum,* but with green pepper and cucumber flavours, this plant offers beautiful coin-like, small, blue-green leaves that grow on tall stems (to 6 feet/2 meters). Use raw in salads, dips, salsa, and bean dishes or roll up in tortillas.

Pepicha (*Porophyllum tagetoides*). Also native to Mexico and South America, this plant is tall, similar to tarragon in height and leaf shape except that it develops interesting pods from unopened flower petals and it tastes strongly of cilantro. It is used medicinally by the Nahauatl (Mexican natives) for bacterial infections and as a detoxifying herb for cleansing the liver. Use with squash, rice, pasta, couscous, potatoes, and egg salad; good with fish and in brothy soups.

Vietnamese Coriander (*Persicaria odorata*). Also called *Rau Răm* or *Vietnamese Mint*, it contains aliphatic aldehydes as well as the alcohol decanol with sesquiterpenes making up about 15% of its oil. A tender perennial with pretty, lance-shaped leaves with red and green markings, this plant is a good container plant. Use fresh as you would cilantro in salads and raw rice rolls, Mexican salsa verde, or with fish or chicken.

Cooking with Coriander Seeds

Like any other spice, coriander seeds are best if purchased dried but as fresh as possible. This means growing your own or finding a spice seller with a high turnover so that the dried seeds have not been stored longer than 3 to 6 months. Replenish coriander and, in fact, all your spices at least once every year because their fragrance and pungency dissipate upon storing. Keep in a dark, air-tight glass container and store in a cool place. Store whole seeds and grind them just before using in recipes. The finer the grind of spices, the stronger the flavour.

Coriander seeds ready for grinding. *Pat Crocker*

Thai Nut Sauce

Makes about 3 cups

2 tablespoons melted coconut oil
1 onion, finely chopped
1 clove garlic, minced
1 tablespoon Curry Spice Blend (recipe follows)
1 can (15 ounce/425 gram) full-fat coconut milk
1 cup natural peanut or almond or cashew butter
1/4 cup coconut nectar or liquid honey
Juice of 1 lime
Water, as required
1/2 cup chopped, fresh flat-leaf parsley or cilantro

In a saucepan, heat oil over medium heat. Sauté onion for 5 minutes.
Add garlic and curry and cook, stirring frequently, for 2 minutes or
until onions are soft and mixture is fragrant.

Add coconut milk and bring to a boil over medium-high heat. Add
nut butter, nectar, and lime juice. Cook, stirring constantly for 1 to 2
minutes or until incorporated and smooth. Add water, if necessary, to
thin the sauce to the desired consistency: thin for a satay or dipping
sauce, thicker for a fish or vegetable sauce. Stir in parsley or cilantro.

Curry Spice Blend

Makes 1/2 cup

3 tablespoons coriander seeds
2 tablespoons fenugreek seeds
1 tablespoon allspice berries
1 stick (4-inches) cinnamon, crushed
10 cardamom pods
2 (or to taste) dried cayenne peppers or other hot chiles, crushed
2 to 3 tablespoons chopped fresh coriander root, optional
2 tablespoons ground dried turmeric
1 small dark glass jar (1/2 cup capacity) plus lid

In a small skillet or spice wok, combine coriander, fenugreek, allspice, cinnamon, cardamom, chiles, and coriander root, if using. Toast over medium heat, stirring frequently for 3 to 4 minutes or until seeds are lightly coloured and fragrant. Remove from heat just as the seeds begin to pop. Do not let the spices smoke and burn. Set aside to cool.

In a mortar (using a pestle) or small electric grinder, pound or grind toasted spices to preferred consistency: coarse or finely ground. Transfer to a bowl, add turmeric and mix well. Transfer to a jar, cap, label, and store in a cool place for up to 3 months.

Coriander Pear Loaf

MAKES 1 LOAF

1 cup all-purpose flour
2/3 cup coconut flour
1 1/2 teaspoons baking powder
1 teaspoon crushed coriander seeds
1 teaspoon orange zest
1 teaspoon sea salt
2 pears, peeled, cored, and coarsely chopped
3 large eggs
3/4 cup granulated sugar
1/4 cup melted coconut oil or extra-virgin olive oil
Juice of 1 orange

CORIANDER GLAZE
1/2 cup confectioners' sugar
1 teaspoon ground coriander seeds
2 tablespoons freshly squeezed orange juice, as required

Preheat oven to 350° F (180° C). Grease the bottom and sides of a loaf pan (8 x 4-inch).

In a large bowl, combine all-purpose flour, coconut flour, baking powder, coriander, zest, and salt. Add pears and toss to coat.

In a bowl, whisk eggs and sugar together until light and creamy. Whisk in oil and orange juice.

Stir egg mixture into flour mixture and mix just until combined. Scrape into prepared pan and bake in preheated oven for 55 to 65 minutes, or until a cake tester inserted into the middle comes out clean. Set aside on a cooling rack for 15 minutes.

Meanwhile, make glaze: in a bowl, combine sugar and coriander. Slowly add orange juice and mix until the glaze is thin enough to drizzle over cake. Remove loaf to a serving platter and drizzle Coriander Glaze over.

Coriander roots with leaves attached. *Pat Crocker*

Pat Crocker is a misocoriandrist. She hates cilantro, but loves coriander seed. Culinary herbalist, lecturer, photographer, and author of several award-winning books including *Coconut 24/7*, *Flex Appeal*, *Preserving*, *The Healing Herbs Cookbook*, *The Vegetarian Cook's Bible*, *The Juicing Bible* and *The Smoothies Bible*, available at bookstores throughout Canada and the United States. Pat Crocker received the IHA Otto Richter Award in 2016. patcrocker.com

Coriandrum sativum 'Slo-Bolt.' *Susan Belsinger*

Coriander and Cilantro:
Reflections and Recipes

Donna Frawley

I HAVE BEEN growing cilantro (*Coriandrum sativum*) for over twenty years. I don't remember what encouraged me to grow it in the first place, maybe just because it was an herb I could grow successfully in Michigan. As with growing all herbs that are new to you, there are several years of trial and error. After learning that the hot weather encourages it to bolt, we realized that one or two plants were not enough, and saving seeds so you can broadcast them where you want them works well. We have a lot of cilantro growing in our garden in the spring and early summer. As it begins to go into flower, we strategically harvest most of it, but let a pre-determined number of plants go to seed, then harvest the beige seeds, called *coriander*, and hand broadcast them all over the garden. Some of the seeds germinate in August so we get a fall harvest of cilantro leaves.

The plants withstand fall and spring rototilling and in the spring the cycle starts over again. It is recommended that you sow seeds every three weeks for a continuous harvest; however, I have found that our hot weather in mid-summer prevents the seeds from sprouting. So when the temperatures cool down a little, the cilantro seeds germinate and start growing. Planting slow-bolting varieties will give you a slightly longer harvest season.

Coriander is an annual that self-seeds if you don't harvest the seeds yourself. *Cilantro* refers to the leaves of a coriander plant which grows two different types of leaves. The lower leaves look similar to Italian parsley leaves while the upper leaves are delicate and finely cut. Later, it bears tiny white flowers touched with lavender which make lovely, flavorful garnishes. The leaves and flowers are edible and have a similar pungent flavor. I use fresh cilantro leaves in a mushroom and cheese omelet, in roasted red pepper soup, in savory muffins, in salsa, snipped into salads, chili or any other Mexican dish, as well as in my Mexican Vinegar and it is especially good in my fish taco recipe.

The dried seeds have a warm, sweet, citrus-like flavor and are used in cakes, breads, marinades, salad dressings, cheese, eggs, chili sauce, guacamole, pickling brines, and may be ground into curries.

Cilantro has become one of the most popular herbs in the past twenty years, close behind basil in popularity. However, in my climate, the cilantro is ready when there are no tomatoes and peppers. Then, when the tomatoes and peppers are ready to harvest for salsa, there is no fresh cilantro. In my experience, either you love cilantro or you hate it, there is no in between, but those who love it, really love it. The flavor is unique.

The following are some of my favorite recipes using cilantro or coriander.

Assembling fish tacos. *Susan Belsinger*

After a trip to California where I ate my first fish taco, I went in search of the perfect fish taco recipe. This is it. I adapted the recipe from one I saw on Michigan Out-of-Doors.

MAKES 12 TACOS

CREMA
I mix this a few hours ahead of time so all of the flavors have a chance to develop.

1 avocado, peeled with seed removed
1 cup mayonnaise
1 cup sour cream
1/4 cup chopped fresh cilantro
1 jalapeño pepper, chopped finely
Juice and zest of 1 lime

In a medium bowl, smash the avocado. Combine remaining ingredients and whisk together. Cover and refrigerate one hour before using.

CORN SALSA
Take this mixture out of the refrigerator 1 hour before using to take the chill off so it doesn't cool down the fish too much. After soaking them in water for 1 hour, I oven roast my corn in their husks in a 350° F oven for 30 minutes.

3 ears corn grilled or roasted in husk, removed from husks OR 1 can
    Mexican-style corn
1/4 cup finely diced jalapeño
Juice and zest from 1 1/2 limes
1/4 teaspoon salt
2 tablespoon finely chopped fresh cilantro
1/3 cup finely diced red onion

In a bowl, combine all ingredients with the corn and mix thoroughly. Set in refrigerator until one hour before using.

CABBAGE
The citrus gives the cabbage a nice bright flavor.

4 cups Napa or any other cabbage you would like, shredded
Juice of 2 oranges
Juice of 2 limes
1/2 teaspoon salt

Put shredded cabbage in a bowl and dress it with orange juice, lime juice, and salt right before you start frying the fish.

FISH
I like to use cod. It holds together when fried and is the focal point of the tacos. The panko crumbs give the fish a nice crunch, adding to the textures in the taco. Marinated tofu may be substituted for fish.

2 cod filets, about a pound, patted dry and cut into 3/4 inch- to 1-inch
    strips, crosswise
1 cup flour
3 eggs, whisked in a bowl large enough to fit filet strips
1 cup panko bread crumbs
Vegetable oil, enough to fry fish

Coat fish strips in flour on all sides. Dip fish in whisked eggs and then coat in bread crumbs. Sauté for a couple minutes on each side, or deep fry in 350° F oil for 3 minutes. Place fish in a shallow pan to keep warm while you fry the tortillas.

If using tofu, squeeze out liquid, slice and fry on both sides until browned. Assemble as instructed below.

TORTILLAS
8 flour tortillas, 4-inch OR 8-inch
Vegetable oil

In a small frypan (big enough to hold the size of tortilla you are using), heat oil. Lightly fry tortilla on both sides, just until pliable. Set aside on paper towels until all tortillas are done.

TO ASSEMBLE FISH TACOS
Crema
Tortillas
Cooked fish or tofu
Corn salsa
Cabbage

Place about 1 tablespoon crema on each tortilla. Place 2 fish or tofu strips on each tortilla. Spoon 3 to 4 tablespoons corn salsa on each filet. Place 3 to 4 tablespoons of dressed cabbage over all. Enjoy.

Orange Marmalade Bread

*This recipe is from my **Herbal Breads Cookbook**. This bread is great toasted.*

MAKES 4 LARGE LOAVES OR 8 SMALL

2 packages active dry yeast
2 tablespoons sugar
2 cups warm water
11 cups flour
3 eggs
1/2 cup oil
1 cup dried skim milk powder
1/2 cup wheat germ, optional
1 teaspoon salt
2 tablespoons ground coriander seed
1 pound jar orange marmalade

In a bowl, dissolve yeast and sugar in warm water. Add 3 cups of flour and all other ingredients. Beat vigorously for 2 minutes until smooth and well blended. Stir in additional flour as needed. Turn out onto a floured board and knead 10 minutes.

Place dough in a greased bowl and cover with a damp towel; let rise until doubled, about 1 hour. Punch down; turn over; let rise again for 1 hour. Turn out onto greased board. Let rest 10 minutes. Form into loaves and place in greased bread pans. Let rise until doubled in bulk, about 1 hour.

Bake at 350° F for 50 minutes until brown and they leave pan easily.

Variation: Substitute cranberries for the orange marmalade using 3 cups berries, 1 cup orange juice, and 1 cup sugar.

Cheese Omelet with Cilantro

I am a very lucky girl in that my husband makes me breakfast every morning. This is one of my favorites.

MAKES ONE SERVING

2 eggs
1 tablespoon milk
2 tablespoons butter
1/4 cup sliced mushrooms
1/4 to 1/2 cup grated Swiss cheese
Fresh cilantro, snipped

In a small bowl, blend egg and milk. Melt butter in a small frying pan and sauté mushrooms, then move to plate. Reheat pan that you cooked mushrooms in and cook egg mixture on one side, then flip over. Put cheese, mushrooms, and cilantro on one half. Turn other half on top and serve.

Cilantro. *Yvonne Sisko*

Quick Guacamole

Used with permission of Theresa Loe, first published in The Herbal Home Companion.

MAKES ABOUT 2 CUPS

2 ripe avocados, peeled and pit removed
2 tablespoons fresh lemon juice
1/2 onion, finely chopped
2 to 4 tablespoons chunky salsa
1 tablespoon freshly chopped cilantro
Salt

Chop the avocados and place in a medium-sized bowl with the lemon juice. Use a fork to mash the avocados. Add the onion, salsa, and cilantro. Mix well. Add salt to taste. Store covered in the refrigerator until ready to serve.

Donna Frawley started her business Frawley's Fine Herbary in 1983. She began by selling at her local Farmers' Market and that fall opened a home-based business which continues today. Donna majored in Home Economics and worked at a private country club in Minnesota. She used that interest and skill to develop 60 culinary herb mixes, several blends, 8 herb flavored vinegars, and 8 herbal teas. She carries over 100 bulk culinary herbs and spices plus fresh herbs that are sold at Midland, Michigan's local Farmers' Market from May through October and a local specialty store during the growing season. She has authored three books, *The Herbal Breads Cookbook*, *Our Favorite Recipes*, and *Edible Flowers Book*, has a DVD "Cooking With Herbs", writes a monthly herb column in her local newspaper, and has written for *Herb Companion*. Donna teaches cooking classes and speaks on many culinary herb topics through her shop and has talked to many outside groups over the years. She is a regular instructor at Whiting Forest where she has taught over 28 classes. Donna is a member of the Valley Herb Society, the Great Lakes Herb Business Association, the Michigan Herb Associates, and the International Herb Association (IHA).

Upper cilantro leaves. *Alicia Mann*

Alicia's Shrimp Ceviche

Alicia Mann

Fresh cilantro right from the garden makes this a refreshing and easy summer salad for a sultry summer evening, especially if you thaw a bag of already cooked shrimp. If you find the ceviche a little too acidic, drain off some marinade, add a little more avocado or some olive oil and/or a little more salt. Substitute 2 teaspoons of paprika for the chile if you want a milder effect. Pretty blue borage flowers look lovely and accentuate the cucumber taste.

SERVES 4 TO 6

1 pound medium to large cooked shrimp, peeled and deveined
3/4 cup lime juice (juice from 3 to 4 limes)
3/4 cup lemon juice (juice from 2 to 3 lemons)
1 cup finely chopped red onion
1 serrano or jalapeño pepper, ribs and seeds removed, minced
1 cup chopped fresh cilantro
1 cucumber, peeled and diced into 1/2-inch pieces
1 avocado, peeled, seed removed, cut into 1/2-inch chunks
1/4 cup herbal leaves and flowers: borage, lemon balm, lemon verbena,
     bee balm, mint, etc.

Cut each piece of shrimp in half, or into inch-long pieces. Place shrimp in a glass or ceramic bowl. Mix in the lime and lemon juice. Cover and refrigerate for a half hour.

Mix in the chopped red onion and serrano. Refrigerate an additional half hour. Right before serving, mix in the cilantro, cucumber, and avocado. Top with borage flowers or other herbs and flowers.

Alicia Mann is a classically trained artist, a metalsmith at Heritage Metalworks in Downington, Pennsylvania, and a novice organic gardener. It is important to her to always start with a drawing, no matter what the medium, even if it is just scribbles, to help grasp the overall idea and the end result. She graduated from Maryland Institute College of Art in 2011 as a sculpture major with heavy emphasis on life drawing, metalwork, and figurative sculpture. She has been pursuing and interweaving her interests in art and horticulture. As the garden teaches the ephemeral qualities of nature, Alicia takes these lessons right back to the drawing table and the kitchen.

Salsa with Cilantro. *Susan Belsinger*

Celebrate Children and Cilantro with a Salsa Garden!

Jane L. Taylor

MANY CHILDREN DO not have a natural liking for the taste of cilantro. An easy introduction may be through a favorite condiment—salsa. The word *salsa* comes from the Italian and Spanish terms for sauce. It's this very popular sauce that can encourage kids to want to grow their own ingredients and plant a Salsa Garden.

Plant all the Salsa Garden theme ingredients together in one spot, so the children can make the connection with the plants and the final yummy product. You will need to grow the following plants.

Cilantro is very fast growing herb and, if planted at the same time as the rest of the veggies needed to make salsa, it may be long gone to seed production, so you will need to replant fresh seeds every few weeks. Some newer slow bolting varieties do last longer. 'Slo-Bolting', 'Santo' and 'Calypso' are three.

For any Salsa Garden, **tomatoes** are a must. The paste type 'Roma' or 'San Marzano' are best and they can be staked or grown in a cage.

The **sweet bell pepper** 'Yolo Wonder' is green at first and will later turn red. 'Flavorbust' is a very tasty yellow bell pepper. 'Lunchbox' comes in several colors, but they are smaller so you may want to add more than one or two to the recipe.

For a little zing, plant the **jalapeño pepper** 'Early Jalapeño'. Make sure the children handle these peppers with rubber gloves and are careful not to touch their eyes while preparing the pepper.

Plant a few **onions** and for fun you might try growing 'Egyptian Walking' onions. These perennial onions produce a small shallot-like onion that can be harvested or the bulblets may also be used.

Don't forget the **garlic**. The hardneck garlics 'German White' or 'Music' have nice plump cloves.

To prepare the Garden Fresh Summer Salsa, it is great fun to do it outside right in the garden using a manual (hand crank) food processor. As fresh fruits come into season, these can be added to the salsa, for example, strawberries, melons, peaches, and apples.

When the cilantro goes to seed, gather them and store in a dry place for about three weeks. The seeds, called *coriander*, are considered a spice and have a lemony, citrus flavor. When ready to use, let the kids crush the seeds in a mortar and pestle and add to chili, sprinkle on top of roasted vegetables, or add to a spice rub for meats.

Children love to make salsa. *Jane Taylor*

MAKES 6 SERVINGS

5 ripe tomatoes, cored
1 small onion, peeled
1 garlic clove, peeled
1 bell pepper of any color, seeded
1 jalapeño chile pepper, seeded
1/4 cup fresh cilantro
1/4 teaspoon salt
1 tablespoon fresh lime juice

Place the vegetables and cilantro in the hand-crank food processor and have kids take a turn at the crank. If you do not use a food processor, then chop all the ingredients on a cutting board. If children chop, young ones can use a plastic lettuce knife. Mix in salt and fresh lime juice. Serve with tortilla chips in the garden and enjoy!

Guacamole

If avocados are available, make some guacamole which most kids adore.

MAKES 6 SERVINGS

2 ripe avocados
1 fresh paste tomato, washed, cored and chopped
1 small onion, chopped
1 heaping tablespoon fresh cilantro leaves, chopped into little pieces
1 jalapeño, seeded and finely chopped (use less if you want it milder)
1/2 fresh lime
Pinch of salt

Gently scoop out the avocados and mash in a mortar and pestle. The rest of the ingredients may also be chopped in a manual food processor.

In a bowl mix the tomato, onion, cilantro, and jalapeño into the mashed avocado. Squeeze fresh lime juice and salt over the top.

Salsa ingredients. *Susan Belsinger*

RECOMMENDED BOOKS

Bayless, Rick. *Salsas that Cook*. Fireside, 1998.

Curtis, Susan D. *Salsas and Tacos*. Gibbs Smith Pub., 2006.

Reynolds, Aaron. *Chicks and Salsa*. Bloombury Books, 2007.

Seed sources for the varieties mentioned can be obtained from Sow True Seed at sowtrueseed.com/ or Johnny's Selected Seeds at johnny-seeds.com/.

Jane L. Taylor was the Founding Curator of the Michigan 4-H Children's Garden and adjunct faculty in the Department of Horticulture at Michigan State University. She has served on the board of the Michigan Herb Associates for 28 years and been a contributor to the *Michigan Herb Journal* for that time as well as author and co-author of several MSU Extension publications, magazine, and journal articles. In 2000 she received the first Jane L. Taylor Award, a namesake award from the American Horticultural Society. She presented the IHA Otto Richter Memorial Award Lecture in 2015.

Scintillating Cilantro, Captivating Coriander

Rosemary Roman Nolan

I HAVE TAUGHT food folklore and culinary arts for over ten years, and I relish nothing more than introducing students to new spices and fresh herbs that they may have fearfully bypassed in their markets or gardens.

Fresh cilantro is devilishly fun in that it is a "love/hate" herb to spring on a novice cook. I had always known that some people could not abide this aromatic plant, but it was one of my students who informed me that the aversion to cilantro is not that of a fussy eater—it's actually genetic.

The first thing everyone does in class is assume I am holding up parsley. No, it's sometimes called *Chinese parsley*, I say, but here is regular Italian parsley held up for comparison. See the difference? Now, smell the difference. The reactions to a first sniff of cilantro are priceless. Either students' eyes light up, or an expression of incredible disgust and revulsion appears. Eyes narrow, noses wrinkle, people back away as from a bouquet of poison ivy. "I don't want to cook with THAT!"

Well, I explain, we always put it minced up on the side in a mixed group class, so that students may season and garnish their finished dishes at will. For the brave who are not sure, I have them eat some fresh cilantro after the sniff test. Some reactions I have collected over the years:

"I want to try it! Do you mean you can actually buy this in the supermarket?"

"This is disgusting. It tastes like dish soap."

Grimacing and spitting, "This tastes like licking a roll of dirty nickels."

"Is this an ingredient in bug repellent?"

"I love this! How do I grow it?"

"Eeuw! People actually eat this? It smells like skunk spray!"

"Oh I love cilantro. I could eat it by the handful!"

As you can see, there is no one on the fence when it comes to cilantro, so it's best to have the waivers ready in your kitchen for guests to sign if you're cooking with it!

The next surprise comes when students learn that the ground coriander they have been using in their spice cookies and pumpkin bread is the ground seed (actually the plant's fruit, not a seed) produced by this pungent malefactor of the herb world. The aromas of the fresh leaves and the dried seeds are indeed dramatically different.

Coriander has been used both in Europe and America to flavor distilled liqueurs and strong spirits—among them gin, Chartreuse, absinthe, and Benedictine. The Romans, those sometimes inadvertent botanists, brought coriander to Northern Europe, from whence it eventually took ship for North America. The Spanish introduced the plant to the southern part of the New World, hence its prevalence in Mesoamerican and South American cuisine. It was documented in New England in the 1600s, but never achieved prominence in our native cooking. It spread to India, China, and Southeast Asia, where it is probably utilized more widely than anywhere else in the world.

Cilantro grows easily as a self-seeding annual in the Northeast where I live; buy one packet of seeds and you are set for the next several seasons. Not terribly fussy about soil, it does prefer full sun and adequate water to produce lush foliage. Hot dry weather will cause the plant to become leggy almost overnight, bolt faster, and put all its energy into producing fruits. The umbrella-like sprays of round green fruits are weighty when unripe and make the entire plant droop to the ground if not tied up.

If the end of the growing season is near, I don't bother to strip the seed-fruits off and store them. Since coriander dislikes being uprooted or transplanted, I simply bend the plants sharply in half in clumps so that the fruits will fall into the earth as they dry. In the spring I clear the dried plant stems, make sure all the fruits have dropped off, and soon a new patch of cilantro will appear with no cultivation whatsoever.

If you like cilantro, clip and pinch it back frequently whenever you need some for the kitchen to keep it from bolting. Alternatively, let it go to seed, save the fruits of the first crop, and sow a second crop which will rapidly provide you with more fresh foliage before cold weather sets in.

Medicinally, coriander is a carminative (aiding digestion) and a tea made from it was frequently used as "gripe water" for colicky babies and upset stomachs in the same fashion that we use dill and mint. The entire plant is useful in the treatment of inflammatory conditions such as ulcers, skin eruptions, inflamed eyes, and fever. Coriander has also been used as an herb to relieve labor pains. The essential oil is antiseptic and is also used in the manufacture of perfumes and colognes.

If you cannot abide fresh cilantro, try to bring ground coriander into your life: it is ambrosial as an addition to baked goods, as part of a spice rub for roast chicken or lamb, and in curry of any sort. I usually add a good pinch of coriander and also nutmeg to classic tomato sauces to deepen and enrich the flavor while tempering the acidity of the tomatoes, without resorting to a laggardly use of sugar.

In other words, coriander/cilantro is not just some stinky green stuff that ends up in your salsa or guacamole. This herb has traveled a long path with us and offered nothing but sustenance. In one form or another, it will serve you well. For those of you who cannot stand it fresh, seek out the dried seeds in whole or ground form and you will not be sorry!

The term "pesto" here refers mainly to the means of production. This all-purpose flavor paste can be used as a marinade for chicken or seafood, a topping for steamed rice or hot noodles, a dipping sauce for steamed or raw veggies, a salad dressing for cooked potatoes, or served by the side of steamed Asian dumplings—use your imagination and customize the final result to your own tastes! Unlike Italian parsley, whose stems are tough and bitter, fresh cilantro stems are tender and can be used along with the leaves. I merely trim the rough and dry ends off the bottom of the bunch.

MAKES APPROXIMATELY 1 1/2 CUPS

1 bunch fresh cilantro, stem ends trimmed, roughly chopped
3 cloves garlic, chopped
Dash Thai fish sauce
Fresh juice of half a lime
2 tablespoons sesame seeds or pepitas (green pumpkin seeds)
Fresh Italian or Thai basil leaves from 3 stems, about 5 inches long
Fresh mint leaves from 3 stems, about 5" long
2 tablespoons toasted sesame oil
About 1 cup peanut oil or extra virgin olive oil: enough to blend
    smoothly in food processor
1/3 cup dry-roasted peanuts or other nuts, such as macadamias, pecans,
    or walnuts
Salt and freshly ground pepper

Simply combine all the ingredients in food processor except peanut or olive oil and process to desired consistency while adding a thin stream of olive or peanut oil. If you want a more soupy consistency, add more oil; if you want a more chunky consistency, use less oil and pulse only until the ingredients are blended.

Can be frozen, but is best stored in an airtight container in the fridge and used up within 7 to 10 days.

SERVES 6 TO 8

FILLING
3 tablespoons peanut or vegetable oil
1/2 cup chopped shallots
3 cloves minced garlic
1/2 pound ground pork, chicken, or turkey
1 tablespoon tamarind pulp, dissolved in 2 tablespoons warm water
2 tablespoons brown sugar
About 2 tablespoons Thai fish sauce
About 1/2 teaspoon salt
1 tablespoon minced fresh ginger
2 tablespoons minced, dry roasted peanuts

WRAPPING AND GARNISHES
24 soft lettuce leaves (such as Bibb or butter lettuce)
1 stalk lemongrass, trimmed and minced
2 tablespoons minced fresh ginger
4 scallions, trimmed and minced
1/2 cup chopped fresh cilantro leaves and stems

To make the filling, heat a deep skillet or wok over high heat and add
the oil. Add the shallots and garlic and stir fry until the mixture softens,
about 3 to 5 minutes. Add ground meat and continue until the meat
begins to turn opaque, about 5 minutes. Add the tamarind, sugar,
fish sauce, and salt and cook until the liquids have reduced, about 5
minutes. Add the ginger and peanuts and cook for one more minute.
Set aside to cool. Adjust seasoning if necessary.

Scoop the warm filling into a serving bowl and plate the lettuce leaves
and garnishes separately so that your guests can help themselves. Take
a leaf and add a scant spoonful of filling, plus desired garnishes. Roll
the lettuce leaf up and devour!

Perfumed Cilantro Rice

You can find asafoetida in Indian groceries or online.

SERVES 4 TO 6

About 1 teaspoon peanut or vegetable oil
3 cloves garlic, minced
2 tablespoons fresh ginger, grated or minced
1 1/2 cups long-grain, jasmine or basmati rice
1 teaspoon ground asafoetida
3 1/2 cups chicken or vegetable stock
One generous handful of cilantro, trimmed, stems and leaves chopped

In a heavy saucepan over medium heat, heat a splash of oil and sauté
the garlic and ginger till slightly softened about 3 minutes. Stir in the
rice and asafoetida and toss to coat with the oil for 1 to 2 minutes.
Pour in the stock, stir to prevent sticking, bring to a high simmer, then
reduce heat to low and cover.

In ten minutes, uncover the pot, stir in the cilantro, then cook covered
until the rice has absorbed the stock, about 15 to 20 minutes more.
Reserve a little of the fresh cilantro as a garnish.

Elegant Coconut, Pumpkin and Coriander Bisque

SERVES 4 TO 6

About 1 tablespoon peanut or vegetable oil
3 to 4 shallots, peeled and minced
1 1/2 pounds pumpkin, peeled, seeded, and cubed small (butternut,
     acorn, or other rich winter squash may be substituted)
2 (13- to 14-ounce) cans unsweetened coconut milk
1 cup chicken or vegetable broth
1 cup fresh cilantro, chopped
About 2 tablespoons Thai fish sauce
Salt and ground white pepper
Minced scallions and plain yogurt, for garnish

In a large, heavy saucepan, heat the oil and sauté the shallots and cubed pumpkin, stirring occasionally, until the shallots have softened, about 5 minutes. Add the coconut milk, broth, cilantro, fish sauce, salt and pepper. Simmer over medium heat until the squash is soft. Taste for salt, pepper, and fish sauce and adjust as needed.

For a chunky soup, serve as is. For a semi-chunky soup, smash up a bit with a potato masher right in the pot. For a super silky, elegant bisque, blend in the pot with an immersion blender until completely smooth. Garnish with scallions and a swirl of yogurt if desired.

References

Alford, Jeffrey, and Naomi, Duguid. *Hot Sour Salty Sweet: A Culinary Journey through Southeast Asia*. Workman Publishing, Inc., 2000.

Bremness, Lesley. *Herbs*. DK Publishing, Inc., 1994.

Castleman, Michael. *The Healing Herbs*. Rodale Press, 1991.

Duke, James A., Ph.D. *The Green Pharmacy*. Rodale Press, 1997.

Gordon-Smith, Clare. *Basic Flavorings: Chiles*. Running Press, 1996.

Hazen, Janet. *Turn It Up!* Chronicle Books, 1995.

Keville, Kathi. *Herbs: An Illustrated Encyclopedia*. Michael Friedman Publishing, Inc., 1994.

McIntyre, Anne. *The Medicinal Garden*. Henry Holt and Co., Inc., 1997.

Personal notes. *Proceedings* of the 4th International Herb Symposium, Norton, MA. 1998.

Personal notes. *Proceedings* of the 6th International Herb Symposium, Norton, MA. 2002.

Stewart, Amy. *Wicked Plants: The Weed That Killed Lincoln's Mother & Other Botanical Atrocities*. Algonquin Books, 2009.

Tiwari, Maya. *Ayurveda: A Life of Balance*. Healing Arts Press, 1995.

Rosemary Roman Nolan, LMT, grew up in a family of herbalists and green thumbs and maintains a messy but vibrant organic garden in Central Massachusetts. When not finding new excuses to avoid weeding, and planning for the next big endeavor—beekeeping and chickens—she is a Massachusetts licensed massage therapist and Reiki Master. She has also been an adult education teacher for over ten years, offering food folklore classes, Tribal Fusion belly dance, and many hands-on workshops including soapmaking, cheesemaking, and papermaking. To learn more about her or to obtain contact information, visit her website at amtamembers.com/rosemarynolan.

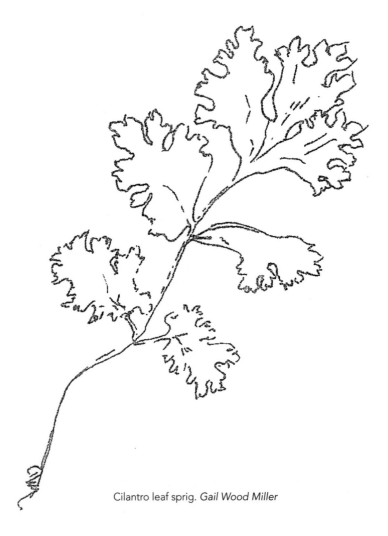

Cilantro leaf sprig. *Gail Wood Miller*

The Little Herb That Could: West Meets East with Coriander

Gail Wood Miller & Peter Miller

It ALMOST LOOKS like Queen Anne's Lace in miniature: delicate, white flowers—small bundles of petals fanned with larger ones—gracefully erect on long stems. Leaf blades, particularly the high ones, are usually shaped in triplets, forming miniature fleurs-de-lis. Isn't it appropriate that the symbol of French royalty—the fleur-de-lis lily motif—is in that elegant European cousin of parsley, coriander?

Coriandrum sativum, so pretty it is used as an ornamental, traveled north and west from the Mediterranean, arriving in Britain about 1,000 B.C., through migration or invasion, possibly coming from Spain and Portugal. It's now as popular in Latin America as it is in Europe. Where would guacamole be without cilantro?

It's also a friendly plant. Our friends Paul and Karen Volckshausen, of Happy Town Farm, Maine, grow cilantro along with dill to attract pollinating insects. Their organic vegetables and flowers increase, and so, especially, does their cilantro.

All of the coriander is edible—the smooth-tasting leaves; the tiny, lacey flowers that honeybees like, too; the stems appearing and tasting like delicate celery; the root (popular in curries and salsas); and the fruits, or seeds, richer in vitamin C than the leaves—living up to its pharmaceutical name of *fructus coriandri.* The Romans used its anti-bacterial quality to help preserve meats. Hippocrates used coriander as a medicine.[1]

---

1 "Take two spoons of dry coriander seeds every day to tonic your blood circulation" was Hippocrates' advice, according to "Coriander (*Coriandrum sativum*)" in *Hippocrates Medicine* (http://www.hippocratesmedicine.com/coriander/).

From 1820 to 1980, coriander was listed in the U. S. Pharmacopoeia. Yet, today, according to the University of California at Los Angeles's Louise M. Darling Biomedical Library, coriander has not been "adequately evaluated" medicinally, although noting its reputation in "folk remedies" as a healing herb. An example is coriander's carminative quality from its volatile oil, helping with digestion.

Coriander seed is rich in vitamins, the percentages varying according to where it is grown; in the United States, 3.5 ounces of coriander may hold as much as 135% of our recommended daily intake (RDI) of vitamin A, and, of vitamin K, as much as 388%. *The Times of India* promotes coriander as helping to balance cholesterol levels, to stimulate insulin secretion, to lower blood sugar levels, to treat conjunctivitis, arthritis, and more (Sinha). Currently, coriander is an ingredient in most cough medicines in India. Historically, it has also been used for curing meat (as in corned beef), distilling spirits (French Chartreuse and Belgian beers), and, sugar-covered, as candy (comfits)—sometimes thrown in celebration before there was paper confetti.

Cilantro is so often in cuisine from China, where it was thought to bring about immortality, that it has been called *Chinese parsley*. And in the Middle Ages, the seed was used in love potions.

Maybe that's why Peter uses the whole plant so authoritatively and insistently in our kitchen. It's a staple ingredient in almost every dish he prepares, leaning toward Middle Eastern and Chinese flavors. A particular favorite of friends and family is his *baba ganoush* with cilantro. And his marinade with cilantro has our grandchildren asking for seconds of scallops.

Along with its adoption into Middle Eastern and Latin American cuisine, ubiquitous cilantro has found its place in Asian cooking, particularly with respect to vegetables and seafood. For most of my adult life, eating in Chinese restaurants, I have always been served steamed whole fish with the traditional ginger and scallions. More recently the dish has appeared with tiny julienned slivers of ginger with a healthy sprinkling of cilantro leaves and stems. Cilantro's pungent, delicate flavor adds wonderfully without interfering with the delicate flesh of the steamed fish. A recent recipe for this dish appears online at *Epicurious*, from *Viet-*

namese Home Cooking by Charles Phan with Jessica Battilana (Random House/Ten Speed Press, 2012).

Middle Eastern Baba Ganoush with Caramelized Onions and Cilantro

This variation of the silky eggplant appetizer, baba ganoush, is emboldened by the addition of caramelized onions and cilantro which give the dish a smokier, more muscular flavor while still retaining the traditional, delicate balance of eggplant, lemon, garlic, and tahini. The cilantro is added just at the end to capture its full effect. The recipe is for a rather large quantity, but one can reduce the ingredients proportionally. We serve it with Middle Eastern flat bread, toasted briefly and slightly charred over a low gas flame, cut in half and then into triangles.

SERVES 8 TO 10

3 pounds firm eggplant
2 medium-size yellow onions, chopped
4 to 6 cloves garlic, minced
2 tablespoons olive oil
1/2 teaspoon salt
1 1/2 tablespoons tahini
3 tablespoons lemon juice
1/2 cup cilantro, chopped coarsely

Prick eggplants with a fork and place on a baking sheet lined with foil. Roast at 400° F for at least an hour until they are charred and collapsed. Alternatively, you can put them on burners over a very low gas flame and rotate regularly until they are charred and collapsed. Either way, the eggplant should be very soft and blackened.

Allow the eggplants to cool. Split them lengthwise with a sharp knife and scoop out the flesh with a tablespoon. Pull out and discard any pockets of dark seed, which make the eggplant bitter. Chop and mash the eggplant to a fine texture and transfer to a bowl. Alternatively, use a blender to get your desired consistency.

While the eggplants are roasting, chop the onions into small pieces and mince the garlic. Heat 1 tablespoon of olive oil and cook in a sauté pan the onions and garlic slowly over a low flame, adding salt and stirring occasionally until the mixture is golden brown and caramelized, about 45 minutes.

Stir the cooked onions and garlic into the eggplant. Add the tahini and lemon juice, stirring the mixture to achieve consistency throughout. Let the *baba ganoush* rest in the refrigerator for about an hour, so the ingredients have time to settle and blend.

Just before serving, mix in the chopped cilantro, reserving some for the top. The full strength of the cilantro begins to fade rather quickly.

Cuban Marinade with Cilantro

I discovered this marinade years ago while reading the menu outside a Cuban restaurant. It is simplicity itself. The restaurant soaked slices of grilled chicken breast in it, but I have found that it is also a delicious marinade with scallops. I added cilantro to the marinade because it seems a perfect foil for the cumin. I serve the dish by itself in the winter and combine it with a tossed salad in the summer.

YIELDS ENOUGH MARINADE FOR 1 TO 2 POUNDS OF MEAT OR SCALLOPS

Juice from two limes
1 tablespoon ground cumin
2 cloves garlic, minced, then smashed flat and minced finer
2 tablespoons minced cilantro

In a bowl, combine the ingredients, stirring together. Pour the marinade over the chicken or scallops and let it sit in the marinade for about half an hour. Turn occasionally.

Grill the chicken or scallops. Serve separately or cut up in a tossed salad.

References

Ask a Master Gardener. "Coriander." *Penn State Extension.* http://extension.psu.edu/ plants/gardening/ herbs/coriander.

De la Foret, Rosalee. "Coriander Benefits." *Herbs with Rosalee.* http://www.herbalremediesadvice. org/coriander-benefits.html.

Gernot Katzer's Spice Pages. "Coriander Seed and Cilantro Herb." http://gernot-katzers-spice-pages.com/engl/Cori_sat.html.

Home Farm Herbery. "A Little History of Coriander©." Home Farm Herbery Blog, *Local Harvest*, Feb. 2013. http://www.localharvest.org/blog/48630/entry/a_little_history_of_coriander.

Louise M. Darling Biomedical Library. "Coriander (Cilantro)." *Spices: Exotic Flavors & Medicines.* History & Special Collections, University of California at Los Angeles, 2002. http://web.archive.org/ web/20070225092627/http://unitproj.library.ucla.edu/biomed/spice/index.cfm?displayID=8.

Our Herb Garden. "Coriander." 2016. http://www.ourherbgarden.com/herb-history/coriander.html.

Sinha, Seema. "Coriander has multiple health benefits." Life & Style, *Times of India.* Feb 15, 2014. http://timesofindia.indiatimes.com/life-style/health-fitness/health-news/Coriander-has-multiple-health-benefits/articleshow/30452697.cms.

Skip the Pie. "Nutritional info of Coriander (Cilantro) Leaves (Raw) vs. Parsley (Raw)." http://skipthepie.org/vegetables-and-vegetable-products/coriander-cilantro-leaves-raw/compared-to/parsley-raw/.

The World's Healthiest Foods. "Cilantro & Coriander Seeds." http://www.whfoods.com/genpage.

Gail Wood Miller cooks for health; Peter Miller cooks for flavor. The herbs they use are generally chosen accordingly: Peter's dry herbs in small, carefully labeled glass jars or fresh herbs refrigerated in large glasses of water; Gail's in dry bunches in baskets or wrapped in toweling in the refrigerator. Gail eyeballs ingredients. Peter measures carefully. His specialties include appetizers, meats, salads, wok-prepared vegetables. Hers include fish, soups, and puddings. They live in lower Manhattan, both as retired college English professors. They shop regularly at the Union Square Farmers' Market and enjoy cooking together. Peter is co-author of *Becoming a Writer* (St. Martin's, 1986) and *4,000 Years of Chinese Calligraphy* (Univ. of Chicago Press, 1990). Gail, a health coach, is author of a young adult novel, *Good Girl* (Lasso, 2016), a self-help book for teens about A.D.D. and nutrition, disguised as a mystery.

'Slo Bolt' flowers. *Susan Belsinger*

Baking with Cilantro:
Cypriot Olive Bread

Marge Powell

I AM THE bread maker for my family. It has been years since we have bought a commercial loaf. The exception, of course, is if we are traveling, especially in France, where we thoroughly enjoy all of the local breads. Normally I use the autolyze method which is easy and uncomplicated and lets me make many loaves at a time. But when I want something special, I go to this recipe. Cypriot Olive Bread is interesting, full of flavor, has a lovely crust, and generally delights the bread eaters. I adapted the recipe many years ago from *Food & Wine Magazine*. According to the magazine, this bread is found only in the town of Laraka on the island of Cyprus.

The original recipe calls for baking this bread in a covered, unglazed clay pot that has been soaked in water for at least 15 minutes. That works well, but I have also made this recipe in a covered Le Creuset pot and a covered Pyrex dish, all of which have provided very satisfactory results. The pots should be in the 3- to 4- quart size range.

A note on the cilantro: Cilantro is a cool weather crop here in North Florida and available fresh from the garden only in January and February. In order to have cilantro available throughout the year for the many recipes that call for it, I lightly process fresh cilantro leaves in a blender with a little olive oil, then put about half a cup of this mixture into a zip-lock freezer bag which I seal and pat flat. These little bags stack nicely in the freezer, and when I have a recipe that calls for cilantro, I open the baggie and break off an appropriately-sized piece of the frozen "cilantro pancake." I find that this method results in very little flavor deterioration.

Cypriot Olive Bread

Makes 1 loaf

2 cups bread flour
1 1/2 teaspoons instant yeast (granulated, not cake)
1/2 teaspoon sugar
1/2 cup high grade olive oil (extra-virgin, cold-pressed)
2/3 cup warm water
3/4 cup chopped cilantro
1/2 cup finely chopped onion
1/2 cup oil-cured black olives, pitted and chopped coarsely
2 teaspoons black sesame seeds

In the bowl of a standing mixer, use a dough hook to combine flour, yeast, and sugar. Add 1/3 cup of the olive oil and mix until the dough resembles fine crumbs. Add the water and mix until a soft dough forms. Gently fold in the cilantro, onions, and olives until well combined. Transfer the dough to a very lightly floured work surface and knead lightly until smooth about 8 to 10 minutes.

Use some of the remaining oil to coat the inside of a large bowl. Place the dough in the bowl and turn to coat with the oil. Cover the bowl and let it stand at room temperature until the dough is doubled in size, about 1 1/2 hours.

After the dough has risen, transfer it to a work surface. Lightly oil your hands and shape the dough to fit your baking pot. Let the dough rest for 15 minutes. Meanwhile, if you are using an unglazed clay pot for baking, soak it and its lid in water for 15 minutes. After 15 minutes, drain and dry the glazed pot and lid. Whatever pot you are using for baking should be oiled inside.

Transfer the rested dough to your baking pot and sprinkle with sesame seeds. Cover with a lid and place in a cold oven. Turn the oven temperature to 475º F. Bake for 45 minutes, then remove the cover and bake for 10 more minutes until the crust is golden brown. Remove the bread from the baking pot and let cool for at least 4 hours before slicing.

Marge Powell has been an herbalist for over 25 years and an avid plant person her entire life. Her herbal interests span the culinary, medicinal, and cosmetic uses of herbs as well as the cultivation of herbs. She completed a medicinal herbal apprenticeship with Susun Weed and was introduced to herbal body care in workshops conducted by Rosemary Gladstar.

Marge is a passionate cook and most of her cooking is herb-enhanced. She teaches classes in cooking with herbs and has recently developed a presentation on the nutritional value of herbs. Other popular workshops are "Making Herbal Salves & Lotions", "Basic Soapmaking with Herbs", and "Making Your Own Medicine". She has conducted hands on workshops on a variety of herbal topics across the United States.

She is currently a board member of the International Herb Association (IHA) and the International Herb Association Foundation (IHAF) and is past president of IHA's former Southeastern Region. She has had numerous herbal articles published in IHA's annual Herb of the Year™ publications as well as their quarterly newsletters.

Cilantro leaf. *Susan Belsinger*

Cilantro seeds drying in a bag. *Susan Belsinger*

Blueberry Liqueur

Jim Long

This can be made from either fresh or frozen blueberries. Use the liqueur over ice cream, in drinks, in lemonade, with tonic water and a slice of lime, or simply as a pleasant after-dinner sipping beverage served in one-ounce liqueur glasses. Vegetable glycerin is available in cooking stores, some pharmacies, and online. While not essential to the liqueur, it is highly recommended as it adds a smooth, silky finish to the beverage.

SERVING SIZE: MOST PEOPLE SERVE A HALF-OUNCE WHILE OTHERS GIVE A LARGER 2-OUNCE SERVING. I LIKE TO MIX AN OUNCE INTO CLUB SODA OVER ICE WITH A TWIST OF LEMON.

4 cups frozen or fresh blueberries
1/2 cup water
1 (1.75 liter) bottle of inexpensive 80 proof vodka
    (or 100 proof if you have it on hand)
1/8 teaspoon coriander seeds
2 whole cloves
1-inch piece stick cinnamon
5 cups sugar
2 cups additional water
1 tablespoon vegetable glycerin, optional but recommended

Combine blueberries and half a cup water in a saucepan and bring to a boil, then simmer until berries soften, about 2 minutes. Remove from heat and allow to cool.

Pour the berries and liquid into a glass canning jar and fill to the top with the vodka. Add the coriander, cloves, and cinnamon. Set aside for 2 months in a dark place such as a pantry.

Strain the berries and spices from the liquid.

In a saucepan, add the 5 cups sugar with about 2 cups water; heat, stirring until the sugar has just dissolved. Cool.

Add the sugar water to the vodka. Then add the vegetable glycerin and stir.

Bottle your liqueur in clean, sterilized bottles and close securely with a cork. The liqueur will keep 1 to 2 years stored in a pantry.

Read Jim's bio on page 22

Cilantro is an often overlooked herb to highlight recipes. *Susan Belsinger*

Let Them Eat Cilantro!

Tamara Huron

As a child I spent many days with my grandma tending her beautiful garden. She grew a great variety of vegetables and herbs. My love for cilantro developed later while living in Colorado, managing restaurants that specialized in southwestern cuisine.

Cilantro was the star of many dishes served at those restaurants. To me cilantro brings a refreshing addition with a hint of zesty citrus undertone. Cilantro is an herb that can enliven anything from an appetizer to a dessert.

Cilantro can be an overlooked herb for highlighting recipes. My cooking classes at the Huntsville Botanical Garden use fresh herbs. I encourage folks to use cilantro in an array of recipes. Cilantro can surprise many people with its qualities and end up as an excellent herb to add to your recipes.

The recipes below come from *Organic Herbal Cooking, Inc.* © 2016.

Grilled Romaine with Cilantro Vinaigrette

This salad is unique because most people don't grill their lettuce. A quick turn on the grill gives the romaine a slightly smoky flavor. The cilantro vinaigrette creates a delightful balance that brings the salad together. If you don't have a grill, a broiler can be substituted.

SERVES 4

2 romaine hearts
1 shallot, chopped
1/4 cup balsamic vinegar
1 tablespoon honey

2 tablespoons minced cilantro
1 cup olive oil plus 2 tablespoons olive oil
Pinch salt and pepper
1 cup crumbled feta cheese
1/2 pint cherry tomatoes, halved

Wash romaine and dry well. Remove outer leaves if wilted or brown. Slice each romaine in half lengthwise and set aside.

In a blender or food processor, add shallot, vinegar, honey, and cilantro. Process until smooth. Slowly add 1 cup olive oil and pulse to blend mixture.

Preheat grill to medium. Brush romaine with remaining olive oil. Season with salt and pepper. Grill romaine for 4 minutes turning frequently. Romaine will be slightly charred, but not heated thoroughly. Remove from grill and place on serving platter. Top with feta cheese. Place tomatoes around romaine. Drizzle with cilantro vinaigrette.

Cilantro and Asparagus Salad

This salad is a must for cilantro fans. The uncooked fresh asparagus and cilantro pair beautifully. The balance of the dressing with the crunch of the peanuts is exceptional. This recipe exemplifies my love for cilantro! Use only cilantro with crisp stems and vibrant leaves.

SERVES 6

1/4 cup olive oil
1 shallot, thinly sliced
1 bunch fresh cilantro
1 bunch whole asparagus spears, tough ends removed
1/2 teaspoon soy sauce
1 teaspoon honey
1/2 cup peanuts, toasted
1 tablespoon sesame seeds, toasted

Place the olive oil in a small saucepan over medium heat. Add the shallot and cook, stirring often, for 6 minutes. Remove from heat.

Wash cilantro well and place on paper towels to dry. Trim tough stems from the cilantro and chop leaves. Slice the asparagus into 1-inch pieces on the diagonal. Whisk together soy sauce, honey, and shallots with the oil.

Place the asparagus, cilantro, peanuts, and sesame seeds in a large bowl. Drizzle the dressing over the salad. Gently toss. Serve immediately.

Zucchini Noodles with Cilantro and Shrimp

Following a healthy Paleo diet has become increasingly popular. I was fascinated with the ingredients and preparation of many recipes, so I purchased a spiralizer and have never looked back. What a fun kitchen gadget! If you do not have a spiralizer, cutting the zucchini into thin threads works, but will not give the same noodle consistency.

SERVES 4

4 medium zucchini, spiralized or cut into thin threads
1/4 teaspoon salt
1 tablespoon coconut oil or olive oil
2 cloves fresh garlic, minced
1 pound medium shrimp, peeled and deveined
Juice of 1/2 lemon
1/2 cup fresh cilantro, finely chopped
Pinch salt and pepper

Place zucchini noodles in a colander. Sprinkle with 1/4 teaspoon salt. Set aside for 15 minutes. Rinse zucchini well and drain. Place on paper towels to absorb moisture.

Heat a large skillet over medium heat. Add coconut oil and garlic. Add shrimp and stir well. Cook for 4 minutes stirring occasionally. Remove shrimp from skillet to a bowl.

Heat skillet and add zucchini noodles. Sauté for 4 minutes stirring often. Add cooked shrimp, lemon juice, and cilantro. Cook 1 minute to heat through. Add a pinch of salt and pepper. Serve immediately.

Spinach and Chicken Enchiladas with Cilantro Cream Sauce

I fell in love with this cilantro sauce featured at a favorite restaurant. I knew I could duplicate the recipe with a few tries. The cilantro cream sauce is comforting and complements these enchiladas wonderfully. Black beans can be substituted for the chicken for a vegetarian dish.

SERVES 4

FILLING
2 tablespoons olive oil
1 small onion, minced
2 garlic cloves, minced
1 pound white mushrooms, chopped
1/4 cup chicken broth
10 ounce bag fresh spinach, coarsely chopped
4 ounces cream cheese, softened
2 cups cooked chicken, shredded (rotisserie chicken works well)

SAUCE
Juice of 1 lime
3/4 cup chicken broth
1 tablespoon garlic powder
Reserved mushroom from the filling
1 cup sour cream
1/2 cup fresh cilantro, chopped

ASSEMBLY
8 (6-inch) flour tortillas or soft taco size
1 1/2 cups Monterey jack cheese, shredded
Cooking spray

Preheat oven to 350º F.

For the filling, heat the olive oil in a large skillet over medium heat. Add the onions, garlic, and mushrooms. Sauté and stir occasionally about 7 minutes. Remove half of the mushroom mixture and set aside for the sauce. Add the chicken broth and cook for 2 minutes. Add the spinach and cook until spinach has wilted. Stir in the cream cheese until melted. Add the chicken and stir to cover with the sauce.

For the sauce, combine in a small saucepan the lime juice, chicken broth, and garlic powder. Add the reserved mushroom mixture, sour cream, and cilantro. Reduce heat to simmer until sauce just begins to thicken.

Spray a 9- by 13-inch baking dish with cooking spray. Divide filling evenly among the 8 tortillas, fill, roll and place them seam side down in the prepared pan. Pour sauce over enchiladas, top with shredded cheese, and bake 15 minutes.

Cilantro Lime Dessert Bars

This recipe originally was a tart and delicious dessert bar. My fondness for fresh herbs in desserts led me to modify this dessert bringing cilantro to the center of the stage. Lime and cilantro make a winning combination. Serve these bars cold or at room temperature.

SERVES 8

2 sticks (1 cup) unsalted butter, at room temperature
1/2 cup powdered sugar
2 cups all-purpose flour
Pinch salt
3 large egg yolks
1 1/2 teaspoons grated lime zest
1 (14 ounce) can sweetened condensed milk
2/3 cup fresh lime juice (about 8 limes)
Handful fresh cilantro, minced

Preheat oven to 350º F degrees and spray a 9- by 9-inch baking dish with cooking spray.

With mixer on high, beat the butter and powdered sugar together in a bowl until well combined and fluffy, about 2 to 3 minutes. Add the flour and salt and mix until just combined. Press the dough into the pan and bake until lightly golden, about 25 minutes.

While the crust is baking, prepare the lime mixture. Beat the egg yolks and lime zest on high speed until very thick, about 5 minutes (a stand mixer with the whisk attachment works great here). Turn the speed down to low on the mixer and add the condensed milk in a slow stream, mixing constantly; then, raise the speed back up to high and mix until thick, about 3 minutes. Add the lime juice and cilantro, and mix until just combined.

Once the crust is done, take it out of the oven and spread the lime mixture on top. Return to oven and bake until the filling is just set, about 25 to 30 minutes.

Cool the bars completely and refrigerate at least 4 hours. Cut into squares and enjoy!

Tamara Huron, BA, MA, is a graduate of Nazareth College and the University of Kansas. Originally from Binghamton, New York, and living for many years in Colorado, she now calls Alabama her home. Tamara furthered her culinary knowledge working at country clubs and restaurants. She creates recipes that highlight herbs and has written for numerous magazines and publications. Tamara's fondness for herbs and cooking led her to develop Organic Herbal Cooking, Inc. Her company offers an organic herb of the month, which arrives with beautiful photo recipe cards. She writes Organic Herbal Cooking's blog and shares the benefits of using herbs in simple healthful cooking. Tamara enjoys doing cooking shows and teaching her audiences about fresh herbs. Look for her cooking videos on YouTube and follow her on Facebook and Pinterest. She is a member of the Huntsville Herb Society and is chair of the Tea Bed at the Huntsville Botanical Garden. Fresh herbs are a must and incorporated into every meal that Tamara prepares.

Culantro or Cilantro:
No, It's Not the Same!

Angela Lugo

Culantro (*Eryngium foetidum* L., Apiaceae) is both a cooking and a medicinal herb well known in the Caribbean, West Indies, and the Far East. It is a biennial herb indigenous to continental tropical America and the West Indies. The herb is commonly found along moist or shaded pathways and in heavy soils. In these areas, it proliferates like a weed. However, here in the United States, outside ethnic neighborhoods, it is not very well known. Most confuse it with the now ubiquitous cilantro found in tacos, salads, and many things Mexican. Some of culantro's common names are *shado beni* and *bhandhania* (Trinidad and Tobago), *chadron benee* (Dominica), *coulante* (Haiti), *recao* (Puerto Rico), and *fitweed* (Guyana).

In Vietnam and the rest of Asia, culantro is also known and is most popular in Thailand, Malaysia, and Singapore, where it is commonly used with or instead of cilantro for soups, noodle dishes, and curries. I have not found how culantro got to these regions, but there is a huge presence of Indians and Asians in the islands mentioned above, so it is easy to see how it could have been transported to the Asian countries. Today, the presence of increasingly large West Indian, Latin American, and Asian immigrant communities in the metropolises of the United States, Canada, and the United Kingdom has created a large market for culantro, and large quantities are exported from Puerto Rico, the Caribbean, and Trinidad in the West Indies to these areas.

Every time I cut or cook with *recao*, my mind flashes back to my childhood. As a child, my family and I moved to New York from the island of Puerto Rico. In the city, we continued our food traditions, gravitating towards bodegas that had all our spices and herbs to flavor foods or concoct remedies for various ailments. Recao was definitely something we always had in our kitchen. Every two weeks my mother would buy onions, garlic, *ajicitos dulces* (sweet miniature peppers), tomatoes, cumin, and recao for our *sofrito*, the seasoning that goes into everything—in our beans, soups, fricassees, yellow rice, stews, etc. My mother would peel the onions and garlic, cube and chop the vegetables and culantro, and put all through a manual meat grinder (the food processor of yore). She would then season the sofrito with salt, cumin, and oregano and put it into a glass jar and refrigerate. She always had extra recao leaves which she would add to the various dishes at the last minute for added flavor. So, recao was not an exotic herb for me; it was a staple.

Recao has an aroma and taste similar to the popular cilantro. In fact, if cooks cannot find culantro for sofrito, they substitute cilantro. However, recao has a stronger smell to it and its leaves are tougher. Also known as *broad leaf* or *spiny coriander*, its leaves, long and broad with serrated edges, can grow up to 10 inches in length. It can grow in poor soil with little fertilizer, but it also does well in pots. Culantro plants are hardy and prefer partial shade, even though they tolerate full sun. Some growers feel that cutting the shoot that contains the seeds will encourage leaf production, while others do not.

To harvest, cut the leaves at the soil line with a knife or scissors, leaving the new, inner leaves to continue growth. I usually just pinch the leaves I need for a dish but use scissors or a knife when harvesting a big bunch. A word of caution: its spiny leaves sometimes make it uncomfortable to harvest without gloves. Also, because of its tough leaves, if I do put it in my salad, I cut it into thin ribbons; otherwise, I use cilantro and leave the culantro for teas or cooking. The plant throws out what looks like a green straw with a floret at the end; this floret is what contains the seeds which can be stored for subsequent plantings. In the tropics, it is self-seeding. I plant my seeds here in central New Jersey in late spring, and I make sure I bring my plants in before first frost.

In the garden, recao attracts ladybugs, lacewings, and other beneficial insects. It also seems that aphids do not like this herb.

Culantro is rich in iron, riboflavin, calcium, and carotene. Its leaves are an excellent source of vitamins A, B2, B1, and C, powerful antioxidants which increase vitality and immunity. The leaves also contain phosphorous for strong bones.

Medicinally, the leaves and roots are boiled for fevers, chills, vomiting, diarrhea, colds, and convulsions. The water is taken for pneumonia, flu, diabetes, constipation, and malarial fever. In chutneys, the leaves are used as an appetite stimulant. Culantro is anti-inflammatory and contains large amounts of plant sterols, so it can help with asthma, arthritis, and swelling. It also contains trimethylbenzaldehyde, a powerful pain reliever. Culantro tea can soothe earaches, stomachaches, and headaches. In some countries, culantro is also called *fitweed* because it is said to help prevent or soothe away epileptic fits.

Since the United States and other parts of the world do not know much about culantro, there is not a lot yet written about this herb. However, like cilantro, culantro is slowly becoming better known and easier to find. Many Asian farmers' markets carry it and you can definitely find in any Latino market. If you like cilantro, you need to try culantro.

Basic Sofrito

A heaping tablespoon will usually be enough for any dish for two people. However, depending on your taste, you may add more. This should be enough sofrito for about 10 servings. It stores well in the refrigerator for a couple of weeks. But, if I am going away or make a bigger batch, I freeze it.

YIELDS 10 SERVINGS

2 big Spanish onions
1 head garlic
2 small tomatoes
1 red pepper
15 fresh recao leaves
1 tablespoon dried oregano
1 teaspoon ground cumin
1 teaspoon sea salt
2 tablespoons olive oil
Tomato sauce or tomato paste, if desired

Rough chop onions, garlic, tomatoes, pepper, and recao in food processor, then mix in oregano, cumin, and salt. Put into glass jar and refrigerate.

When making any dish, heat some olive oil, put 1 tablespoon of sofrito into the heating oil, add 2 to 3 tablespoons tomato sauce or 1 teaspoon to 1 tablespoon (maximum) tomato paste, stir and slowly sauté. After 5 minutes, just add to your dish. If you like a fresher recao taste, add a couple of leaves about 2 minutes before the dish is done. Enjoy!

References

Benedetti, Maria Dolores Hajosy. *Earth & Spirit Healing Lore and More from Puerto Rico*. Waterfront Press,1989.

Haider, Paul, Dr. "Culantro (Recao)—A Wonderful Healing Herb and Spice." *Relax to Success*. December 17, 2013. https://paulhaider.wordpress.com/2013/12/17/culantro-racao-a-wonderful-healing-herb-and-spice/. Accessed May 25, 2016.

Lozada, Eliab. "Culantro." *Just4Growers*. http://www.just4growers.com/stream/troubleshooting/culantro.aspx. Accessed May 25, 2016.

Nunez, Esteban Melendez, Ph.D. *Plantas Medicinales De Puerto Rico*. Editorial De La Universidad De Puerto Rico, 1982.

Ramcharan, Christopher. "Culantro: A Much Utilized, Little Understood Herb." Accessed May 25, 2016. https://hort.purdue.edu/newcrop/proceedings1999/v4-506.html.

Sanchez, Beverly Anne. "Culantro: Jewel of Caribbean/West Indian Cuisine and Its Medicinal Applications." Knoji. Accessed May 25, 2016. https://natural-herbal-remedies.knoji.com/culantro-jewel-of-caribbeanwest-indian-cuisine-and-its-medicinal-applications/.

Angela Lugo is an Associate Professor of English at Middlesex County College in Edison, New Jersey. She is also on the board of Raices Cultural Center in New Brunswick, NJ, a non-profit organization dedicated to eco-culture, seed saving, and eco-cultural archivism. She was born in San Sebastian, a small mountain town on the island of Puerto Rico, and comes from a long line of *curanderos*; her grandmother Cecilia was the go-to person for folk and natural remedies for both spiritual and physical ailments. Angela grew up hearing about the native herbs of the island and their uses from both her grandmother and her father. Today, she continues to learn about and research these foods and herbs for both culinary and medicinal uses.

In Confusion—
Cilantro or Coriander?

Skye Suter

WHILE THE OFFICIAL Latin binomial for this Herb of the Year is *Coriandrum sativum,* coriander has a number of confusing but interesting common names. In the United States the word *coriander* refers to the seed while *cilantro* indicates the leaf of the coriander plant. The word *cilantro* is derived from the Spanish word for coriander. In the United Kingdom the seed is known as *coriander seed* while the leaf and stalk are known as *coriander* or *coriander leaf.* Other common names for the coriander herb are *Chinese parsley, Japanese parsley,* and *dizzycorn.* While variety abounds in the English language, there are countless names for coriander in other languages. And to add further confusion with names, there are other species of plants with the word *coriander* used in their descriptions.

A few other notable plants bear the name *cilantro* because they have a very similar scent and taste. These plants are used in similar fashion to the official coriander plant both in cooking and in medicine. Culantro, also known as *Mexican coriander* or *long coriander,* is actually *Eryngium foetidium,* for which the Latin translation is "foul smelling thistle." This prickly cousin (in name) is often referred to as *spiny* or *serrated coriander,* which describes the leaf shape. Culantro is used in Asian, Latin American, and Caribbean cuisines and is more pungent than *Coriandrum sativum.* Other plants bearing the cilantro name are the *Polygonum odoratum,* or *Vietnamese cilantro* (or *Vietnamese coriander*), and *Porophyllum ruderale,* or *Bolivian coriander.* The Vietnamese coriander is often used interchangeably with peppermint or *Coriander sativum* in Vietnamese recipes. Bolivian coriander is combined with rue and cilantro and other South American herbs in salsas, tacos, and soups.

Love it —Hate it

Setting aside the nomenclature confusion, we can see that themes pertaining to scent and taste run through the common names. In this arena strong and emphatic terminology is frequently used in describing coriander. Coriander is probably the most loved or hated herb in the herb world. Even within families, love/hate lines are strongly drawn. In my own family I count my eldest child and myself as cilantro lovers while my husband and younger child have historically found the leaf unpalatable. The strange thing is that my husband has had somewhat of a turnaround in recent years as I have exposed him to a lot of Indian and Mexican style food. He now actually appreciates and tolerates cilantro (in modest doses) in the appropriate culinary applications.

The haters of this herb are reacting to the coriander leaf, or cilantro; they have a perfectly sound excuse for intensely disliking it. It's genetic! Olfactory receptor genes which influence the sense of smell cause cilantro haters to experience a disagreeable, soapy taste in the mouth when the leaf is eaten. If cilantro haters do not actually have the sensitivity receptor, they can learn to appreciate cilantro given time and the right circumstances. They just have to unlearn influences from cultural eating habits or bad culinary experiences. I think this scenario is the explanation for my husband's turnaround.

Native to Europe and the Near East, coriander has a long and deserved reputation for its scandalous smell as evidenced by descriptions from ancient Rome to Greece and Medieval Europe. The 15th century herbalist John Gerard described the leaves as "a very stinking herb". On the positive side, the seeds lose their unpleasant scent as they dry, the fragrance sweetening. During the medieval era, the plant's perceived unpleasant odor when it was handled gave coriander a reputation for being poisonous. That odor also made coriander a handy ingredient for charms to ward off evil.

Cilantro fans love the taste as well as the aroma. When ripe, the seeds have a bright, aromatic, sweet scent, slightly floral. When eaten, cilantro offers a lemony undertone as part of the taste experience. The leaves have been described as piney, slightly soapy (which cilantro lovers enjoy), green, and citrusy; overall, they are more piquant than the seeds. Both seeds and leaves combine well with heavily spiced, pungent dishes.

In India the seeds are ground or used whole in curries, vegetable dishes, and spice combinations. Coriander seed is also used on the sub-continent for its anti-inflammatory properties and the leaves are a popular household remedy for digestive upsets and urinary tract infections. Mexico, other South American countries, and Middle Eastern countries heavily favor coriander, culantro, and Vietnamese cilantro in their cuisines.

In Thailand, even the roots of coriander plants are used as a flavoring agent for curries and other dishes. Fans during the Medieval and Renaissance eras added all parts to love potions as an aphrodisiac. Robert Turner, 17th century physician, epitomizes the medieval take on coriander in the *Brittish Physician*, "[W]hen taken with wine, coriander stimulates the animal passions."

Old Recipes

I am fascinated by old recipes and enjoy reading them and reading about them. Deciphering some of the ingredients and methods of cookery can be challenging, like figuring out a puzzle. Whether recipes were composed for medicinal purposes, for household chores, or for the table, they all have a background story with a purpose behind ingredients and preparations, however archaic and outlandish.

Below, a typical example of an old recipe calls for coriander in a deviled or "stuffed egg" recipe. It describes splitting a hard-boiled egg with a thread. Such a practical idea! Descriptive terms used for combining the stuffing ingredients like "kneading" and "pounding" are amusing but sound a little off kilter to the modern ear.

The Making of Stuffed Eggs. *Take as many eggs as you like, and boil them whole in hot water; put them in cold water and split them in half with a thread. Take the yolks aside and pound cilantro and put in onion juice, pepper and coriander, and beat all this together with murri, oil and salt and knead the yolks with this until it forms a dough. Then stuff the whites with this and fasten it together, insert a small stick into each egg, and sprinkle them with pepper, God willing.*

The Spice Mixture. *One part pepper, two of caraway, three parts dry coriander; pound all that and sift and use. And those dishes in which they are* *used separately, throw in separately, God willing.* 13th century *An Anonymous Andalusian Cookbook* (Charles Perry, trans.).

Coriander Comfits and Other Medicinal Uses

Comfits, in the context of days gone by, were small sugar-coated seeds, nuts, or berries. The most popular seeds included coriander, anise, cardamom, and caraway. Comfits were made by coating the seeds in boiled sugar syrup giving them a hard candy coating. Coriander comfits were considered medicinal and used for breath fresheners as well as relief from excess flatulence. During the Regency period in England, decorative comfit boxes similar to snuff boxes were carried around. Colorful, candy coated coriander and fennel seeds are offered after an Indian meal both as a breath mint and digestive aid for all that rich spicy food.

Various forms of the coriander plant from the powdered fruit and liquid extract to essential oils have been used as flavoring to disguise unpalatable medicines. It has also been used in ointment form to relieve rheumatism and arthritis. *Banckes' Herbal* states that "the seed thereof is good to do away the fevers that come the third day."

Cookery

Ancient cookery made good use of coriander. Columella, historic writer and epicure from the Roman Empire, recommended sowing coriander seed in spring and fall to take advantage of a continued crop. During the summer months, coriander seed was pressed and mixed with vinegar for preserving meat. Ancient Roman recipes called for coriander to be ground with salt as a rub on meat or fish. Coriander was part of the combination of herbs that make up the famous fish sauce *garum*.

Historically, such varied dishes as lamb, mutton, pigeon, duck, eggplant, salad, beer, "good fine white clareyt", meatballs, sausages, "calves feete" jelly, casseroles, "bisket breads", oysters, eels, prawns, hares, compost (actually a pickle or relish), and many other culinary concoctions have called for the seed or leaf of coriander. Recipes from Italy, Spain (especially Andalusia), England, the Netherlands, Germany, and other surrounding countries offer numerous recipes that can inspire today's cooking.

Recipes

Fresh cilantro leaves may be substituted for parsley and vice versa where one is not available. Flat leaf parsley and cilantro are also very similar in appearance and can sometimes be confused. If in doubt, use your nose to smell the difference. For coriander aficionados, the seed makes a great table spice; put in a peppermill, it can be freshly ground just like pepper. Medieval cookery, Indian cuisine, friends, and other influences inspire the recipes below.

Coriander-Paprika Herb Salt

There are many fun ways to combine herbs with salts to create wonderful seasonings for your cooking efforts. While other herbal salt recipes are good with sweet or savory applications, this one is better suited to savory dishes. Very good as part of a barbecue rub or on grilled fish, it blends nicely in the soup recipe below. Give away the extra salt to your friends and family.

MAKES ABOUT 2 CUPS

1 cup kosher salt
1/4 cup fresh sage leaves, washed and patted dry
1/8 cup dried savory leaves
1/4 cup whole coriander seed
1/8 cup dried rosemary
1 tablespoon paprika
1/2 cup coarse sea salt

Combine the kosher salt, fresh sage, savory, coriander seeds, rosemary, and paprika in a food processer. Pulse and grind ingredients until an even, fine consistency has been achieved. Add the coarse sea salt and pulse to combine. Empty the herbal salt mixture into a large bowl or onto a cookie sheet to air-dry for at least two hours to overnight. This allows fresh herbs to dry out before storing away in a cupboard or spice shelf Once dry, pack into glass jars and label. It will stay fresh for more than a year.

Recipes for carrot soup are found in numerous ancient texts, but the soup seems to have a distinctive connection to the British Isles, perhaps because it has become a Lenten fare staple. Classic versions of carrot soup (or soop) tend to stick with carrots and coriander but I like to add parsnips and fresh herbs from the garden. Melted cheese, crispy bacon bits, cheese bread sticks, and croutons are some traditional options to add to the final presentation. This soup would be delicious made with sweet baby carrots fresh from the garden. Sometimes the flavor of cumin can be overwhelming. If you don't like it, leave it out. Herb salts are a way to add additional herbal goodness to a recipe. They can be used to flavor the croutons or used as a finishing salt before serving.

SERVES 4 TO 6

SOUP
About 1 tablespoon grapeseed oil or olive oil
1 medium onion, quartered
1/2 teaspoon cumin, toasted and ground, optional
1 teaspoon coriander, ground
1 pound carrots, peeled and cut into 1-inch chunks
1 or 2 parsnips, peeled and cut into 1-inch chunks, optional
1 large potato, peeled and diced into 1-inch chunks
1 large bunch fresh cilantro, roughly chopped, some set aside for
    garnish
1 cup vegetable stock, plus more if needed
Sea salt and freshly ground pepper
Fresh snipped chives for garnish

CROUTONS
1 to 2 cups Italian loaf or French bread cut into 1-inch cubes
1 to 2 tablespoons olive oil
Herbed salt or sea salt to taste (optional)

To prepare the soup, heat the oil in a large pan and sauté the onions for four to five minutes. Stir in ground cumin and coriander. Add the carrots and parsnips. Sauté until softened, about three to four minutes. Add the potato. Stir in a handful of cilantro and a cup of vegetable stock, season with salt and pepper, then bring to a boil. Simmer uncovered until the vegetables are tender.

The soup can be blended into a smooth consistency with an immersion blender, in a regular blender, or in a food processor. Taste for seasoning and add a bit more stock to thin, if need be.

To make the croutons, spread the cubed bread onto a foil-lined baking sheet. Drizzle with the olive oil and sprinkle with herbed salt or other preferred seasoning. Place under a broiler and closely watch, turning cubes until they are brown and crispy. Set aside to cool.

To serve, reheat soup and stir in reserved coriander leaves. Garnish with chives and croutons, and serve hot.

Pesto, Salsa Verde, and Other Green Sauces

Pesto sauce is an incredibly versatile creation with infinite variations. It can be tossed into a bit of pasta for a flavorful hot meal or incorporated into cold pasta or potatoes to enhance flavor. Spread it on a crispy cracker, flatbread, or crostini for a delicious appetizer. Drizzling pesto over steamed veggies makes for a unique and flavorful side dish. When combined with cheese and sour cream, pesto creates a fantastic dip for vegetables.

A basic pesto is made from fresh basil or other uncooked greens, nuts, a quality olive oil, and a good, hard cheese. Some elements like the cheese or nuts may be omitted, but more often additional ingredients are added to a pesto. Pesto bases or green sauces can be made from just about any raw leafy green and/or herb combination. Arugula, basil, mint, oregano, rosemary, lemon verbena, chives, savory, sorrel, spring onion, garlic, spinach, fennel, roasted pepper, kale, scallions, salad burnet, coriander, and parsley, plus many more greens, work wonderfully as the base. Pine nuts, although traditional, are not a requirement; use whatever nut is handy in the cupboard. Pistachios, hazelnuts, walnuts, or almonds are all good choices. The best cheeses for a pesto are hard cheeses such as Asiago, Parmigiano-Reggiano, Parmesan, or Pecorino Romano. Pesto can be buzzed or blended to a smooth or chunky consistency, depending on your preference.

The ratio of ingredients for basic pesto consists of 1 cup of nuts, 2 cups of packed fresh leafy herbs and greens, 1/2 cup of grated cheese, 2 large cloves of garlic, 1/2 to 1 cup of olive oil, and sea salt and freshly ground pepper to taste. This yields from 1 1/2 to 2 1/2 cups of pesto depending on how many ingredients you keep adding. Use approximately 1/2 cup of pesto per person. Extra pesto can be stored in the refrigerator, or put away in the freezer for future use.

Columella-Inspired Pea and Cilantro Salsa Verde

Columella, the ancient Roman agriculturist and epicurean, recorded a wonderful recipe for a "salad" in which many greens (including cilantro) were ground together, then served, drizzled with olive oil and sprinkled with a grated cheese. The similarity of ingredients and preparations of his recipe inspired the Roman pesto or green sauce below.

YIELDS 1 1/2 TO 2 CUPS

2 large roasted garlic cloves, peeled or 1 small shallot, peeled and
    quartered
1/2 cup toasted almonds
1/2 teaspoon toasted cumin seeds
1/2 cup frozen peas, thawed
1/2 cup packed fresh cilantro leaves, heavier stems removed
1/2 cup packed, fresh flat leaf or curly parsley, stems removed
2 teaspoons fresh winter savory
3 tablespoons fresh herbs from garden (lemon verbena, salad burnet,
    chives, and so on)
1 tablespoon apple cider vinegar
1/2 teaspoon whole coriander seeds
1/2 cup Parmigiano-Reggiano cheese, or other hard grating cheese
1/2 to 1 cup plus extra virgin olive oil, as needed
Coarse sea salt and freshly ground black pepper

Place garlic clove or shallots on foil-lined pan in oven at 350° F (175° C) for 15 to 20 minutes, or until soft. Set aside to cool. In the meantime, toast almonds and cumin in a small cast iron pan. Set aside.

In a food processor, add thawed peas, cilantro, parsley, the fresh garden herbs of your choice, roasted garlic or shallot, almonds, cumin, coriander seeds, vinegar, 1/2 cup of the olive oil and blend. Process, and then keep drizzling in oil to get the desired consistency. Process ingredients on a constant speed for a smoother blend or pulse for a chunkier consistency.

Use tossed on cooled pasta like farfalle or medium shells for a summer salad, or in hot pasta like spaghetti or rigatoni for a hot meal. Grate a good-quality hard cheese, like Locatelli or Parmigiano-Reggiano, over the finished pasta before serving.

References

Arrowsmith, Nancy. *Essential Herbal Wisdom: A Complete Exploration of 50 Remarkable Herbs*. Llewellyn, 2009.

The Epicenter. *What is Coriander?* http://theepicentre.com/spice/coriander/. Accessed 5/3/16.

Folkard, Richard. *Plant Lore, Legends, and Lyrics: Embracing the Myths, Traditions.* E-book, digitized edition. London : S. Low, Marston, Searle, and Rivington, 1884. Accessed 5/5/16.

Gallowglass.org. *Local Spices: Savory Seeds in the Middle Ages.* http://www.gallowglass.org/jadwiga/herbs/seeds.html. Accessed 5/26/16.

Heilmeyer, Marina. *The Ancient Herb*. The J. Paul Getty Trust, 2007.

Hoffman, David. *The Complete Herbs Sourcebook: An A to Z Guide of Herbs to Cure your Everyday Ailments.* Sterling: 2013.

Internet Archeology. *7 Discussions of individual taxa.* http://intarch.ac.uk/journal/issue1/tomlinson/part2.html. Accessed 8/25/16.

Medieval Cookery. *Stuffed eggs—food and old recipes.* http://medievalcookery.com/recipes/claret.html. Accessed 6/9/16.

Ody, Penelope. *Home Herbal*. Dorling Kindersley, Inc., 1995.

Our Herb Garden. *History of Coriander: Name Origin.* http://www.ourherbgarden.com/. Accessed 5/3/16.

The Regency Redingote. *Comfits-Regency Tic-Tacs ®.* Posted 1 May 2009. https://regencyredingote.wordpress.com/2009/05/01/comfits-regency-tic-tacs/. Accessed 5/26/16.

The World's Healthiest Foods. *Cilantro and Coriander Seeds.* http://www.whfoods.com/genpage.php?tname=foodspice&dbid=70. Accessed 6/9/16.

Watts, D.C. *Dictionary of Plant Lore.* Google Books. Academic Press. Accessed 5/3/16.

Culantro pixie. *Skye Suter*

Skye Suter has been involved with plants and illustration for most of her life. She worked as an editorial art director for the *Staten Island Advance* where she also wrote and illustrated a gardening column and wrote art reviews. Skye spent ten years at the Staten Island Botanical Garden as educational director where she worked on educational projects, graphic design, and much more.

She keeps connected to herbs and the subjects she loves through writing, illustrating, and gardening as well as keeping her hand in with local arts groups and nature organizations. After serving six years as president of the Staten Island Herb Society, she now concentrates her time teaching subjects related to nature and herbs, illustrating, graphic design, and writing projects such as articles and newsletters for organizations such as the IHA. She has her own e-newsletter about herbs called *The Herbal Leaf.* Write to her at theherballeaf@gmail.com to sign up for this free, bi-monthly newsletter.

The Curious Conundrum of Coriander

Ann Sprayregan

NAIVELY, I HAD always assumed that *coriander* referred to the small dry berries or, when ground, the fragrant, tannish-brown powder. However, I have learned that *Coriandrum sativum* actually refers to the whole plant. The leaves are called *cilantro*. Often the leaves and seeds not only have different tastes and fragrances, but also different nutritional values.

First, when you're researching or talking about coriander, you have to understand that what must be specified is exactly what the subject might be. My problem was exacerbated by the lack of clarity in some writings I'd assembled because their titles stated *coriander*, but, as I happily read along, thinking I actually understood the subject—coriander seeds—I would be suddenly brought up short by the brief or casual mention of a leaf. Sometimes, there was no direct mention, only implication, so, after all my research, I remained clueless—and misinformed.

Second, how does one describe the taste and fragrance of coriander seeds? Coriander has been described variously as *lemony, earthy, mellow, subtle, pleasant, piney, warm,* and *sweet*.

The ground seeds are usually used together with various spices in a curry mix—cumin, turmeric, fenugreek, pepper, cloves, cardamom, cinnamon, ginger, to mention a few. I have always experienced coriander as something that would "brighten" the taste of a dish when it might have gotten too dark or heavy.

In view of the above, I often marvel at the lengthy, detailed, and complex descriptions of wines and beers that have proliferated on restaurant, bistro, and bar menus these days, sometimes approaching phone book dimensions. And, trying to hide my plebian, unsophisticated gourmet-challenged palate and limited vocabulary, I wonder: Are they for real? Do I really have such concrete taste buds?

At any rate, I see that, around the world, coriander seeds, whole or ground, are used in curries, stews, soups, pastes, rubs, sauces, pickling, even hot chocolate! (A Brooklyn chef swears by it).

As is the case with many other spices, toasting the seeds brings out the oils, the full taste.

Experiment with coriander and "brighten" your cooking!

Spicy Ground Lamb

Coriander evokes flavors enjoyed from North Africa to the Indian continent—and beyond! Serve this dish with or over rice or pasta. Important to note: these quantities are estimates. Determine quantities and proportions of different spices according to your taste. The lamb dish is enhanced when accompanied by a simple cucumber salad: sliced cucumber topped with onions, tomatoes, chopped parsley, a touch of chopped mint, salt and pepper, vinegar, and olive oil.

SERVES 4

1 heaping tablespoon curry powder (I use Madras, Mild)
1 heaping teaspoon ground coriander
1/2 teaspoon ground cinnamon
1/2 teaspoon ground cloves
1/2 teaspoon garlic powder, optional
Pinch ground cayenne, optional
3 to 4 tablespoons extra virgin olive oil
1 pound ground lamb
Small handful (about 1/2 cup) dried currants
1/2 teaspoon lemon zest, or very finely chopped lemon peel
1/4 cup water, if needed
Salt and freshly ground pepper
Small handful (about 1/8 to 1/4 cup) lightly toasted pine nuts, optional

In a 10- or 12-inch cast iron skillet on low heat, spread the curry powder, ground coriander, cinnamon, cloves, garlic, and cayenne, if using. Heat spices in the skillet a few minutes or until the spice fragrances reach you. Then add 3 to 4 tablespoons olive oil and mix well with the spices.

Stir in the ground lamb. Press the meat down and cook until the bottom layer begins to brown. Then turn the meat over and break into pieces to help the meat cook evenly and allow the spices to spread throughout.

When the meat looks as if it will soon be done, after about 10 to 15 minutes, add the currants and lemon zest. Cover and cook for about 10 to 15 minutes, but keep checking to see if the meat looks too dry. Cooking with a cover may bring out the moisture, but if, after the first 5 minutes, that doesn't seem to be happening, add tiny amounts of water, according to how loose you prefer your sauce.

Cover and continue to cook for 10 to 15 minutes. Taste to see if you want to adjust the spices. Add salt and pepper to taste.

You may want to lightly toast some pine nuts to sprinkle over the lamb before you serve it.

Ann Sprayregen, an Associate Professor, retired from NYCCT, City University of New York, where she worked as a counselor in educational opportunity programs (EOP). Long interested in all aspects of herbs, she concomitantly ran a small herbal and health food retail business. When the college day care center was defunded during a recession, they had a ready source of products for sale to the college community—a financial help to the Center and a learning experience for all. Membership in the IHA has provided further invaluable learning as well as camaraderie. Ann has served on the International Herb Association Foundation (IHAF) for over ten years and was awarded the IHA Professional Award in 2014.

"Slo-Bolt." *Susan Belsinger*

The Nutritional and Medicinal Benefits of Cilantro and Coriander

Carol Little

CILANTRO? IT'S NOT one of those gentle herbs on the sidelines that everyone likes. If you're in the cilantro (*Coriandrum sativum*) fan club, you may be interested to know that it is a powerful herbal ally. If you're not fond of it, you may want to find ways to add it to your meals as it is of great benefit.

In North America, the fragrant, leafy green above-ground parts are known as the herb *cilantro*, while the nutty seeds are the spice called *coriander*. In the United Kingdom and other parts of Europe, however, the whole plant is called coriander.

Low in calories but high in nutrients, cilantro has many health benefits. Cilantro is a good source of antioxidants, dietary fiber, essential oils, vitamins A, C, and K as well as the minerals calcium, iron, magnesium, manganese, potassium, beta carotene, folic acid, niacin, and riboflavin. The substantial mineral content helps to regulate heart rate and blood pressure. Cilantro's high iron content is thought to help counteract anemia as iron is essential for red blood production.

Cilantro shows potential as a natural chelation agent, especially for those who have been exposed to high levels of mercury in dental fillings or seafood (Omura and Beckman). In the mid-1990s, Dr. Omura, MD, published two papers regarding research with people ingesting cilantro in a popular Vietnamese soup. In those studies, participants with symptoms of excess mercury noted relief after regular consumption of large amounts of cilantro.

Chelation helps to rid the body of toxic chemicals. Picture cilantro as a cartoon character in the body reaching out a hand to a heavy metal molecule and helping it exit the body via a blood vessel. In natural medicine, cilantro has been effectively used to help the body to release heavy metals like mercury, lead, aluminum, and other toxins, literally binding to these substances, then removing them from blood, organs, and tissue through elimination channels.

In a two-week, detoxifying formulation, Dr. David Williams combines chlorella, bentonite clay, and cilantro to make the elimination process more effective. Since cilantro may release more heavy metals than the body can remove, and to prevent metals from being deposited in the colon, he recommends taking 1 to 2 teaspoons of a form of the clay mixed with water three times a day between meals. For an even more effective chelation, some herbalists suggest adding two cloves of garlic to fresh cilantro and chlorella. As with many herbal traditions, these protocols are based on experiential evidence and notes from years of hands on consultations, passed from teachers to students. Always check with your health practitioner before beginning any health regimen.

Cilantro has been shown to ease hormonal premenstrual mood swings and to relax cramping during menses. Cilantro's antibacterial action appears to protect against painful urinary tract infections. It acts as a natural antiseptic and antifungal agent for skin disorders like fungal infections and eczema. Cilantro is known to have the ability to clear up recurring infections, both viral and bacterial, especially when eaten with omega-3 rich foods like nuts.

James A. Duke, Ph.D., former botanist at the U.S. Department of Agriculture, author of *The CRC Handbook of Medicinal Herbs,* and longtime IHA member, states that cilantro has been shown to settle the stomach. He recommends drinking a cup of the tea made from a handful of the leaves when experiencing any form of stomach discomfort.

In the kitchen, cilantro can be used as an edible garnish, added to salads, finely minced and sprinkled onto fish, eggs, vegetables, grains, pasta, or used to create fresh salsas. My favourite ways to use cilantro all year long are in the forms of paste and pesto. They are easy to make and then freeze in ice cube trays. Add to many dishes for extra nutrition and flavor. This is a super way to preserve and have cilantro on hand all year long.

The aromatic, brownish coriander seeds are an integral part of my culinary spice collection. Both nutty and sweet, these seeds have been enjoyed in cuisines around the world and in well-respected traditional medicine since before Biblical times. Coriander seed is highly nutritive and a good source of dietary fiber, iron, and magnesium as well as a rich source of phytonutrients and flavonoids. Revered in both Traditional Chinese Medicine (TCM) and Ayurvedic traditions, coriander seed is an ancient and versatile plant remedy.

As a digestive aid, coriander seed helps to prevent flatulence, soothe nausea, and settle a queasy stomach. It helps the alimentary tract to produce enzymes and increase production of digestive juice. Additionally, it stimulates digestion through peristaltic action. You can drink straight coriander tea or combine with allspice, cardamom, cloves, cumin, fennel, garlic, ginger, and/or turmeric for a more sophisticated concoction.

As an anti-inflammatory herb, it can reduce minor swelling and may alleviate inflammatory conditions like arthritis. Additionally, it can lower the LDL (bad) cholesterol and support the HDL (good) cholesterol. Coriander's antibacterial properties have been shown to be effective against salmonella bacteria. For this reason, it can help to relieve diarrhea caused by microbial infections.

Coriander helps to promote healthy liver function and to stimulate the endocrine glands. It can help with insulin secretion and to regulate blood sugar. Its diuretic qualities aid in detoxification. Made into a strong tea, coriander compresses can ease conjunctivitis. Coriander tea or syrup can help when an expectorant is needed during cough season.

The following recipes offer several delicious ways to add cilantro and coriander to your diet.

Cilantro Pesto #1

This one is a basic recipe and the one I make most. I always use fresh herbs when making pesto.

Yields 1 cup

1 clove garlic
1/4 cup walnuts or almonds
2 cups fresh cilantro leaves
1/4 cup olive oil or walnut oil
1/2 cup Parmesan or bleu cheese, optional
Sea salt and freshly ground black pepper

In a food processor, pulse the garlic and nuts until coarsely chopped. Add the cilantro and pulse until chopped, about a minute. Add the oil slowly to mix with the contents of the food processor. Stop and scrape down the sides of the bowl. Add more oil if mixture appears dry. Add cheese, if using, and process to combine. Season with salt and pepper to taste. Store in refrigerator for up to a week.

Cilantro Pesto #2

This recipe has more ingredients and a little heat for a kicked up version!

Yields 1 cup

1 to 3 cloves garlic crushed
1/4 cup chopped or crushed walnuts
1 1/4 cups fresh cilantro leaves
About 1 1/2 tablespoons olive oil
2 tablespoons (about 1 ounce)
    dry-packed sun-dried tomatoes, chopped
1 teaspoon white wine vinegar
2 tablespoons grated Parmesan cheese
1/2 teaspoon chile pepper flakes, optional
Sea salt and freshly ground black pepper

In a food processor, pulse the garlic and nuts until coarsely chopped. Add the cilantro and pulse until chopped, about a minute. Slowly add one and a half tablespoons olive oil to mix with the contents of the food processor. Stop and scrape down the sides of the bowl. Add the sun-dried tomatoes, oil, vinegar, and chile flakes. Add more oil if mixture appears dry. Add the Parmesan cheese and process to combine. Season with salt and pepper. Store in refrigerator for up to a week.

Chilean Pebre

I loved this Chilean staple from the first bite. While there are as many recipes as there are towns, my favourite recipe comes from my Valparaiso friend Sandra. Serve with crackers or a good bread, as a side dish, or add to sandwich fillings.

4 TO 6 SERVINGS

1 bunch fresh cilantro greens, chopped
1 medium tomato, chopped
3 garlic cloves, chopped finely
1 tablespoon onion, chopped
1 chile pepper, chopped, fresh or dried (optional)
2 to 3 tablespoons olive oil
Sea salt and freshly ground black pepper to taste

Chop the cilantro, tomato, garlic, onion, and chile (if using). Mix together in a medium-sized bowl. Add the olive oil and mix together well. Add a little more oil as needed to reach smooth consistency, then season to taste. This is best served the same day but will keep for 2 days in the refrigerator.

Herb Paste 101

Herbs like cilantro, chives, mint, parsley, or basil harvested at their peak can be blended with olive oil into an aromatic and delicious paste to enliven any meal. Use as a marinade, topping, or dip, or add to mayonnaise, mustard, and salsa to create exciting new condiments. Use a good quality olive oil for the best results.

YIELDS 2 TO 4 SERVINGS

Large handful of fresh cilantro, alone or with other aromatic herb(s)
About 1 tablespoon olive oil

Pinch the leaves from the stems of the chosen herb. Add the leaves to a food processor. Pulse the machine briefly to chop the herbs. Add a drizzle of olive oil while continuing to process the herbs. It doesn't take long before the oil and herbs form a paste. Store in the refrigerator up to a week.

Orange, Cilantro and Black Bean Salad

If you're short on time, substitute 1 1/2 cups of drained canned mandarin oranges for the fresh orange segments in this flavourful side dish, but make sure they're packed in their own juices.

YIELDS 4 SERVINGS (3/4) CUP SERVINGS

1/2 teaspoon olive oil
1/2 medium red onion, cut into thin wedges
2 medium garlic cloves, finely chopped
1/2 teaspoon ground cumin
1 cup cooked black beans, rinsed and drained if canned
2 tablespoons fresh, chopped cilantro
2 teaspoons red wine vinegar
2 medium-sized seedless oranges, peeled, broken into segments and
    chopped in half
1/4 teaspoon table salt
1/4 teaspoon black pepper

In a large skillet, warm oil over medium-high heat. Add onion and sauté 2 minutes. Add garlic and cumin and cook 1 minute more. Stir in black beans and cook just until heated through. Transfer bean mixture to a medium-sized bowl and stir in cilantro, vinegar, and oranges. Season with salt and pepper and serve.

Wise Water Tea

This trio of seeds increases digestive ability and makes a tasty tonic before or after meals. In herbal medicine, the tea is used specifically to help the body strengthen and clear toxins after chemotherapy. Crush or toast seeds first for the best flavor.

YIELDS 4 CUPS

1 quart water
1 teaspoon coriander seed
1 teaspoon cumin seed
1 teaspoon fennel seed

Boil 1 quart of water. Pour into a non-plastic thermos or 1-quart canning jar with a lid. Add coriander, cumin, and fennel seeds. Let steep for about 15 minutes. Strain and drink a cup before breakfast and sip the rest throughout the day.

Garam Masala

One of India's most popular blends, it's used as a final flavouring near the end of a dish or sprinkled on top just prior to serving. I like to include a dash in autumn and winter soups or stews or in grain dishes.

YIELDS 4 CUPS

4 tablespoons coriander seed
2 tablespoons cumin seed
1 tablespoon caraway seed
2 tablespoons cardamom seed
1 tablespoon black peppercorns
1 3-inch cinnamon stick, broken into small pieces
1 teaspoon whole cloves

In a small, heavy skillet, over medium heat, pan roast the first 5 ingredients until slightly browned and aromatic. Turn the seeds often as they cook to avoid burning. Set aside to cool.

Cut or break the cinnamon stick into very small pieces. Process the cinnamon in a grinder or a small food processor. Add the cloves and the roasted seeds to this mixture and process the whole thing until it becomes a fine powder. Store in glass jar, labeled, in a cool, dark cupboard.

Aromatic Roasted Chickpeas

Yields four servings

3 (15 ounce) cans chickpeas
3 tablespoons olive oil
1 to 2 large cloves garlic
1 to 1 1/2 teaspoons *garam masala*
Sea salt
Lime juice, optional

Preheat oven to 350° F.

Rinse the chickpeas well with cold water, removing any loose skins. Drain in a colander for 5 minutes. Pat dry with a dish towel and spread onto a baking sheet. Toss with the olive oil and garlic, coating well, then use a wooden spoon to spread them into a single layer.

Roast for approximately 40 minutes; turn 2 to 3 times with spoon until lightly browned. They may split. Remove from the oven and toss with the spice mix and salt. Taste and adjust the seasonings if needed.

Serve warm or cold. A little lime juice can be sprinkled over, just before serving for a brighter taste.

Coriander Rub #1

A tasty addition to meat dishes, spice rubs are easy to make. Use with free range chicken or pork tenderloin. Slather on meat for at least 20 minutes, then follow your favorite recipe.

Yields enough for 2 to 3 pounds of meat

1 tablespoon coriander seeds
2 teaspoons each of dried sage, rosemary, and thyme
1 bay leaf, crushed
1 or 2 garlic cloves
1 teaspoon sea salt
1 teaspoon black pepper
1 teaspoon olive oil

Combine all ingredients in a food processor until the consistency of a paste. Store in the refrigerator for 2 to 3 days.

Coriander Rub #2

This rub adds colour and flavour to your pork, chicken, and lamb. If you use hot paprika in place of the sweet paprika, use about half the amount. Slather on meat for at least 20 minutes, then follow your favorite recipe.

Yields enough for 2 to 3 pounds of meat

1 tablespoon coriander seeds
1 teaspoon ground cumin
2 teaspoons turmeric
1 teaspoon sweet paprika (if hot paprika, use less)
1 inch piece gingerroot, grated
1 teaspoon garlic, chopped
1/2 teaspoon hot red pepper flakes
1 tablespoon olive oil

Combine all ingredients in a food processor until the consistency of a paste. Store in a jar in the refrigerator for 2 to 3 days.

References

Duke, James. *The Handbook of Medicinal Herbs.* CRC Press, 2002.

Omura, Y. and S. I. Beckman, S.I. 1995. Role of mercury (Hg) in resistant infections and effective treatment of *Chlamydia trachomatis* and *Herpes* family viral infection (and potential treatment for cancer) by removing localized Hg deposits with Chinese parsley and delivering effective antibiotics using various drug uptake enhancement methods. *Acupunct Elecrother Res.* 50: 195-229. Accessed August 12, 2016.

Omura, Y., Shimotsuura, Y., Fukuoka, A., Fukuoka, H. and T. Nomoro.1996. Significant mercury deposits in internal organs following the removal of dental amalgam, and development of pre-cancer on the gingiva and the sides of the tongue and their represented organs as a result of inadvertent exposure to strong curing light and effective treatment. *Acupunct Electrother Res.* 21: 133-160. Accessed August 12, 2016.

Dr. David Williams. "Searching the World for Better Health: Using Cilantro and Clay for Detoxification." http://www.drdavidwilliams.com/cilantro-clay-for-detoxification/. Accessed October 29, 2016.

Carol Little, R.H. is a traditional herbalist in Toronto, Canada, where she has a private practice working primarily with women. Her easy-to-digest weekly blog posts offer quick take-away ideas to help readers feel their best (www.studiobotanica.com). Carol is a past board member and current professional member of the Ontario Herbalists Association. She combines her love of travel and passion for all things green to write about both. Carol has written for *Vitality Magazine*, contributes to the monthly online *Natural Herbal Living Magazine* (bit-ly/herballivinginfo) as well as the quarterly IHA newsletter and annual *Herb of the Year™* series. In addition, she monitors the IHA Facebook page. Check out her active Facebook community at facebook.com/studiobotanica.

Choosing Cilantro —
Creative Cooking

Karen O'Brien

CILANTRO WAS NOT an herb I grew up with. I'm not sure when I became involved with this tasty treat, but it was probably when I traveled westward and ate at some authentic Mexican restaurants. Happily, I do not have the genes that preclude enjoyment of this herb, even though my ethnic background (eastern European) is most likely not one where this herb would have been used or even known about.

I love cilantro and use it frequently in salsas, guacamole, and other south of the border dishes like fish tacos. I tend to put in as much cilantro as will fit, as I really enjoy the pungent flavor. One of my favorite condiments is to mix liberal amounts of cilantro with lime juice and equal parts mayonnaise and sour cream–this is delicious on chicken burgers.

But I have branched out, using my favored herb in salads and soups, mixing cooking styles and flavors from around the world and using *Coriandrum sativum* to achieve cilantro nirvana.

Cilantro. *Yvonne Sisko*

Roasted ground coriander adds a wonderful depth of flavor to dishes. I use it almost exclusively over regular ground coriander. You can make your own or buy it. It blends well with cumin, turmeric, cardamom, and many other spices.

SERVES 6 TO 8

2 cups red quinoa
4 cups water
1/2 pound fresh asparagus, cut into 1/2 inch lengths
1 can water chestnuts, diced
2 mangoes, peeled and chopped
1 teaspoon roasted ground coriander
1 teaspoon turmeric
1/2 teaspoon ground cardamom
1/2 cup extra virgin olive oil

If the quinoa has not been pre-rinsed, wash, rinse, and drain it twice to remove the saponins.

Otherwise, you will have soapy tasting quinoa.

In a medium saucepan, cook the quinoa in 4 cups of water; drain and set aside in a large bowl.

Meanwhile, steam the asparagus until tender—about 6 minutes. Drain and add to the quinoa, along with the water chestnuts and mango. Sprinkle the coriander, turmeric, and cardamom into the quinoa mixture and mix well, ensuring that the spices coat the quinoa. Drizzle olive oil over, a small amount at a time until the quinoa is well coated.

This dish is best made ahead of time to give the ingredients time to blend. Serve cold.

This dish comes together quickly and is a good way to use up extra cooked pork or chicken. I make it with a large amount of cilantro as I love it. Adjust the amount according to your fondness for the herb.

SERVES 4, OR 8–10 AS AN APPETIZER

2 large onions, sliced thinly into rings
3 tablespoons olive oil
8 whole wheat tortillas
Extra olive oil for coating tortillas, about 1/4 cup
3 mangoes, peeled, and sliced thinly
2 cups cooked pork loin, sliced thinly, or 2 cups cooked chicken breast,
    shredded
3 cups shredded cheddar cheese
1 to 2 cups chopped cilantro
Sour cream
Guacamole

Sauté onions in oil until soft and set aside.

Place four tortillas on cookie sheet sprayed or coated with oil. Layer each tortilla with onions, mango, and pork then sprinkle each with cheese and cilantro. Top with another tortilla and spray or brush with oil.

Cook in 350° degree oven until cheese is melted, about 15 to 20 minutes. Serve with sour cream and/or guacamole for dipping.

Coriander and dill seed umbels drying in the herb garden. *Susan Belsinger*

Seeds

Shirley Russak Wachtel

Coriander seeds swim in the palm of my hand

They are unmiraculous

Tiny ovals of yellow brown

Their faces deformed by vertical ridges

Anonymous as dirt.

And yet released into air

They sing their scents

A peppery sweetness

At once nutty and pungent

Lemon and orange

Fragrant as a flower

Yet subtle as a breeze

A hodgepodge of contradictions resurrected

To a new identity

Wheat beer

Dhana dal

Garam masala

Coriander seeds swim in the palm of my hand

Inspired.

Coriander seed in suribachi. *Susan Belsinger*

Shirley Russak Wachtel is a college English professor living in New Jersey. She holds a D.Lit from Drew University. She is also the author of a book of poetry, *In the Mellow Light*, several books for children, and a series, *Spotlight on Reading*, a college-level text. Her personal essays have been published in *The New York Times* OpEd section. Her short stories and poems have appeared in *Middlesex*, *biostories*, *River Poets Journal*, *Haiku Journal*, *emerge*, *Leaves of Ink*, *Whisper*, and other literary journals. Her acclaimed memoir, *My Mother's Shoes*, follows her mother's journey during the Holocaust and as a new citizen in America. Wachtel's latest book, *The Music Makers*, is the story of five individuals living in upstate New York who are drawn together by a mysterious young boy.

Medicine
Aromatherapy
Ethnobotany

Cilantro flowers in the garden. *Peter Coleman*

Cilantro/Coriander:
Use it Liberally!

Rosemary Gladstar

I'M A HUGE fan of cilantro, and love the fresh leaves chopped fine in salads or added to Asian and Mexican dishes. Yum! Obviously, I'm not one who finds the smell or taste of cilantro offensive, but am rather addicted to the flavor. I love knowing as I eat it that it's helping to clean my body of toxins that might be accumulating and helping to boost my immune system.

One of my favorite ways of eating it is cilantro pesto. Of course, one would have to be a lover of cilantro to eat it this way as it is quite strongly flavored. For those less enamored with the taste, mellow the flavors by blending cilantro half and half with parsley and/or basil in your traditional pesto recipe.

Traditional Uses

Cilantro belongs to the large and well-known Apiaceae family which includes such notables as dill, anise, carrot, cumin, parsnip, and fennel. Interestingly, both the leaf (cilantro) and the seed (coriander) are equally popular. Both have distinctive flavors and are used for different, though similar purposes. While most people enjoy the aromatic seeds, the leaves elicit a more varied set of responses in people. Most people love them, as witnessed in cilantro's popularity in world cuisine. But there are some people who have a fairly strong aversion to cilantro. It seems to be a love or hate relationship with the leaves of *Coriandrum sativum*: either "use it liberally" or "skip the cilantro"!

Like other members of this aromatic family, cilantro's long and colorful history as a food and medicine dates back several thousand years. It is mentioned in the Old Testament a number of times, and is even supposed to resemble the manna served in the desert in one Biblical passage, perhaps because of its sweet digestive properties. It was cultivated in the Middle East over 7,000 years ago and is still found in many of the most popular Middle Eastern dishes. In fact, cilantro and its counterpart, coriander, are among the most popular spices in the world today when one considers how many world cuisines and recipes they are included in.

Native to the Mediterranean and Middle Eastern regions, cilantro's popularity spread rapidly. It was cultivated in ancient Egypt and mentioned in Sanskrit texts dating back over 1500 years ago. Coriander seeds were among the items found in the tomb of Ramses II, which gives some perspective of how important this spice was; one didn't bury just anything with a king who was also considered a god. The seeds were also used to help preserve meat and to cover up the scent of rotting flesh, which may be another reason why it was found buried in the tombs of kings.

The Greek and Romans were also fond of cilantro and its aromatic seeds, and it was a popular spice as well as a medicinal herb in both cultures. The early physicians, including Hippocrates, used coriander as a digestive aid and as an aromatic stimulant. It was also considered a fairly potent sexual stimulant by several early cultures, often found in aphrodisiac formulas. One such popular drink, Hippocras, was formulated with coriander, cardamom, clove, ginger, and cinnamon, and was commonly served at weddings and romantic rendezvous. This recipe spread rapidly and was exported by the Crusaders to Europe, and later by the Spaniards to South America. But it was considered to be so rousing that it was banned by the church in several countries; perhaps one of our earliest examples of sexual censorship? (I'd love to know what else was in that formula!)

Coriander was also mentioned in *The Arabian Nights* (also known as *One Thousand and One Nights*), a book over 1000 years old. In the story, coriander was part of a mixture that supposedly helped a childless man to have children. Ah! Even the ancient Arabs knew of its famed aphrodisiac properties! In Traditional Chinese Medicine, coriander also had a reputation as an aphrodisiac and was included in sexual tonics and formulas.

Coriander was one of the first plants (along with dandelions) to be brought to the Americas from Europe. By the mid-1600s, cilantro could be found growing near many of the settlements, including the Massachusetts Bay Colony. You can be certain that coriander was included in herbal decoctions for digestive issues, in the early "meetin' seeds" that were used to calm the children's stomachs during those long meetings, and as a flavoring aid to mask other, less tasty herbal medicines. Coriander was also a popular carminative, a remedy used to ease digestion and to help expel gas from the intestines. This remains, still, one of its most popular uses.

In Ayurvedic medicine, an ancient system that developed in India several thousand years ago, coriander is considered an aphrodisiac, digestive aid, anti-flatulent, tonic, and mild diuretic.

Modern Medicinal Uses

Both the leaves and seeds of *Coriandrum sativum* contain essential oils that have medicinal properties that are known to help expel gas, soothe upset stomachs, and aid digestion. The seeds have antispasmodic properties that help with stomach cramps and spastic muscles. They can also alleviate mild tension headaches. Coriander seeds can be made into an infusion and the resulting tea used for strained, tired eyes. In Ayurvedic medicine, the seeds are considered a fine tonic for the kidneys and used as a mild diuretic. The leaves, which are used in many Asian, Mexican, and Middle Eastern dishes, are considered one of the best remedies for detoxifying heavy metals such as mercury or lead from the system. Both the leaves and seeds have mild stimulating properties that stimulate digestion, and according to ancient legend, can also stimulate libido. I'm sure it's no match for Viagra, but it's worth a try! Try the recipe for Hippocras below.

Please note: information below will state whether it is the leaf (cilantro) or seed (coriander) that's used as they have different properties. Although cilantro and coriander come from the same plant and have many similar properties, their flavors are very different and should not be substituted for each other.

Antibiotic properties

The antibiotic compound, dodecenal, found in cilantro has showed impressive results. This compound has been shown in laboratory tests to be twice as effective as the commonly used antibiotic drug gentamicin at killing the food-borne bacteria, salmonella. However, keep in mind, these are laboratory findings with single isolates of plants, which do not always work the same way as whole plants on the human body.

Anti-Microbial Properties

Cilantro contains important volatile oils that have antimicrobial properties, which make it useful for fungal, bacterial, or yeast infections.

Cholesterol-Lowering Ability

Studies have shown that cilantro, when consumed on a regular basis, can lower LDL ("bad cholesterol") and increase HDL ("good cholesterol"). It seems to work by reducing the amount of damaged fats (lipid peroxides) in the cell membranes and by serving as an anti-inflammatory agent.

Digestion

Coriander seeds promote assimilation of food and healthy digestion. They also help expel gas and calm spastic digestive muscles. The seeds can be chewed, made into tincture or tea, or used to season and flavor food while enhancing over all well-being.

Eyesight

The high beta-carotene and antioxidants in cilantro make it good for eye health, and also for helping to alleviate eye problems. In addition, it also helps reduce the threat to our eyes posed by age-related vision disorders such as macular degeneration and cataracts.

Heavy Metal Detoxifier

Cilantro is one of the very few herbs that is used as a heavy metal detox agent, to detoxify mercury, lead, aluminum, and other heavy metals. You can use it juiced; in tinctures; or in cilantro pestos. Eat it regularly for this purpose.

Poultice

Fresh cilantro leaves make a cooling, soothing poultice for insect bites and rashes. Blend in a blender, or crush in a mortar and pestle, with a small amount of water or yogurt. Apply directly to the site, and leave on for 30 to 45 minutes. Apply twice a day, until heat is gone and rash is better.

Safety Profile

Cilantro and coriander are generally considered safe and benign. However, some people are allergic to members of the Apiaceae family and can have an allergic reaction to coriander (itchiness, watery eyes, and/or rash). And, as mentioned, some people have an aversion to the taste of cilantro; they find it repelling rather than tasty. Even Parkinson himself, a great herbalist writing in 1640, found cilantro repulsive: "The whole plant, seede and all while it is green and growing hath a strong and loathsome savour scarce to be endured; but when the seede is full ripe and dry it is of reasonable good scent and taste without offence."

Hippocras

Like many of these ancient herbal recipes, there are many variations of Hippocras. This is one favorite. Hippocras was at one time one of the most famous aphrodisiac formulas in the world. I think, perhaps, people then had more time for sex or fewer sexual problems, as aphrodisiacs seemed to be far less powerful and medicinal than they are now, and were more flavorful and fun. Use the wine of your choice: red seems better as an aphrodisiac, but white seems to blend better with the flavor of coriander.

1 bottle white or red wine
1 ounce coriander seeds (freshly crushed)
1/2 ounce cinnamon
1/2 ounce ginger (fresh grated preferably, but dried will work)
1/4 ounce cardamom (freshly crushed preferably, but ground will work)
1/8 ounce lemon or orange peel (organic and unsprayed)
Honey (as little or much as you like)
Place all ingredients in a saucepan and over a very low heat, simmer (do not boil) for 30 to 45 minutes. Turn off the heat, cover, and let sit over night to allow flavors to merge. Strain and add honey to taste.

You can either warm it over low heat and drink warm or serve chilled on the rocks. Turn down the lights, bring out the candles, play your favorite music, and sip this ancient formula. Allow time for the warm stimulating flavors to entice you into romance. This is more about the "slow sex movement" than "fast sex"!

Rosemary Gladstar is a star figure in the field of modern herbalism, internationally renowned for her technical knowledge and stewardship in the global herbalist community. She has been learning, teaching, and writing about herbs for over 40 years and is the author of eleven books. Her work includes *Medicinal Herbs: A Beginners Guide*, *Herbal Healing for Women*, *Rosemary Gladstar's Herbal Recipes for Vibrant Health*, and *The Science and Art of Herbalism*, an extensive in depth home study course.

She lives and works from her home, Sage Mountain Herbal Retreat Center and Botanical Sanctuary—a 500-acre botanical preserve she founded in Central Vermont. She is also the Founding President of United Plant Savers, director of The New England Women's Herbal Conference, and founder and past director of the International Herb Symposium. sagemountain.com

Cilantro flowers in the garden. *Stephanie Parello*

The Medicinal Properties of Coriander

Daniel Gagnon

IN THE UNITED States, the leaf of *Coridandrum sativum* is commonly called *cilantro* while the fruit is commonly called *coriander seed*. In this article, to prevent confusion and to use the common parlance, I refer to cilantro or cilantro leaf as coriander leaf and coriander fruits as coriander seeds. In many countries of the world, it is also called Chinese parsley.

Other Common Names

Ayurvedic: Dhanyaka (seed)
Chinese (Pinyin name): Yuan sui zi (seed)
Italian: Cilantro (leaf), Coriandolo (seed)
French: Coriandre
German: Koriander
Spanish: Cilantro
Unani: Kazbura
United Kingdom and Australia: Coriander leaf, coriander seed

Part Used

Seed and leaf

Coriander and History

Coriander has a long history of use. It is mentioned in the *Papyrus of Ebers* dating around 1500 BCE. Coriander is also mentioned in the writings of Cato the Elder (234–149 BCE) as well as Pliny the Elder (23–79 CE). It has also been reported that coriander seeds were known in England before the Norman Conquest (around 1066 CE). Pliny the Elder, a

Roman author, naturalist, and natural philosopher, used the name *cori-andrum* for this herb. The name is thought to be derived from the word *koros* (a bug) in reference to the strong smell of the fresh leaves (Grieve 1971). Some individuals have a distinct aversion to the smell and taste of fresh coriander leaves. When bed bugs are crushed, the insects emit a smell that is reminiscent of fresh coriander leaf. That may, in part, explain the origin of the name coriander.

Coriander's Constituents

The chemical composition of foods is of interest to individuals who may want to gain a better understanding of how herbal constituents may influence the function of the body. The following are some of the known constituents found in the seeds and leaves of coriander.

The leaf has appreciable amounts of vitamins A, B (including folic acid, and B6), C, and K. The leaf is also a rich source of dietary fiber and minerals including calcium, iron, magnesium, manganese, and potassium (Kirschmann 1996). Fibers and minerals provide important dietary factors that help us maintain our health. Dietary fibers are essential for intestinal regularity and to maintain healthy cholesterol and blood sugar levels. Potassium is an important component of cells and body fluids that help regulate heart rate and blood pressure. Iron is essential for healthy red blood cell production. Manganese is used by the body as a co-factor to manufacture the antioxidant enzyme *superoxide dismutase*. Coriander leaf also contains powerful antibacterial compounds including α-pinene, β-phellandrene, cineole, and borneol.

Coriander seed contains between 0.1 to 2.0 percent of volatile oil depending on the seed variety. The constituents of the essential oil of coriander seeds can be broken down into four major groups: 1. alcohols including linolool (60–80%), geraniol (1.2–4.6%), terpinen-4-ol (3%), and α-terpineol (0.5%); 2. hydrocarbons including γ-terpinene (1–8%), r-cymene (3.5%), limonene (0.5%–4.0%), camphene (1.4%), and myrcene (0.2%–2.0%); 3. ketones including camphor (0.9–4.9%); and 4. esters including geranyl acetate (0.1–4.7%) and lynalyl acetate (0–2.7%) (Mandal 2015). Since the seeds are rich in fats (16–28%) and protein (11–17%), their residues at the end of the distillation process can be used as animal feed (Evans 1989).

Coriander seed essential oil is pale yellow or colorless, has the scent of coriander, and has a mild aromatic taste. The fruit contains malic acid, tannins, and fatty acids including linoleic acid, palmitic acid, oleic acid, and stearic acid. Before starting the distillation process, the seeds are crushed; this allows more essential oil to be extracted (Grieve 1971).

One of the major constituents of coriander seed oil is linalool. When isolated from the oil, linalool is used for a variety of purposes. It is estimated that linalool finds its way into 60 to 80% of all commercial perfumed hygiene products and cleaning products including soaps, shampoos, body lotions, and detergents. It is also used as a chemical intermediate, leading to the manufacturing of such products as vitamin E. Additionally, pest management professionals use linalool as an insecticide against fleas, fruit flies, and cockroaches (Evans 1996).

Coriander leaf essential oil contains approximately 44 compounds mainly aromatic acids containing 2-decenoic acid (30.8%), E-11-tetradecenoic acid (13.4%), capric acid (12.7%), undecyl alcohol (6.4%), tridecanoic acid (5.5%), and undecanoic acid (7.1%) as major constituents (Bhuiyan 2009). In the last decade, the essential oil of coriander leaf has been gaining in popularity as more people use essential oils in their everyday lives.

Agricultural Production

The primary producers of coriander seeds are Egypt, India, Morocco, and the United States. Smaller quantities are also produced in Hungary, Poland, Czech Republic, Holland, France, Italy, Turkey, the Balkans, Germany, China, Iran, as well as some countries of Central and South America (Teuscher 2005). Two varieties of seeds dominate the market, *Coriandrum sativum* var. *vulgare* which yields seeds that measure 3 to 5 mm in diameter while *Coriandrum sativum* var. *microcarpum* yields seeds that measure only 1.3 to 3 mm in diameter (Teuschler 2005). The seeds from Morocco and India are primarily of the *vulgare* variety and are larger (75 to 100 seeds per gram) while seeds from Eastern Europe are primarily of the *microcarpum* variety and are smaller (>130 seeds per gram) (Teuscher 2005). The seeds that come from the smaller seed varieties contain higher levels of essential oils (up to 2.0%). The varieties that produce larger seeds yield less essential oil (0.1 to 0.3%). That explains why growers who produce seeds destined for the distillation of essential oils favor small seed production. During the Communist regime, the U.S.S.R. was the major producer of coriander seed essential oil and controlled the world price and supply. Today, Ukraine continues the legacy and is still one of the primary producers of coriander seed essential oil (Evans 1996).

Coriander seeds and leaves have significant medicinal properties and offer substantial health benefits to mankind.

The Medicinal Properties of Coriander Seeds

There are seven major areas within which the healing power of coriander seeds can be tapped.

Coriander seeds and strong-tasting herbs

For hundreds of years, coriander seeds have been added to numerous formulations with the goal to soften the assault of bitter-tasting herbs on the taste buds (Leclerc 1976). They are excellent at masking the taste of very strong herbs. They are often added to laxative-based products that contain such bitter-tasting herbs as cascara sagrada, buckthorn, senna, jalap, and aloin latex. They are also added to formulas that contain barberry, Oregon grape root, quassia bark, as well as many other bitter or strong tasting herbs (Van Hellemont 1986). With the help of coriander seeds, herbal mixtures containing strong-tasting herbs taste better, much better. Thus, a greater number of individuals become willing and able to take their "bad tasting" medicines.

Coriander seeds and gastrointestinal gas

Although most people prefer not to talk about this subject, flatulence can be a serious annoyance and cause serious embarrassment. Not only is it socially unacceptable, but it can cause serious gastrointestinal pain. Coriander seeds offer their considerable carminative properties to individuals afflicted with this health annoyance. Carminative herbs help prevent or stop gas production throughout the entire digestive system. The seeds can be lifesaving for individuals who have constant burping or experience significant amount of flatulence, especially when they eat certain foods (milk and other dairy products, onion, garlic, cabbage, cauliflower, green peppers, Brussels sprouts, beans, lentils, etc.) or after eating particularly rich meals. Although coriander seeds may not be as strong as anise seeds, fennel seeds, or dill seeds, for most individuals, they offer excellent relief when an episode of gastrointestinal gas flares up (Van Hellemont 1986). A tea can be made by mixing whole coriander, anise, and fennel seeds together and crushing them just before making the tea. The freshly prepared tea is a very pleasant addition to the end of a meal.

Coriander seeds and stomach tissues protection

Coriander seeds possess substantial stomach protective properties. These properties may be useful when a person experiences digestive cramps after eating certain foods or when significant stress manifests as stomach upsets or digestive disturbances. Coriander seeds decrease or stop stomach spasms, production of gastrointestinal gas as well as excess or insufficient production of digestive juices. Recently, researchers found that coriander seeds increase the production of a gastric compound by the stomach that protects its epithelial (surface) layer from the harsh digestive juices (Zaidi 2012). It is used in Europe both to increase the digestive juice secretion when they are low and as an effective calmative when stomach acids are too elevated (Van Hellemont 1986).

Individuals who experience considerable stress in their lives initially see their production of digestive juices decrease substantially. During stress, the body protects itself by shunting blood away from the digestive tract. This results in a decreased production of digestive juices manifesting as difficulty digesting meals and increased fermentation in the digestive system manifesting as gas. A tea or tincture of coriander seeds taken 20 minutes *before* meals will increase the secretion of digestive juice and facilitate digestion (Witchl 2004).

However, when stress continues over a long period of time, the opposite may occur. Secretions may increase but, unfortunately, because of the stress, it doesn't occur at meal times. This leads to inflammation of the stomach lining. Stomach burning, esophageal reflux, and ulceration may occur. For those types of digestive discomforts, drink one cup of tea *after* meals. Coriander seeds stimulate the digestive function but do not aggravate the acidity that may already exist. It actually gets rid of the inflammation and supports the return to proper digestive function (Pole 2006).

Another area where coriander seeds may be of use is in *Helicobacter pylori* infections. It is estimated that up to 50% of the world's population is infected to a certain degree with *H. pylori*. Researchers from Pakistan noted that coriander seeds decrease the production of inflammatory substances such as IL-8 or ROS, factors known to inflame the stomach (Zaidi 2012). These researchers recommend that coriander seeds be added to the diets of patients faced with stomach ulcers. The seeds are both soothing to the gastric membranes and calming to the gastric inflammation.

Coriander seeds and stress

As noted above, stress can wreak havoc on the digestive system. Its negative influence can be felt throughout a person's life. Some of the symptoms that accompany stress include sleep disturbances, anxiety, muscle tension and aches, headaches, fatigue, mood swings, edginess, and forgetfulness. Research suggests that one of the ways that coriander seeds can be helpful for stress is that they seem to exert a muscle-relaxant effect (Rabbani 2011). The seeds were nearly equivalent to diazepam as a substance that reduces anxiety (Mahendra 2011). They also exerted numerous positive effects to those afflicted with stress (Koppula 2012). Add in the help that coriander seeds offer in sleep issues and anxiety (Andalib 2011), and you discover an herb that clearly belongs in your medicine cabinet.

Coriander seeds and diabetes

In many countries around the world, countless diabetics choose to use herbs either as a primary treatment for, or as an adjunct to, the treatment of their diabetes (Otoom 2006, Srinivasan 2005). One of the main herbs used for this purpose is coriander seeds. Animal studies have demonstrated that using the seeds modifies glucose regulation in a positive way (Gray 2007). In a human study, a group of 20 volunteers each took 2.5 grams of ground coriander seed twice a day for 60 days. Another 20 volunteers did not take coriander seeds and served as a control group. At the end of the trial, the treatment group had a significant reduction in fasting blood sugar levels. In addition, they also experienced a healthy rise in their beta carotene, vitamin A, vitamin C, vitamin E, and glutathione levels. The control group did not see any improvements of these parameters (Rajeshwari 2011). As a word of caution, if you are a diabetic and choose to use coriander seeds to supplement your diabetes care plan, be sure to monitor your blood sugar closely and talk with your doctor about your usage of coriander seeds for that purpose.

Coriander seeds, kidneys, and blood pressure

Coriander seeds have been used for centuries as a diuretic to help the kidneys get rid of excess water (Fournier 1948). Laboratory studies using animals have confirmed the value of using the seeds for that purpose (Aissaoui 2008). Additional research by the same university group showed that, in animals with high blood pressure, the use of coriander seed tea helped lower the blood pressure (Jabeen 2009). What makes coriander seeds attractive is the fact that this herbal medicine spares potassium. Most diuretic drugs not only eliminate sodium but also potassium. Proper amounts of potassium are essential for healthy cardiac function. When large amounts of potassium are eliminated from the human body, the deficiency of this essential mineral may lead to irregular heart beat (arrhythmia). Since coriander seeds barely increased the elimination of potassium, they are thought to be safer than the diuretic drugs used for that purpose. Some individuals, in order to minimize the side effects experienced with the diuretic drugs, supplement their diet with coriander seeds. As a word of caution, if you have high blood pressure and choose to use coriander seeds to supplement your hypertension care plan, monitor your blood pressure closely and talk with your doctor about your usage of coriander seeds for this purpose.

Coriander seed essential oil and skin health

Coriander seed essential oil is used as a topical treatment for chronic wounds, impetigo, and herpes simplex outbreaks (Abascal 2012). The seed oil is also used as a liniment for rheumatism and painful joints (Witchl 2004). The oil reduces the production of inflammatory compounds both in the skin and in the joints, and is a safer alternative to NSAIDS (nonsteroidal anti-inflammatory drugs) (Abascal 2012).

The Medicinal Properties of Coriander Leaf

Coriander leaf and heavy metal detoxification

Starting in the early 1990s, the use of coriander leaf has been advocated as a strategy to eliminate heavy metal accumulations, particularly those of mercury, from the human body. The putative rationale behind this use is that coriander leaf constituents are thought to attach to heavy metals and promote their excretion out of the body. Much has been written about this controversial therapy. Proponents are staunchly adamant that ingestion of coriander leaf results in a lessening of heavy metal load while opponents of the therapy argue that there is no scientific basis for the claims made by those advocating its use.

In 1995 and 1996, Dr. Omura, MD, published two papers where he introduced the use of a new bidigital O-ring test claimed to measure heavy metal levels in the body. He also proposed a protocol to remove heavy metals from the human body. In his clinical practice, Dr. Omura observed mercury blood levels rise after his patients had mercury dental amalgams removed. He had also noted that individuals who ate Vietnamese soup made with coriander leaf experienced increasing excretion of mercury, lead, and aluminum. From these two observations, he started to treat patients exhibiting high heavy metal loads with 100 mg coriander leaf tablets four times a day He claimed that levels of heavy metals dropped substantially (Omura 1995, Omura 1996).

In the United States, Dr. Deitrich Klinghartd, MD, became a proponent of Dr. Omura's method and began teaching health professionals about his own specific protocol for heavy metals removal. However, no other clinical papers or human clinical trials have been published to show the efficacy of using coriander leaf to remove heavy metals once they are deposited in human tissues. The lack of published clinical studies lies at the center of the controversy.

However, keep in mind Dr. Omura's observation that eating coriander leaf may reduce the absorption of heavy metals when it occurs at the same time as the heavy metal exposure. There is strong evidence in animal studies that coriander leaf used either prior to or at the same time as heavy metal or toxin exposure may protect the liver and other tissues. In an animal study where mice were fed lead and coriander leaves, the study showed that ingestion of coriander leaf reduced the negative effects of lead on liver enzymes, testosterone levels, and sperm density as well as the concentration of lead in the mice's gonads (Sharma 2010). In another animal study, mice were exposed to lead in their drinking water. The study concluded that coriander leaf seemed to contain some type of unidentified chelating agent, an agent that binds and stimulates the excretion of another substance. Coriander leaf was shown to suppress lead deposition in the mice's bones and kidneys (Aga 2001). Another animal study showed that feeding coriander leaf extract to rats prior to exposing them to liver toxins offered significant liver protection (Sreelatha 2009).

The long and short of these studies is the implication that eating coriander leaf with foods that contain elevated amounts of heavy metals or toxins may prevent their absorption in our body. For example, eating coriander leaves with tuna or other fish that contain significant amounts of heavy metals may protect you from the heavy metals found in these foods. Given that high levels of heavy metals are increasingly found in all types of foods, it is certainly an excellent idea to incorporate the regular use of coriander leaf into our everyday diet.

Preparation and Dosage

Internally
Coriander Seed: Coriander seeds make a good tasting tea. To make the tea, steep one tablespoon of crushed coriander seeds in a cup of hot water for 10 to 15 minutes and filter. Take 2 or 3 cups per day.

To use powdered coriander seed: Take 1/2 teaspoon per dosage mixed well in water or juice, from 2 to 5 times a day (Van Hellemont 1986).

Coriander Leaf: Take 30 drops of the liquid herbal extract in warm water 2 or 3 times a day at meal times. Add approximately 1 tablespoon of the fresh leaves to your meal when you consume foods that may have an elevated heavy metal load, such as seafood, tuna, or other fish located higher on the food chain.

Externally
Coriander seed essential oil can be mixed in a carrier oil such as sweet almond oil. Stir 1 ounce of coriander seed essential oil into 10 ounces of sweet almond oil. Mix well. Apply to the skin or joints as needed (Bartram 1998).

Safety

The Botanical Safety Handbook classifies coriander seed and leaf as a Class 1 herb, an herb that can be safely consumed when used appropriately (Gardner 2013). Other researchers have also concluded that coriander seeds are very safe, even when taken in very large doses (Mahendra 2011).

Contraindications

Coriander seed and leaf have no known contraindications (Van Hellemont 1986).

Side Effects

A few isolated reports of allergic reactions to coriander seed and leaf have been reported (Manzanedo 2004).

Drug Interactions

The Botanical Safety Handbook has classified coriander seed and leaf as a Class A herb, an herb for which no clinically relevant interaction are expected (Gardner 2013).

Kitchen Tips

Do not buy powdered coriander seeds as they will lose their aroma and essential oils very quickly. Buy whole seeds and crush or powder them just before use. By following these recommendations, you access the full medicinal qualities of the seeds when you need them.

Whole dried seeds will keep for years when they are stored in hermetically-sealed glass or metal containers in an area low in moisture and free of light (Witchl 2004).

Coriander leaf will keep for a relatively long time in the refrigerator when it is placed as a whole plant with whole washed roots in a vase filled with water. Cover the plant and the vase with a plastic bag. Regularly remove the leaves that are turning yellow. Stored in that way, the plant will stay fresh for many weeks (Teuscher 2005).

References

Abascal, K. and E. Yarnell 2012. Cilantro—Culinary herb or miracle medicinal plant. *Alternative and Complementary Therapies.* 18(5): 259-264.

Aga, M., Iwaki, K., Ueda, Y., Ushio, S., Masaki N., Fukuda, S., Kimoto, T., Ikeda, M. and M. Kurimoto. 2001. Preventive effect of *Coriandrum sativum* (Chinese parsley) on localized lead deposition in ICR mice. *J Ethnopharmacol.* 77: 203-208.

Aissaoui, A., El-Hilaly, J., Israili, Z.H. and B. Lyoussi. 2008. Acute diuretic effect of continuous intravenous infusion infusion of an aqueous extract of *Coriandrum sativum* L. in anesthesized rats. *J. Ethnopharmacol.* 115(1): 89-95.

Andalib, S., Vaseghi, A., Vaseghi, G. and A. Motavallian. 2011. Sedative and hypnotic effects of Iranian traditional medicinal herbs on the treatment of insomnia. *EXCLI J.* 10: 192-197.

Bartram, T. (1998) *Bartram's Encyclopedia of Herbal Medicine.* London, England: Constable and Robinson Ltd.

Bhuiyan, N.I., Begum, J. and M. Sultana. 2009. Chemical composition of leaf and seed essential oil of *Coriandrum sativum* L. from Bangladesh. *Bangladesh J Pharmacol* 4: 150-153.

Evans, W. 1989. *Trease and Evans' Pharmacognosy,* 13 ed. London, England: Bailliere Tindall.

Evans, W. 1996. *Trease and Evans' Pharmacognosy,*14 ed. London, England: WB Saunders Co. Ltd.

Fournier, P. 1948. *Le livre des plantes medicinales et vénéneuses de France.* Lechevalier, Paris, France.

Gardner, Z. and M. McGuffin. editors. 2013. *Botanical Safety Handbook,* 2 ed. CRC Press, 2013.

Gray, A.M. and P.R. Flatt. 2007. Insulin-releasing and insulin-like activity of the traditional anti-diabetic plant *Coriandrum sativum* (coriander). *Br J Nutrit* 81(03): 203-209.

Grieve, M. *A Modern Herbal.* Dover Publications, Inc., 1971 (reprint of 1931 ed.).

Jabeen, Q., Bashir, S., Lyoussi, B. and A.H. Gilani. Coriander fruit exhibits gut modulatory, blood pressure lowering and diuretic activities. *J. Ethnopharmacol.* 122(1). 123-130.

Kurshmann, G.J. and J.D. Kirshmann. *Nutrition Almanac,* 4 ed. McGraw-Hill, 1996.

Koppula, S. and D.K. Choi. 2012. Anti-stress and anti-amnesic effects of *Coriandrum sativum* Linn (Umbelliferae) extract—an experimental study. In rats. *Trop J Pharmaceutical Res.* 11: 36-42.

Leclerc, H. *Précis de phytothérapie.* Masson, 1976.

Mahendra, P. and S. Bisht. 2011. A daily use spice with great medicinal effect. *Pharmacognosy J.* 3:84:88.

Mahendra, P. and S. Bisht. 2011. Anti-anxiety activity of *Coriandrum sativum* assessed using different experimental animal models. *Indian J Pharmacol.* 43: 574-577.

Mandal, S., and M. Mandal. 2015. Coriander (*Coriandrum sativum* L.) essential oil: Chemistry and biological activity. *Asian Pac J Trop Biomed.* 5(6): 421–428.

Manzanedo, L., Blanco, J., Fuentes, M., Caballero, M.L. and I. Moneo. 2004. Anaphylactic reaction in a patient sensitized to coriander seed. *Allergy.* 59(3): 362-363.

McGuffin, M., Kartesz, J.F., Leung, A.Y. and A.O. Tucker. *Herbs of Commerce,* 2 ed. American Herbal Products Association, 2000.

Omura, Y, and S.I. Beckman. 1995. Role of mercury (Hg) in resistant infections and effective treatment of *Chlamydia trachomatis* and *Herpes* family viral infection (and potential treatment for cancer) by removing localized Hg deposits with Chinese parsley and delivering effective antibiotics using various drug uptake enhancement methods. *Acupunct Elecrother Res.* 50: 195-229.

Omura, Y., Shimotsuura,Y., Fukuoka, A., Fukuoka, H. and T. Nomor. 1996. Significant mercury deposits in internal organs following the removal of dental amalgam, and development of pre-cancer on the gingiva and the sides of the tongue and their represented organs as a result of inadvertent exposure to strong curing light and effective treatment. *Acupunct Electrother Res.* 21: 133-160.

Otoom, S.A., Al-Safi, S.A., Kerem, Z.K. and A. Alkofahi. 2006. The use of medicinal herbs by diabetic Jordanian patients. *J. Herb Pharmacother.* 6(2): 31-41.

Pole, S. *Ayurvedic Medicine: The Principles of Traditional Practice.* Churchill Livingstone Elsevier, 2006.

Rabbani, M., Vaseghi, G., Sajjadi, S.E. and B. Amin. 2011. Persian herbal medicines with anxiolytic activity. *J Med Plants* 39: 7-11.

Rajeshwari, C.U. and B. Andallu. 2011. Oxidative stress in NIDDM patients: Influence of coriander (*Coriandrum sativum*) seeds. *Res J Pharmaceutical Biol Chem Sci.* 2: 31-41.

Rudrappa, Umesh. *Cilantro (Coriander Leaves) nutrition facts.* http://www.nutrition-and-you.com/cilantro.html. Accessed 7/23/2016.

Sharma, V., Kansai, L. and A. Sharma. 2010. Prophylactic efficacy of *Coriandrum sativum* (coriander) on testis of lead-exposed mice. *Biol Trace Elem Res.* 136: 337-354.

Sreelatha, S., Padma, P.R. and M. Umadevi. 2009. Protective effects of *Coriandrum sativum* extracts on carbon tetrachloride-induced hepatotoxicity in rats. *Food Chem Toxicol.* 47: 702-708.

Srinivasan, K. 2005. Plant foods in the management of diabetes mellitus: Spices as beneficial antidiabetic food adjuncts. *Int J Food Sci Nutr* 56(6): 399-414.

Teuscher, E., Anton, R. and A. Lobstein. *Plantes Aromatiques.* Editions Tec et Doc, 2005.

United States Department of Agriculture. Agricultural Research Service. National Nutrient database for Standard Reference Release 28. 2016. https://ndb.nal.usda.gov/ndb/foods/show/2931?manu=&fgcd. Accessed 7/23/2016.

Van Hellemont, J. 1986. *Compendium de Phytotherapie.* Brussels, Belgium: Association Pharmaceutique Belge.

Wichtl, M. (Ed.) *Herbal Drugs and Phytopharmaceuticals.* 3 ed. CRC Press, 2004.

Zaidi, S.F., Muhammad, J.S., Shahryar, S. Usmanghani, K. and A. Gilani. 2012. Anti-inflammatory and cytoprotective effects of selected Pakistani medicinal plants in *Helicobacter pylori*-infected gastric epithelial cells. *J. Ethnopharmacol.* 141: 403-413.

Daniel Gagnon, Medical Herbalist, MS, RH (AHG) is a French-Canadian from Ontario who relocated to Santa Fe, NM in 1979. He has been a practicing Medical Herbalist since 1976. Daniel is the author of *The Practical Guide to Herbal Medicines*, a book designed to provide herbal health care options. He is also the co-author of *Breathe Free*, a book on healing the respiratory system. He regularly teaches herbal therapeutics both nationally and internationally. Daniel is the owner of Herbs, Etc., an herbal medicine retail store and manufacturing facility. herbsetc.com. Daniel can be reached at botandan@aol.com.

Coriander flowers. *Susan Belsinger*

Coriander essential oils. *Susan Belsinger*

Scent Blending with Cilantro and Coriander Essential Oils

Marge Powell

I LIKE TO think of essential oils as exactly that, the essence of a plant. But we need to carefully distinguish essential oils from fragrance oils. Fragrance oils are created chemically in a laboratory. Essential oils are created by the plant, are generally considered to have therapeutic value, and have a scent that seems to blend well with our bodies. When I am conducting a soapmaking or a scent blending workshop, I ask the participants to join me in a small experiment. First I pass around a small bottle of fragrance oil. I ask them to sniff it and then to be aware of their body's reaction to the scent. I watch their faces and I see a number of frowns and grimaces. Almost always unanimously, the participants report an unsettling reaction from their bodies, like an assault on their sense of smell. Next I pass around a small bottle of an essential oil and ask them to register their body's reaction. This time their faces are smiling and many have their eyes closed. The participants report a pleased reaction and many report that the scent was not only pleasing but seemed to blend with their body.

The point is this: Fragrance oils are synthetic and should be avoided while essential oils are a gift from the plant. Essential oils are potent and need to be used carefully after much research and should never be placed directly on the skin without some type of carrier oil. But they are beneficial in both their scent and their therapeutic value (aromatherapy). The drawback is that fragrance oils are much less expensive than essential oils which tempt many crafters like soapmakers to use them. However, I believe that to be a false economy and, personally, I would never make or use a product that contained fragrance oil.

As we know cilantro and coriander are the same plant (*Coriandrum sativum*) but the essential oils of cilantro and coriander are not the same. Cilantro essential oil is steam-distilled from the fresh leaves of the cilantro plant. It has a fresh, herby scent that is reminiscent of the leaves. In fact, one use of cilantro essential oil is to give or boost the cilantro taste in foods, an application beyond the scope of this article. On the other hand, coriander essential oil is steam-distilled from the fresh, ripe seeds of the cilantro plant. Its scent is much more complex than that of the cilantro essential oil, somewhat herby but with more depth and a very slight citrus note.

While we are concerned here with blending scents to make a pleasing combination, we need to recognize that the scents we are using do have therapeutic or aromatherapy effects. Very little is written about the aromatherapy value of cilantro essential. However, recent studies indicate that cilantro essential oil may have antimicrobial, antioxidant, anxiolytic, hypoglycemic, hypolipidemic, analgesic, anti-inflammatory, and anticonvulsion activities.

On the other hand, quite a bit has been written about coriander essential oil. Jeanne Rose in her book *375 Essential Oils and Hydrosols* says the major component of coriander essential oil is linalool (75%) and she indicates that its anti-inflammatory action can be used for stress, anxiety, and insomnia as well as in a massage oil to ease arthritis and migraine headaches. The majority of experts recommend coriander essential oil as a carminative to aid digestion; however, Kathi Keville in her book *Aromatherapy Healing for the Body and Soul* mentions coriander essential oil as one of the oils that contain a hormone-like substance related to estrogen and as such recommends its use during menopause to relieve hot flashes

Note that the beneficial effects of essential oils are not gained through ingestion. Our skin absorbs these volatile oils easily in the form of massage oils, perfume blends, and lotions and soaps scented with essential oils, or just plain inhalation. This brings us to our primary topic of blending scents.

Why blend scents? The easy answer is to create unique and pleasing aromas. The more complete answer is that each essential oil has a *note*.

There are top notes, usually citrus and herb scents, whose scents you notice first; there are middle notes, the florals and spices, which smooth out the blend and add depth; and there are base notes, deep scents like patchouli. Base notes are the scents that linger; they add fullness to a blend and "fix" the scent. A scent blend is created using essential oils from each group of notes.

Normally a blend will contain 10 to 30% top notes, 30 to 60% middle notes, and 15 to 30% base notes. Both cilantro and coriander essential oils are top notes. Coriander is especially nice because of its complex herby scent. Primarily, I use scent blends as a personal perfume and to scent the soaps and lotions I make. You can make similar scents for these applications but the process is different for personal scents (perfumes) than it is for soap making. When making a perfume, the essential oils are diluted with either an oil such as jojoba or perfumers or formulators alcohol (a pure alcohol available on line). The standard constituency of personal scents is seen in Table 1:

TABLE 1

Formulation	Essential Oil	Perfumers Alcohol	Formulators Alcohol	Distilled Water Or Distillate
Perfume	20 – 30%	65 – 80%	65 – 80%	0 – 5%
Cologne	15 – 20%		70 – 85%	5 – 10%
Room Freshener Or Linen Spray	3 -- 7%		20 – 30%	63 – 77%

Considerations in Scenting Soaps or Lotions

When making scent blends for soaps or lotions, there is no dilution. You need much more scent for soap making than for perfumery (from 2 to 4% of the total oil weight) so you will probably use less expensive essential oils which will limit the palette but both coriander and cilantro essential oils are some of the least expensive essential oils. Lotion scents can be between 1 to 3% of the total batch weight depending on personal taste.

You have to consider that the lye in soap making will destroy some of the scent power of the essential oil.

The temperature of your soap batch will affect the scent. The higher the temperatures, the more scent that will be needed because of the volatility of the essential oil. Try to use a lower temperature when you are adding essential oils. The same is true of scenting lotions: add the scent blend when the temperature has cooled but the batch is still pourable.

Essential Oils of Coriander Perfume Blends

Mix the essential oils with alcohol or oil according to the table above.

Table 2

Starry night* Drops	Essential oil	Note	%
2	patchouli	base	29%
1	vetiver	base	
6	sandalwood	base	
3	lemongrass	mid	13%
1	basil	mid	
6	coriander	top	58%
6	lavender	top	
4	lime	top	
2	grapefruit	top	

*from the former Snowdrift Farm Company

Table 3

Drops	Essential oil	Note	%
20	vanilla**	base	50%
2	clove bud	mid	10%
2	cinnamon leaf	mid	
10	sweet orange	top	40%
3	peppermint	top	
1	spearmint	top	
1	fennel	top	
1	coriander	top	

**to reduce the cost of using vanilla resin you can use vodka that has been infused with vanilla beans for 6 weeks These blends could also be used to formulate a room freshener using the ratios in Table 1.

The following blend is more expensive to make than the first two blends but the result is a light floral I find very pleasing to wear as it reminds me of spring.

Table 4

Drops	Essential oil	Note	%
48	vetiver	base	49%
20	patchouli	base	
8	Benzoin tincture	base	
36	rose absolute	mid	36%
14	jasmine	mid	
6	melissa (lemon balm)	mid	
10	cedarwood	top	15%
6	juniper berry	top	
8	coriander seed	top	
156			

Scent Blends for Soaps and Lotions

Some tips for scenting soaps

1. Make your blends ahead of time and let them age.
2. As your soap cures, wrap the batch loosely in a paper such as blank newsprint.
3. As your soap cures, place some of the scent on cotton balls and place the balls with the batch.
4. Store like-scented soap together.

The following scents would be blended and added directly to the soap or lotion batch with no dilution. Note that these blends are measured in ounces rather than in drops.

Cinnamon Rose Blend

YEILD: 4.6 TOTAL OUNCES

Essential Oil	Quantity
almond oil (for superfatting)	0.8 ounces
cinnamon	1.2 ounces
rose geranium	1.2 ounces
peru balsam resin	0.4 ounces
coriander	0.2 ounces
black pepper	0.2 ounces
palma rosa	0.2 ounces
bois de rose	0.2 ounces
cassia	0.2 ounces

Healing Angels Blend

YEILD: 7.8 TOTAL OUNCES

Essential Oil	Quantity
clary sage	2.0 ounces
basil	1.0 ounces
patchouli	1.0 ounces
elemi	0.2 ounces
lavender absolute	1.0 ounces
coriander	0.6 ounces
grapefruit	2.0 ounces

Eve's Bower

YEILD: 4 TOTAL OUNCES

Essential Oil	Quantity
almond oil (for superfatting)	0.8 ounces
sandalwood	0.4 ounces
rosemary	0.6 ounces
lavender	0.6 ounces
ylang ylang	0.4 ounces
juniper berry	0.6 ounces

jasmine	0.4 ounces
coriander	0.2 ounces

Fresh Fields

YEILD: 5 TOTAL OUNCES

Essential Oil	Quantity
patchouli	0.75 ounces
basil	0.5 ounces
lemongrass	1.0 ounces
lime	1.0 ounces
cilantro	0.75 ounces
coriander	1.0 ounces

Please consider these blends as starting points for your own creativity. And remember *always* to test for any skin sensitivity. While I have never encountered any skin sensitivity with any of these blends, our bodies are all different, so be sure to listen to what your body is telling you.

References

Dodt, Colleen K. *The Essential Oils Book.* Storey Publishing, 1996.

Keville, Kathi, *Aromatherapy Healing for the Body & Soul.* Publications International,1998.

Rose, Jeanne. *375 Essential Oils and Hydrosols.* Frog, Ltd., 1999.

Schnaubelt, Kurt, Ph.D. *The Healing Intelligence of Essential Oils.* Healing Arts Press, 2011.

Wormwood, Susan and Valerie Ann Wormwood. *Essential Aromatherapy.* New World Library, 2003.

Marge Powell has been an herbalist for over 25 years and an avid plant person her entire life. Her herbal interests span the culinary, medicinal, body care, and growing aspects of herbs. She completed a medicinal herbal apprenticeship with Susun Weed and was introduced to herbal body care in workshops by Rosemary Gladstar.

Marge has conducted hands on workshops on a variety of herbal topics across the United States. Her most popular workshops include Making Herbal Salves & Lotions, Blending Scents, Basic Soapmaking with Herbs, and Making Your Own Medicine. In 2000 she founded her body care and soap company, Magnolia Hill Soap Company, Inc. Her products are available at magnoliahillsoap.com.

Currently a board member of the International Herb Association (IHA) and the International Herb Association Foundation, and past president of IHA's former Southeastern Region, Marge has had numerous herbal articles published in IHA's annual Herb of the Year™ publications as well as their quarterly newsletters.

Coriander in suribachi. *Susan Belsinger*

Coriander: A Culinary Cure

Dorene Petersen

CORIANDER (*CORIANDRUM SATIVUM* L.) has a long history of both culinary and medicinal use in many countries. In India, it is known as *dhanya*, meaning "rich one," and it is used as a primary ingredient in daily cooking.

The fresh leaves are commonly called cilantro, and the plant is a parsley lookalike so you may also see it by other names, like *Mexican parsley*.[2]

Coriandrum sativum has traditionally been used for a variety of bodily discomforts, including everything from poor digestion to insomnia to painful joints.[3]

Coriander is from the family Apiaceae. The name *coriandrum* was used by Pliny the Elder, a Roman naturalist (AD 23-79), and is derived from the Greek word *koros*, a bug, implying that the leaves have an unpleasant smell, like bed bugs.[4, 5] Contemporary writers tend to take the opposite view, however, commonly describing the plant's aromatic qualities with words like "sweet," "spicy," and "herbaceous."

This explains why coriander seed essential oil is used in perfume and soap making in addition to its more well-known culinary, Ayurvedic, herbal medicine, and aromatherapy uses. It is also sometimes used in the

---

2 Other common names include *Arab parsley, Chinese parsley, dizzycorn*, and *Japanese parsley*.

3 GLOBinMED (2011). *Coriandrum sativum*. Global Information Hub On Integrated Medicine. Retrieved from http://www.globinmed.com/index.php?option=com_content&view=article&id=79073:coriandrum-sativum-linn-umbelliferae&catid=705:c#21.

4 Grieve, M. (n.d.). *A Modern Herbal*: "Coriander." *Botanical.com*. [Online] Retrieved from https://www.botanical.com/botanical/mgmh/c/corian99.html.

5 Small, E. *Culinary Herbs*, 2 ed. NRC Research Press, 2006.

pharmaceutical industry as a flavoring agent and has historically been used to flavor tobacco. No wonder it is called "rich one."

How to Identify Coriander

Coriandrum sativum is native to southeastern Europe. However, you can find it growing wild in many countries, and it is cultivated worldwide.[6]

Coriander is an annual that grows one- to two-feet tall and has compound leaves (many parts joined to a single stem). Medicinal and culinary value are found in the fresh or dried leaf (cilantro) and in the seed (coriander). Both the leaves and the seeds are also steam distilled to capture their potent essential oil.

The seed is globular shaped and quite small (five to seven millimeters in diameter[7]).

TIP: Don't confuse coriander with the caraway seed *Carum carvi* (L.), though they look similar. Coriander is larger than caraway, and is shaped more spherical than ovoid.

How to Cultivate and Harvest Coriander

Coriander *C. sativum* is hardy to zone 5 in the United States.

Despite having seed that is slow to germinate, it is an easy annual to grow. Replanted from seeds each year, it will flower from June to July. The flowers are hermaphroditic and are pollinated by insects.

The seeds ripen in mid to late summer, from August to September.

---

6 Arctander, S. *Perfume and Flavor Materials of Natural Origin*. Allured Publishing Corporation, 1994. 192.

7 Gunkel, W., Fraser, L.C. and S. C.Bhatia. *Handbook of Essential Oils: Volume 4*. CBS Publishers, 2010. 305.

Coriander is happiest in dry, light soil and generally does well in partial shade; however, if your end goal is essential oil, grow it in a position where it will get maximum sunshine.[8]

Constant moisture and too much nitrogen are enemies to coriander. They encourage it to rapidly grow, flower, and set seed. This reduces the quality of the active constituents (i.e., both flavor and medicinal value).

Other herbs can provide a friendly companion planting environment such as anise *Pimpinella anisum* (L.), dill *Anethum graveolens* (L.), and chervil *Anthriscus cerefolium* (L.) Hoffm. They are all great choices to plant nearby, but avoid planting coriander near fennel *Foeniculum vulgare* (Mill) as it struggles to compete.[9]

Remember, coriander seed is slow to germinate so don't be in a hurry. Start early in the season and sow in April or, using a cold frame, in March, or you can even sow the seed outside in the fall. Coriander planted in the fall is said to grow bigger and produce more seeds.[10] Experimental plantings have shown a yield from 500 to 800 pounds per acre.[11]

If distilling for seed essential oil, it is best to grind or crush the seeds just prior to distillation. The yield increases considerably, by as much as 21%, and the distillation time is reduced from fifteen hours to three to four hours.[12]

TIP: Spent seed material from distillation can be dried and used as cattle feed.

---

8 Plants for a Future Database. (2010). *Coriandrum sativum* - L. [Online exclusive]. Retrieved from http://www.pfaf.org/user/Plant.aspx?LatinName=Coriandrum+sativum.

9 Ibid.

10 Ibid.

11 Gunkel, W., Fraser, L.C., and S. C. Bhatia. *Handbook of Essential Oils: Volume 4.* CBS Publishers, 1994. 306.

12 Ibid.

Why You Might Choose Oil over Herb

Including coriander herb in your regular diet is a great way to ensure ongoing benefits, but how many of us eat coriander or cilantro every day? As an alternative, the essential oil is a convenient way to access this herb's power. For example, a blend of essential oils containing coriander seed can be:

- Added to your morning shower

- Used in an aroma inhaler and sniffed throughout the day

- Added to your car diffusor so you inhale it on your daily commute

You can also use the essential oil whole, unblended in your food; add a few drops to your olive oil and lemon juice to dress up your salad.

Why Coriander is Therapeutically Effective

The most influential active constituent in coriander seed essential oil, by volume, is linalool, though there is an array of important constituents in smaller volumes, too. Linalool is reported anywhere from 20 to 80% (typically 60 to 70%)[13] depending on factors such as where the plant is grown, how it is grown, and maturity of the seed at the time of harvest.

Research carried out in 2007 compared the composition of the oils from seeds in three phases of maturity: immature, intermediate ripeness, and fully mature. Linalool was as low as 11% in immature seed and as high as 87.5% in the fully mature seed.[14]

Other constituents usually present in much smaller percentages also showed variation. Geranyl acetate, an ester, for example, was present at 46.3% in immature seed but at only 0.8% in fully mature seed.[15] (Esters are known for their anti-inflammatory action.)

---

13 Gunkel, W., Fraser, L.C., and S. C. Bhatia, *Handbook of Essential Oils: Volume 3*. CBS Publishers, 2010. 309.

14 Msaada, K., Hosni, K., Ben Taarit, M., Chahed, T., Kchouk, M.E., and B. Marzouk. (2007). Changes on essential oil composition of coriander (*Coriandrum sativum* L.) fruits during three stages of maturity. *Food Chem.*, 102, 1131-1134.

15 Lawrence, B. (2011). Progress in Essential Oils. *Perfumer & Flavorist*, 36.

The bottom line, then, is that if you have a therapeutic end goal, make sure you know what is in your essential oil. Having said that, while it is extremely useful to be aware of the therapeutic uses that are shared by essential oils containing constituents with specific functional groups, be cautious when relying on these trends to determine the pharmacological actions of essential oils. Structure-activity relationships (SARs) have been the focus of both natural product and synthetic chemists for decades, but the pharmacological action of a molecule can be drastically altered by the addition or removal of a single atom, or a simple functional group, such as a methyl group (-CH3). Thus, although functional group trends are a useful means of hypothesizing the pharmacology of an essential oil, they are by no means a definitive answer to their therapeutic action.

We can, however, draw some guiding conclusions. We know linalool is a monoterpenol and, when inhaled, research has shown it has a sedative and anxiolytic effect as well as a number of others.[16]

Though, the above constituents are not the only ones that grant coriander essential oil its therapeutic efficacy; there are several additional active constituents in coriander important to note, including: alpha-thujene, sabinene, beta-pinene, myrcene, para-cymene, limonene, (Z)-beta-ocimene, gamma-terpenine, terpinolene, camphor, citronellal, carvone, terpinen-4-ol, decanal, and geranyl acetate.[17, 18]

This constituent profile provides a wide range of therapeutic possibilities.

For example, coriander can be used as an anthelmintic, anti-inflammatory, anti-amnesic, anti-colitis, antimicrobial, antioxidant, anxiolytic,

16 Linck, V.M., da Silva, A.L., Figueiró, M., Caramão, E.B., Moreno, P.R., and E. Elisabetsky. (2010). Effects of inhaled Linalool in anxiety, social interaction and aggressive behavior in mice. *Phytomedicine*, *17*(8-9), 679-83. doi: 10.1016/j.phymed.2009.10.002. Epub 2009 Dec 3.

17 Coskuner, Y. and E. Karababa. (2006). Physical properties of coriander seeds (*Coriandrum sativum* L). *Journal of Food Engineering*, 80, 408-416. Retrieved from http://www.globinmed.com/index.php?option=com_content&view=article&id=79073:coriandrum-sativum-linn-umbelliferae&catid=705:c#3.

18 Eikani, M.H., Golmohammad, F., and S. Rowshanzamir. (2007). Subcritical water extraction of essential oils from coriander seeds (*Coriandrum sativum* L). *Journal of Food Engineering*, 80, 735-740. Retrieved from http://www.globinmed.com/index.php?option=com_content&view=article&id=79073:coriandrum-sativum-linn-umbelliferae&catid=705:c#3.

carminative, hepatoprotective, hypoglycemic, hypocholesterolemic, and neuroprotective agent, among others.

Translated into everyday language, coriander essential oil has been shown to be an effective support for Alzheimer's disease, diabetes, epilepsy, inflammation (such as irritable bowel syndrome and Crohn's disease), liver support, parasites, skin infections, stress, and oral thrush.

Let's take a closer look at some of these therapeutic actions:

So, What is an Antimicrobial Therapeutic Action?
The term "antimicrobial" is likely more self-explanatory than some therapeutic actions. It simply means coriander has the ability to destroy micro-organisms or suppress their multiplication or growth, such as the Gram-negative bacteria *Escherichia coli* (commonly called *E. coli*) and the yeast Candida, which causes fungal infections.

Results from a 2011 study found coriander essential oil exhibited fungicidal activity against *Candida* spp., which may be useful for Candida protocols.[19]

An additional 2011 study looked at five different plants with antimicrobial properties to determine their ability to inhibit Candidiasis, or oral Candida. The oil from coriander inhibited all *Candida* spp. The essential oil from coriander was also effective against biofilm development when applied at regular intervals.[20]

19 Silva, F., Ferreira, S., Duarte, A., Mendonça, D.I., and F.C. Domingues. (2011). Antifungal activity of *Coriandrum sativum* essential oil, its mode of action against Candida species and potential synergism with amphotericin B. *Phytomedicine*. [Epub ahead of print] Retrieved from http://www.ncbi.nlm.nih.gov/pubmed/21788125.

20 Furletti, V.F., Teixeira, I.P., Obando-Pereda, G., Mardegan, R.C., Sartoratto, A., Figueira, G.M., et al. (2011). Action of *Coriandrum sativum* L. Essential oil upon oral *Candida albicans* biofilm formation. *Evid Based Complement Alternat Med*. Retrieved from http://www.ncbi.nlm.nih.gov/pmc/articles/PMC3108195/?tool=pubmed.

Further, in an earlier study published in *Food Chemistry*,[21] coriander was tested for antimicrobial activity against Gram-positive bacteria (e.g., *Staphylococcus aureus* and *Bacillus* spp.) and Gram-negative bacteria (e.g., *E. coli, Salmonella typhi, Klebsiella pneumonia, Proteus mirabilis,* and *Pseudomonas aeruginosae*), in addition to the pathogenic fungus *Candida albicans.* The oil was shown to be effective against all but one microbe, *P. aeruginosae,* which was resistant.

You might find it interesting to know that coriander essential oil's synergistic effect is currently being evaluated for use in the pharmaceutical industry. Researchers are interested in its synergistic use with antibiotic drugs for the Gram-negative bacteria *Acinetobacter baumannii.* The synergistic effects could prove effective with antibacterial medications for this known drug-resistant strain of bacteria.[22, 23]

So, What is an Antioxidant Therapeutic Action?

The antioxidant properties of coriander essential oil have been established by multiple studies, and they have also been shown to have an exceptional ability to inhibit lipid peroxidation.[24, 25, 26] Other studies show

21 Matasyoha, J.C., Maiyob, Z.C., Ngureb, R.M., and R. Chepkorira,. (2008). Chemical composition and antimicrobial activity of the essential oil of *Coriandrum sativum. Food Chemistry*, *113*(2), 526-529. Retrieved from http://www.sciencedirect.com/science/article/pii/S0308814608009424.

22 Duarte, A., Ferreira, S., Silva, F., and F.C. Domingues. (2012). Synergistic activity of coriander oil and conventional antibiotics against *Acinetobacter baumannii. Phytomedicine*, *19*(3-4), 236-8.

23 Maragakis, L.L. and T.M. Perl. (2008). *Acinetobacter baumannii*: epidemiology, antimicrobial resistance, and treatment options. *Clin Infect Dis., 46*(8), 1254-63.

24 Wangensteen, H., Samuelsen, A. and K. Malterud. (2004). Antioxidant activity in extracts from coriander. *Food Chemistry, 88*(2), 293-297. Retrieved from: http://dx.doi.org/10.1016/j.foodchem.2004.01.047.

25 Darughe, F., Barzegar, M., and M. Sahari. (2012). Antioxidant and antifungal activity of Coriander (*Coriandrum sativum* L.) essential oil in cake. *International Food Research Journal, 19*(3), 1253-1260.

26 Duarte, A., Luis, A., Oleastro, M., and F. Domingues. (2015). Antioxidant properties of coriander essential oil and linalool and their potential to control Campylobacter spp. *Food Control*, 61:115-122. Retrieved from http://www.sciencedirect.com/science/article/pii/S0956713515302127.

that coriander essential oil has potential to counteract not just anxiety, but depression and oxidative stress in Alzheimer's disease.[27]

A 2006 study ranked coriander fourth out of twelve oils tested for antioxidant capacity. It's interesting to note the final ranking: clove *Syzygium aromaticum* (L.), basil *Ocimum basilicum* (L.), bay *Laurus nobilis* (L.), coriander *C. sativum,* nutmeg *Myristica fragrans* (Houtt.), black pepper *Piper nigrum* (L.), helichrysum *Helichrysum italicum* (Roth) G. Don, peppermint *Mentha ×piperita* (L.), marjoram *Origanum majorana* (L.), cinnamon *Cinnamomum zeylanicum* (Blume), sage *Salvia officinalis* (L.), and fennel *F. vulgare.*[28]

In a slightly earlier study, coriander essential oil was shown to inhibit the oxidation of organic compounds (aldehyde hexanal to carboxylic acid). This suggests it may be a useful additive in food products to help inhibit rancidification.[29]

Coriander essential oil has also been shown to inhibit the oxidation of iron and to induce the oxidative degradation of lipids, which contributes to the development of atherosclerosis (when tested with reactive oxygen species like diphenylpicrylhydrazyl radicals).[30]

The antioxidant action coupled with coriander's anti-inflammatory action is also beneficial in cases of inflammation of the digestive tract. This includes Crohn's disease, colitis, and irritable bowel disorder.

A 2016 animal study involving rats validated this traditional use of coriander and was conducted to assess if *C. sativum* could provide protec-

---

27 Cioanca, O., Hritcu, L., Mihasan, M.,Trifan, A., and M. Hancianu. (2014). Inhalation of coriander volatile oil increased anxiolytic–antidepressant-like behaviors and decreased oxidative status in beta-amyloid (1–42) rat model of Alzheimer's disease. *Physiology & Behavior,* 131: 68-74. Retrieved from http://dx.doi.org/10.1016/j.physbeh.2014.04.021.

28 Politeo, O., Jukic, M., and M. Milos. (2006). Chemical composition and antioxidant activity of essential oils of twelve spice plants. *Croatica Chemica Acta.,* 79(4), 545-552.

29 Wangensteen, H., Samuelsen, A., and K. Malterud. (2004). Antioxidant activity in extracts from coriander. *Food Chemistry,* 88(2), 293-297.

30 Misharina, T., and A. Samusenko. (2008). Antioxidant properties of essential oils from lemon, grapefruit, coriander, clove, and their mixtures. *Applied Biochemistry and Microbiology,* 44(4), 438-442.

tion against colitis. Acetic acid was administered rectally in order to induce colitis. The semi-solid seed extract and hydrodistilled coriander seed essential oil were tested. Both were given two hours before colitis induction and supplemented daily for a five-day period. The study showed that the doses of 500 and 1,000 mg of coriander extract and 0.5 and 1 ml of the essential oil provided protection.

These results demonstrate the anti-inflammatory and anti-colitis activities of coriander and validate its traditional use for the management of inflammatory bowel disorders. The effect is due to the anti-inflammatory and antioxidant activities of the constituents, such as linalool and the ester linalyl acetate. Note the effect is dose-dependent (i.e., the effects are changed when the dose is changed) and no real protection was observed when smaller doses were used (250 mg extract and 0.25 ml essential oil).[31]

So, What is an Anxiolytic Therapeutic Action?

Generally stated, anxiolytic agents help to prevent or relieve stress and anxiety. Coriander essential oil and herb (i.e., cilantro leaves), for example, have been tested for anxiolytic effects and were shown to help reduce both anxiety and depression. In a 2012 animal study, the anti-stress effects of coriander seed semi-solid extract were evaluated using forced swimming tests. The extract was given at daily doses of 100, 200, and 300 mg/kg one hour prior to induced stress for five consecutive days. The release of stress hormones (noradrenaline and adrenaline) was lower for the animals that received the coriander extract, which shows a strong influence on stress levels.[32]

Another animal study using diazepam (0.5 mg/kg), a drug prescribed for anxiety, and hydroalcoholic coriander semi-solid extract also showed

---

31 Heidari, B., Sajjadi, S.E., and M. Minaiyan. (2016). Effect of *Coriandrum sativum* hydroalcoholic extract and its essential oil on acetic acid-induced acute colitis in rats. *Avicenna J Phytomed.*, 6(2), 205-214.

32 Koppula, S., and C. Choi. (2012). Anti-stress and anti-amnesic effects of *Coriandrum sativum* Linn (Umbelliferae) extract—an experimental study in rats. *Tropical Journal of Pharmaceutical Research, 11*(1). Retrieved from http://dx.doi.org/10.4314/tjpr.v11i1.5.

positive results. In this study, coriander (100 and 200 mg/kg dose) produced anti-anxiety effects similar to diazepam.[33]

So, What is a Hepatoprotective Therapeutic Action?

The term "hepatoprotective" means the ability to prevent liver damage. Hepatoprotective agents are very valuable for liver health, especially to help prevent damage from free radicals and environmental toxins.

Coriander essential oil was evaluated *in vitro* and *in vivo* for its antioxidant and hepatoprotective effect against damage caused by carbon tetrachloride (CCl_4). Carbon tetrachloride is a man-made chemical compound found in industrial products like dry cleaning agents, refrigerants, cleaners, pesticides, and asbestos. Coriander essential oil was shown to reduce 2,2-diphenyl-1-picrylhydrazyl (DPPH), a free radical, in a dose-dependent manner.[34] This suggests coriander can effectively protect the liver from oxidative damage.

This is also supported by an earlier animal study where powdered coriander seed was added into the diet of rats. The seeds were shown to have an antioxidative effect and suppressed formation of free radicals in the rat livers.[35]

So, What is a Hypoglycemic Therapeutic Action?

This is a term you may already be familiar with due to the influx of diabetes information on the internet. Hypoglycemic agents help to lower blood sugar levels, which can be very useful for diabetes management.

For example, in an animal study a coriander leaf decoction was added into the diet of diabetes-induced mice. The decoction was shown to

33 Mahendra, P., and S. Bisht. (2011). Anti-anxiety activity of *Coriandrum sativum* assessed using different experimental anxiety models. *Indian Journal of Pharmacology, 43*(5), 574. Retrieved from http://dx.doi.org/10.4103/0253-7613.84975.

34 Samojlik, I., Laki, N., Mimica-Duki, N., Đakovi-vajcer, K., and B. Boin. (2010). Antioxidant and hepatoprotective potential of essential oils of coriander (*Coriandrum sativum* L.) and caraway (*Carum carvi* L.) (Apiaceae). *J. Agric. Food Chem., 58*(15), 8848-8853.

35 Anilakumar, K., Nagaraj, N., and K. Santhanam. (2001). Effect of coriander seeds on hexachlorocyclohexane induced lipid peroxidation in rat liver. *Nutrition Research, 21*(11), 1455-1462. Retrieved from http://dx.doi.org/10.1016/s0271-5317(01)00338-4.

lower glucose levels by affecting the metabolism of glucose and increasing the secretion of hormone insulin.[36]

Another animal study demonstrated that adding a coriander seed fluid extract into the diet increased insulin release from pancreatic beta cells and significantly reduced blood glucose levels.[37]

So, What is a Hypocholesterolemic Therapeutic Action?
This is another common term used in the wellness community, and its key is the inclusion of "cholesterol." As you might imagine, hypocholesterolemic agents can help lower cholesterol levels in the blood. This action is especially useful for the management of high cholesterol.

Coriander's hypocholesterolemic action was demonstrated in an animal study where the seeds were added into the diet of rats otherwise fed a high-fat and high-cholesterol diet. The seeds had a significant hypolipidemic effect; they decreased fats (also called lipids) in the blood. When lipids bind with proteins in the blood, they are called lipoproteins or cholesterol. Researchers noticed the level of low density lipoprotein and very low density lipoprotein cholesterol decreased while high density lipoprotein cholesterol (the good cholesterol) increased in the experimental group compared to the control group.[38]

So, What is a Neuroprotective Therapeutic Action?
Neuroprotective agents promote recovery or regeneration of the nervous system. Preliminary results from animal studies suggest coriander's neuroprotective effects support healthy brain function and can be used to manage Alzheimer's disease and safeguard against memory impairment caused by epileptic seizures.

36 Gray, A. and P. Flatt. (1999). Insulin-releasing and insulin-like activity of the traditional antidiabetic plant *Coriandrum sativum* (coriander). *British Journal of Nutrition, 81*(03), 203-209. Retrieved from http://dx.doi.org/10.1017/s0007114599000392.

37 Eidi, M., Eidi, A., Saeidi, A., Molanaei, S., Sadeghipour, A., Bahar, M., et al. (2009). Effect of coriander seed (*Coriandrum sativum* L.) ethanol extract on insulin release from pancreatic beta cells in streptozotocin-induced diabetic rats. *Phytother. Res., 23*(3), 404-406. Retrieved from http://dx.doi.org/10.1002/ptr.2642.

38 Dhanapakiam, P., Joseph, J., Ramaswamy, V., Moorthi, V., and A. Kumar. (2008). The cholesterol lowering property of coriander seeds (*Coriandrum sativum*): mechanism of action. *J Environ Biol, 29*(1), 53-56.

Alzheimer's disease is a very complex condition, and coriander shows promise for providing support for one of the known causes, the increase of the acetylcholinesterase (AChE) enzyme. This results in a decrease or inhibition of acetylcholine (ACh), a neurotransmitter that is essential for the brain and nervous system to process and transmit information from one area to another.

The majority of available studies have been conducted on animals. For example, one animal study looked at how coriander leaves added into the diet may or may not improve cognitive function, total serum cholesterol levels, and brain cholinesterase activity. Young and aged mice fed coriander leaves for 45 consecutive days were shown to have a dose-dependent improvement in memory scores (remember, dose-dependent means the effects change when the dose is changed). Memory deficits were also successfully reversed. In addition, brain acetylcholinesterase activity and total serum cholesterol levels were considerably reduced.[39]

In another memory study, an aqueous extract was evaluated for potential anti-amnesic effects. Amnesia-induced mice given 100, 200, and 300 mg/kg of extract were shown to have improved memory deficits. The researchers suggest that this may be due in part to the antioxidant activity of the extract, which relieves stress by combating oxidative damage.[40]

Further, a recent study showed that exposing the hippocampus (memory center of the brain) to coriander essential oil can significantly decrease catalase activity (an enzyme essential for protecting brain cells from oxidative damage) and increase glutathione levels (an important antioxidant essential for preventing oxidative damage). This suggests coriander can suppress oxidative stress associated with Alzheimer's disease.[41]

---

39 Mani, V., Parle, M., Ramasamy, K., and A. Abdul Majeed. (2010). Reversal of memory deficits by *Coriandrum sativum* leaves in mice. *Journal of the Science of Food and Agriculture, 91*(1), 186–192. Retrieved from http://dx.doi.org/10.1002/jsfa.4171.

40 Koppula, S., and C. Choi. (2012). Anti-stress and anti-amnesic effects of *Coriandrum sativum* Linn (Umbelliferae) extract—an experimental study in rats. *Tropical Journal of Pharmaceutical Research, 11*(1). Retrieved from http://dx.doi.org/10.4314/tjpr.v11i1.5

41 Cioanca, O., Hritcu, L., Mihasan, M., Trifan, A., and M. Hancianu. (2014). Inhalation of coriander volatile oil increased anxiolytic–antidepressant-like behaviors and decreased oxidative status in beta-amyloid (1–42) rat model of Alzheimer's disease. *Physiology & Behavior, 131*, 68-74. Retrieved from http://dx.doi.org/10.1016/j.physbeh.2014.04.021.

It's important to also mention developing research on the use of coriander for reversing memory loss as a result of epileptic seizures. A 2015 animal study on the effects of coriander on seizure-induced rats showed that including an aqueous extract in the diet may reverse temporary memory problems and impairments. There is very promising potential for the use of coriander to help manage memory impairment, but further studies are needed to fully understand the neuroprotective effects of coriander extract during seizures.[42]

How to Use Coriander around the Kitchen
Coriander is a big help in the kitchen. The seed has a long tradition of use and is commonly used ground in curry powder. The fresh leaves are also great in salsas and blended into pesto sauces with garlic, olive oil, and pine nuts.

The essential oil can also be used in food preparation. The oil can be added to sweets (especially combined with bergamot *Citrus aurantium* var. *bergamia* [Risso] in hard candies), pickles, meat products, seasonings, and alcoholic beverages (like gin) for a unique, mildly spicy flavor. It's also highly aromatic, which makes for a well-rounded culinary experience.

If you like to experiment in the kitchen, try an essential oil blend. Coriander's flavor blends well with anise *P. anisum*, cardamom *Elettaria cardamomum* (L.), clove *S. aromaticum*, clary sage *Salvia sclarea* (L.), nutmeg *M. fragrans*, and any sweet fruit flavors.

Tip: Research shows that coriander leaves may be more effective than activated carbon in removing heavy metals (such as lead) from water.[43] If your water is contaminated with heavy metals, place a handful of cori-

42 Elahdadi-Salmani, M., Khorshidi, M., and J. Ozbaki. (2015). Reversal effect of *Coriandrum sativum* leaves extract on learning and memory deficits induced by epilepsy in male rats. *Zahedan Journal of Research In Medical Sciences*, 17(3). Retrieved from http://dx.doi.org/10.17795/zjrms1279.

43 Samojlik, I., Lakić, N., Mimica-Dukić, N., Daković-Svajcer, K., and B. Bozin. (2010). Antioxidant and hepatoprotective potential of essential oils of coriander (*Coriandrum sativum* L.) and caraway (*Carum carvi* L.) (Apiaceae). *J Agric Food Chem.*, 58(15), 8848-53. Retrieved from http://www.ncbi.nlm.nih.gov/pubmed/20608729.

ander leaves in a jug of water overnight and strain off the next day before drinking.

How to Use Coriander Essential Oil in Perfumery
Coriander seed essential oil has a pleasant, woody, sweet yet spicy aroma. Steffen Arctander in *Perfume and Flavor Materials of Natural Origin*[44] describes it as having a floral, balsamic undertone and a peppery, woody top note.

Coriander is also used in perfume and soap making, both personally and commercially. For a cologne-type fragrance, it blends well with clary sage *S. sclarea* and bergamot *C. aurantium* var. *bergamia*. For floral perfumes, try blending it with jasmine absolute *Jasminum grandiflorum* (L.) or honeysuckle absolute *Lonicera caprifolium* (L.), and, for a more Oriental note, try *Olibanum Boswellia* spp. or cinnamon *Cinnamomum zeylanicum* (Blume).

However, there are many other essential oils that coriander blends well with, including: cananga *Cananga odorata* (Lam.) (similar to ylang ylang *Cananga odorata* (Lam.) var. *genuina*); citronella *Cymbopogon nardus* (L.) Rendle; cypress *Cupressus sempervirens* (L.); ginger *Zingiber officinale* (Roscoe); neroli *Citrus aurantium* (L.) var. *amara*; petitgrain *C. aurantium;* pine *Pinus sylvestris* (L.); and sandalwood *Santalum album* (L.).[45]

What Else Can I Make with Coriander?
A coriander infusion can be effective for inflammation in the digestive tract, from mouth ulcers to irritable bowel. To make an infusion, pour one cup of boiling water over one teaspoon of freshly crushed coriander seeds (use a mortar and pestle), and infuse in a covered container for 10 to 15 minutes. When ready, strain the infusion through muslin, cheesecloth, or an unbleached coffee filter and store the infusion in a dark-colored bottle in the refrigerator for no more than three days. Take one tablespoon, three times per day, for 14 days.

---

44 Arctander, S. *Perfume and Flavor Materials of Natural Origin.* Allured Publishing Corporation, 1994. 193.

45 Ibid.

Similarly, a coriander tincture can be used in times of stress and at the first signs of those "senior moments." Although it is ideal as a preventative protocol as well, don't wait to start. You can buy a tincture from your trusted herb shop or from any high-quality natural foods store.

If you want to make your own tincture, the standard recipe I recommend is to mix approximately two ounces of freshly crushed coriander seeds with one pint of alcohol (like vodka) or apple cider vinegar in a glass jar with a tight-fitting lid (like a Mason jar).

Keep the tincture in the jar in a warm spot (but not in the sun) for approximately two weeks. Shake the tincture two to three times every day. After two weeks, strain the tincture through pharmaceutical filter paper, an unbleached coffee filter, cheesecloth, or muslin. You may need to strain your tincture two or even three times to remove all of the herb solids. Leaving solids in your tincture may lead to mold and spoilage. Store your tincture in a dark bottle or cupboard.

Consume approximately 20 to 40 drops of tincture in a quarter cup of water, three times a day.

A Recipe for Better Health: DIY Tea Time

Coriander can be used with other carminative herbs to prepare a tea, including anise *P. anisum*, fennel *F. vulgare*, and caraway *C. carvi*. Carminative agents can help prevent or reduce excessive gas.

To make a carminative tea, blend equal parts coriander, anise, fennel, and caraway. I recommend you start with one teaspoon each. Pour one cup of boiling water onto one teaspoon of the herbal mixture, and allow it to steep for 20 minutes. Then strain. Drink one cup, warm, after a meal.[46]

Potential Cautions to Keep in Mind for Coriander

Coriander herb (seed and leaves) and coriander essential oil are listed on the FDA Generally Recognized as Safe (GRAS) list.[47]

---

46 Weiss, R., and V. Fintelmann. *Herbal medicine.* Thieme, 2000. 77.

47 U.S. Food and Drug Administration. (2013). Everything Added to Food in the United States (EAFUS). [Database]. Retrieved from http://www.accessdata.fda.gov/scripts/fcn/fcnNavigation.cfm?rpt=eafusListing.

However, the essential oil can cause allergic reactions and photosensitivity in some people, like other members of the Apiaceae family (e.g., parsley, celery, dill). It can also cause contact dermatitis (a skin rash caused by contact with a substance).[48] Always conduct a skin patch test before using coriander essential oil to ensure it is safe for use on your body.

Likewise, linalool can cause sensitization and irritation on the skin. In the European Union, linalool-containing essential oils used in either fragrance, cosmetics, or detergents are required to be clearly labeled. Basically, if a linalool-containing essential oil is part of a fragrance in a product, then "perfume" or the name of the essential oil is insufficient. These constituents must be listed. In skin cosmetics, the maximum allowable amount in the end product is 10 ppm. In wash-off cosmetics and household products, the maximum allowable amount in the end product is 100 ppm.[49, 50]

Looking Forward: The Future of Coriander
It's clear why coriander is called *dhanya*, "rich one." It is indeed very rich with therapeutic uses that have been shown effective time and time again.

While its traditional uses, like digestive health, remain reason enough to keep coriander herb and essential oil in your holistic medicine cabinet, there is even more hope to be found in developing research. Recent studies into the effective use of coriander with some of the most debilitating conditions of our time, especially Alzheimer's and diabetes management, show this may be a viable, accessible natural support.

However, to date, the majority of our research is from animal studies, and the implications of the information we have collected are very promising. The next generation of development is human trials to further expand our knowledge of the potential therapeutic efficacy of coriander. While

---

48 Brinker, F. (1998). *Herb Contraindications and Drug Interactions*. (2nd ed.). Sandy, OR: Eclectic Medical Publications.

49 European Commission: Health and Consumers Scientific Committees. (2012). Perfume Allergies. Retrieved from http://ec.europa.eu/health/scientific_committees/opinions_layman/perfume-allergies/en/l-3/4-classification.htm.

50 European Commission: Scientific Committee on Consumer Safety. (2012, June 26-27). Opinion on fragrance allergens in cosmetic products. [PDF] Retrieved from http://ec.europa.eu/health/scientific_committees/consumer_safety/docs/sccs_o_102.pdf.

animal studies can give us a glimpse into important therapeutic actions of specific agents within coriander, human studies are essential for a full perspective on how these constituents thrive within the nuanced systems of the human body.

Coriander essential oil. *Susan Belsinger*

Dorene Petersen, BA, Dip.NT, Dip.Acu, RH (AHG) is President of American College of Healthcare Sciences (ACHS) in Portland, Oregon, a DEAC accredited distance education institution offering certificate, undergraduate and graduate degree programs in holistic health. Dorene has over 35 years of clinical teaching and lecturing experience in aromatherapy, herbal medicine, and other holistic health subjects. She has presented papers on essential oils, herbs, and clinical aromatherapy at the International Federation of Essential Oils and Aroma Trades Annual Conference (IFEAT) in California, USA; the Aroma Environment Association of Japan (AEAJ) in Tokyo, Japan; and the Asian Aromatherapy Conference (AAC) in Delhi, India, among others. Dorene currently serves as Chair of the Aromatherapy Registration Council (ARC).

Cilantro. *Pat Kenny*

Cilantro Mimics:
Species with the Scent and
Taste of Fresh Cilantro

Pat Kenny

THE SIMPLE ACT of looking up the word *cilantro* in Stephen Facciola's *Cornucopia II* set me on the trail of some plants of which I had never heard. Yes, cilantro (*Coriander sativum*) was included, with a listing of eleven cultivars. But, it was the plant I saw in the index listed under "cilantro" that surprised me, *Cilantro peperomia,* and my search was on. None of my dorm room, low-light-tolerant ornamental houseplant peperomias had ever smelled like that and I certainly did not think of tasting them.

The plant family designation of peperomia is usually Piperaceae, sometimes Peperomiaceae, sometimes Piperaceae (Peperomiaceae). Taxonomist Guido Mathieu acknowledges that there are an estimated 1500-1700 species in the genus Peperomia. With the help of friend and plant expert Rex Talbert, I've learned that many peperomia have the chemistry that produces the taste and scent similar to the foliage of cilantro and culantro. Let's look at four edible cilantro-scented peperomia with documented culinary usage.

Peperomia maculosa and *Peperomia pellucida* are two tropical American plants with edible leaves. The first, *Peperomia maculosa,* or "cilantro peperomia", is sold in local ethnic markets and used for flavoring beans and meats. *Peperomia pellucida,* known as the *greenhouse tea plant,* or *sunakosho,* is a small weedy plant with succulent leaves and shoots often eaten in salads or used as a potherb. In the West Indies, its leaves are also brewed into tea (Facciola 168-9).

For *Peperomia maculosa* (L.) 'Hook,' Rex Talbert's caution regarding names holds true. Facciola and Allen agree that *Peperomia maculosa* can also be called "cilantro peperomia". While not much has been written about *P. maculosa,* we did find five herbarium specimens from Cuba, Dominican Republic, and Haiti in 1926, 1936, 1941, and1950, respectively. The collectors described the plant as terrestrial, with fleshy leaves, dark green above, white beneath with curved white stripes or broad pale veins and purplish inflorescence. Collections sites ranged from dense thickets, rocky sites, and shaded limestone ledges. A note in the Harvard University Herbarium was an encouraging find describing the "Juice [as] strongly and pungently aromatic 1967" (Von Reis and Lipp).

Peperomia pellucida (L.), also called *meralla* or *sacha yuyu,* is found mostly in private gardens for medicinal purposes. Besides Facciola's description as a "small weedy plant with succulent leaves and shoots," we found five herbarium specimens, collected in Haiti, Jamaica, and the Dominican Republic in 1902, 1920, 1924, 1929, 1945. The collection sites indicate shady, damp places, thickets on a damp bank, often on the west side, and on stone walls along roads. In his book *The Herbalist in The Kitchen,* Gary Allen lists *Culantro de Montana* as well as *Cang cua, rau cangcua* (Vietnam); *ketumpangan ayer* (Malaysia); *olasiman ihalas, sahica-puti, ulasiman-bato* (Philippines); *pak krasang* (Thailand); *ranu-ranga* (Indonesia); and *suna kosho* (Japan) as common names for *P. pellucida.*

P. pellucida's leaves have been used in herbal teas, in salads, and as a potherb, with Allen saying that "it has an odd odor, smelling as if it were stored with uncooked fish" (Allen 323). That does not sound like cilantro to me, yet we have some friends who would beg to differ. Not everyone likes the scent of cilantro, no matter what plant it comes from.

The medical purposes for *Peperomia pellucida* are many, as acknowledged in the *Journal of Ethnopharmacology,* particularly for its analgesic and anti-inflammatory activities. Jonathan Hartwell lists it as a native medicine called *renren* used for breast cancer in Nigeria. Brazilians pour hot water over the whole plant and drink the tea for metrorrhagia (excessive bleeding from womb). Surinamese use it for everything from athlete's foot to high blood pressure, gum problems, headaches, even to exorcise demons (Duke, Plotkin).

According to Malaysian researchers Lee Seong et al., a decoction of the *Peperomia pellucida* plant can be "useful to treat bone aches and pains. The leaf was also used in headache, fever, eczema, abdominal pain, and convulsions treatments. Elsewhere, this plant served multi-functions, including mental disorder treatment in Bangladesh; haemorrhage treatment in Bolivia, cholesterol reduction in Brazil, and renal problems and uric acid reduction in Guyana and Phillipines." Furthermore, chemical composition analyses of *P. pellucida* validate its antibacterial, anti-inflammatory, analgesic, antifungal, and anti-cancer properties (Wei Lee).

The 2015 World University of Bangladesh study indicates that the leaves of *Peperomia pellucida*, whose common name there is *luchi pata*, possess potential antimicrobial activity against important human pathogens, and have been used as a traditional medicinal remedy for thrombosis, diarrhea, and other ailments.

The third cilantro-scented specimen, *Peperomia acuminata* is known as *Culantro de montana, radiator plant*, and *cilantro de monte* (Caribbean), yet these names usually refer to *Eryngium foetidum*. The leaves have been used as seasoning, either dried or boiled (Von Reis and Lipp; Allen). Allen further notes: "*Peperomia acuminata* is a succulent, distally branched herb, with fleshy but often translucid leaves. It grows in very shadowy areas, in the understory of *Quercus* (oak) forests or montane disturbed forests in the Andean region. It gives off a strong aroma of cilantro, difficult to get rid of even by washing hands." This perennial succulent from Northern South America has now naturalized in Hawaii. *P. acuminate* tastes like cilantro and is used, fresh or dried, as seasoning in the American tropics. Allen cautions that some *Peperomia acuminata* sold in the United States are actually *Peperomia elongata* var. *guianensis* (324).

The final specimen, a perennial herb, *Peperomia hobbitoides* 'T. Wendt,' is a new species with an unresolved name (July 2016 *theplantlist.org*) but known locally in southeastern Veracruz, Mexico, as *cilantro de la roca*, where it grows directly on outcrops of limestone. Its delicate annual stems sprout from small, irregularly shaped corms lying in tiny soil pockets of ledges, depressions, and holes in rock. *Britannica* defines the typical habitat of *Peperomia hobbitoides* as karstic limestone, terrain usually characterized by barren, rocky ground, caves, sinkholes, underground rivers, and the absence of surface streams and lakes.

The leaves are broadly ovate, heart-shaped acuminate (gradually tapering to a sharp point, forming concave sides along the tip) with campylodromous venation, where several primary veins or their branches diverge at or close to a single point running in strongly developed, basally recurved arches which converge toward the apex, reaching it or not (*FTBG Virtual Herbarium Glossary*).

According to Tom Wendt, the herbage of the new species has the strong fragrance and flavor of fresh coriander (cilantro) and is eaten by inhabitants of the area. The fragrance pervades the entire plant, which is often used to enliven the late morning meal. He explains the fanciful resemblance to hobbits: "living in a fairyland-like environment, strongly and faithfully tied to this home substrate [...] spending the greater part of the year [...] as a resting tuber, edible, and, like hobbits, its home is under threat by forces much larger than itself, in this case forest clearing [...] and fires ...." Indeed, it is hard to imagine a family more in need of taxonomic friends than Piperaceae.

Much gratitude goes to Alice Tangerini, celebrated staff illustrator of the Botany Department, National Museum of Natural History, Smithsonian Institution, Washington, D.C., a long-time friend through the Guild of Natural Science Illustrators, and my go-to person for requesting to have access to the National Herbarium. We were immediately able to find many specimens of the two peperomias listed by Facciola.

In conclusion, I got excited about the possibility of tracking down information about some plants we had rarely seen listed, or listed and overlooked. The search could be continued by all who have an interest with me; however, I think we will have to do some traveling southward.

References

Ainslie, J.R. "A list of plants used in native medicine in Nigeria." Institute Paper No. 7, Imperial Forestry Institute, Oxford University. 1937.

Allen, Gary. *The Herbalist in the Kitchen.* University of Illinois Press, 2007. 323-324.

"Campylodromous venation." *Fairchild Tropical Botanic Garden Virtual Herbarium Glossary* . www.virtualherbarium.org/glossary/glossary. php?searchfor=ampylodromous=venation/. Accessed 9/20/16.

Duke, James Alan and Rodolfo Vasquez.

Amazonian Ethnobotanical Dictionary. CRC Press, 1994. 133.

Facciola, Stephen. *Cornucopia II—A Source Book of Edible Plants.* Kampong Publications,1998. 168-169.

Giorgetti, Melina, Lucia Rossi, and Eliana Rodrigues. "Brazilian plants with possible action on the Central Nervous System : A study of historical sources from the 16th to 19th century." Revista Brasiliera de Farmacognosia, Rev. bras. farmacogn. Vol.21 no. 3 *Curituba* May/June 2011. *Epub* Mar 25, 2011. *Google Scholar.* Accessed 4/19/16.

Harris, James G. and Melinda Woolf Harris. *Plant Identification Terminology—An Illustrated Glossary.* Spring Lake Publishing, 1994.

Hartwell, Jonathan L. *Plants Used Against Cancer.* Quarterman Publications, Inc., 1982. 458, 464.

"Karst geology." www.britannica.com/science/karst-geology/. Accessed 9/20/16.

"Natural Products." Journal *MOLECULES* 2012, 17 (9), 11139-11145; doi:10.3390/molecules170911139. *Google Scholar.* Accessed 3/22/2016.

Mabberley, D.J. *Mabberley's Plant-Book, A Portable Dictionary of Plants, Their Classification and Uses, 3 ed.* Cambridge University Press, 2008. 646.

Mathieu, Guido, Samain, Marie-Stephanie, Reynders, Marc, and Paul Goetghebeur. 30 May 2008. "Taxonomy of the Peperomia species (Piperaceae) with pseudo-epiphyllous inflorescences, including four

new species." *Botanical Journal of the Linnean Society* 157, 177-196, London. Accessed *Google Scholar* 9/16/2016.

Plotkin, Mark J. *Tales of a Shaman's Apprentice,* Viking Press, 1994.

Staples. George W. and Michael S. Kristiansen. *Ethnic Culinary Herbs: A Guide to Identification and Cultivation in Hawai'i.* University of Hawai'i Press, 1999.

Von Reis and Frank J. Lipp, Jr. "Drugs and Foods from Little-Known Plants—Notes in Harvard U. Herbarium." Harvard University Press, 1973.

Wei, Lee Seong, Wendy Wee, Julius Yong Fu Siong, and Desy Fitrya Syamsumir. "The Characterization of Anticancer, Antimicrobial, Antioxidant Properties and Chemical Compositions of *Peperomia pellucida* Leaf Extract." *Acta Medica Iranica* 49.10, *Tehran University Medical Sciences* (2011). Accessed *Google Scholar* 4/17/2016.

Wendt, Tom. 2003. "Peperomia hobbitoides (Piperaceae), a New Species of Karstophile from Rain Forests of the Isthmus of Tehuantepec, Mexico." Vol. 6, *Plant Resources Center*, University of Texas at Austin. Austin TX. *Google Scholar* sent via email from Rex Talbert 5-23-16.

Zubair, K.L., Samiya J.J., Jalal, U., and R. Mostafizur. 12-30-2015. In Vitro Investigation of Antidiarrhoeal, Antimicrobial and Thrombolytic Activities of Aerial parts of *Peperomia pellucida.* Archives 2015 vol.3 5-13. 1827-8620. *Google Scholar* 9-19-16.

Coriander flowers. *Pat Kenny*

Pat Kenny has been a medical illustrator (retired from NIH); volunteer herb publicist giving photo-illustrated herb talks and demos neighborhood-to-nation; member of IHA since it was IHGMA; member of The Herb Society of America since 1979; and supporter of the nation's largest public herb garden, the National Herb Garden in Washington, D.C., which has stimulated her curiosity about the world of herbal plants.

Split Personality:
Coriander and Cilantro

James A. Duke, Ph.D

THERE ARE TWO standardized common names for this species: *cilantro* for the leaves, *coriander* for the seed. This will be confusing in places like Peru where this is the temperate species used in the Andes, whereas tropical *Eryngium foetidum,* of the same family, bears the name *cilantro* in the lowlands. AH2 gives culantro as the standardized common name for *Eryngium foetidum.* I suspect that both will serve well and similarly for the many indications listed below. Coriander was used in love potions, its use as an aphrodisiac mentioned in *One Thousand and One Nights.* Still, Argentinans may take it as an anaphrodisiac.

I was a confessed Vienna Sausage eater! Back in my murky past, many times, I heated Vienna Sausage in the hot running water in my motel and saved the ten to twenty bucks and two hours it would have cost me to eat out. Hence my intrigue to read Nakatani's summary of Mori et al's study (Nippon Shokuhin Kogyo Gakkaishi 21: 285-7, 1974): Essential oils of celery, cinnamon, coriander and cumin (all Biblical except the celery) were comparable to sorbic acid at preventing the slimy spoilage of Vienna sausage. (See also Nakatani, N. 1994. Antioxidative and Antimicrobial Constituents of Herbs and Spices. 251–269 "Spices, Herbs and Edible Fungi", Elsevier Science B.V. Amsterdam.)

Roig mentions coriander as a Mediterranean plant, locally grown in Cuban gardens. Cuban Experimental Station trials in the 40s led Roig to conclude that the species did well there, and he published his recommendations for cultivation. Apparently then, if not now, coriander (leaves more than seed) was used less for medicine than for food, to spice black beans, soups and other dishes.

Cilantro leaves. *Susan Belsinger*

Ababıka (Sansk.; KAB); *Allaka* (Sansk.; KAB); *Arabische Petersilie* (Ger.; TEU); *Arab Parsley* (Eng.; AGG); *Behan* (Punjab; DEP); *Biles Cereales* (Fr.; KAP); *Böbberli* (Swiss; POR); *Bopchukuksun* (Rai; NPM); *Brasyal* (Tamang; NPM); *Chamem* (Armenia; POR); *Chhatra* (Sansk.; KAB); Chinese *Parsley* (Eng.; Ocn. Port.; AH2; POR; TEU; USN); *Chinesische Petersilie* (Ger.; POR; TEU); *Chrapfechöörnli* (Swiss; POR); *Cilantro* (Eng.; Scn.; Sp.; Spain; AAH2; EFS; EGG; TEU; USN; VAD); *Coentro* (Port.; POR); *Conzra* (Arab.; GHA); *Coentro* (Port.; EFS; USN); *Col* (Essex; KAB); *Cominos* (Pi.; KAB); *Coriander* (Eng.; Hungary; Scn.; AH2; KAP; NPM; POR; TEU; USN); *Coriandolo* (It.; EFS; POR; USN); *Coriandre* (Fr.; BOU; EFS; TEU; USN); *Coriandro* (It.; POrt.; Sp.; EFS; KAB; POR); *Coriándru* (Romania; POR); *Cosbor* (Malta; KAB); *Culantro* (Cuba; Ocn.; Panama; Peru; Pi.; Sp.; AH2; EFS; IED; JTR; POR; RyM; USN); *Culantro chino* (Ma.; JFM); *Culantro de Cartagena* (Cuba; Ma.; JFM; JTR); *Culantro de castilla* (Cuba; Ma.; JFM; JTR); *Culantro domestico* (Ma.; JFM); *Daaniwal* (Kashmir; POR); *Danga* (Nepal; DEP); *Danyalu* (Tel.; DEP); *Daun Ketumbar* (Malaya; POR); *Debja* (Arab.; BOU); *Dembilal* (Ethiopia; POR); *Dhaanya* (Hindi; POR); *Dhaanyakam* (Hindi; POR); *Dhana* (Bombay; Mar.; Sansk.; DEP; KAB; POR); *Dhanak chi* (Turkey; DEP; KAB); *Dhanayaka* (Sanskrit; POR); *Dhane* (Bengal; ADP; DEP; KAB; KAP; POR); *Dhaneyaka* (Sansk.; KAB); *Dhania* (Bengali; Hindi; India; Oriya; Punjab; Urdu; AGG; EFS; KAP; POR); *Dhania Saabut* (Hindi; POR); *Dhanika* (Sansk.; KAB); *Dhaniya* (Bhojpuri, Danuwar, Gurung, Magar, Mooshar, Nepali, Sunwar, Tam.; Tharu; Urdu; Yunani; KAB; KAP; NPM; POR; SUW); *Dhaniyaa* (Hindi; Urdu; POR); *Dhaniya dhap* (Tamang; NPM); *Dhaniyaka* (Sansk.; KAB; POR); *Dhaniyaalu* (Tel.; POR); *Dhaniyalu* (Tel.; ADP); *Dhanna* (Mar.; ADP); *Dhano* (Sind.; DEP; KAB); *Dhanya* (Hindi; Mar.; Sansk.; DEP; KAB; POR); *Dhanyabija* (Sansk.; KAB); *Dhanyaka* (Ayu.; Sansk.; ADP; AH2; DEP; KAB; KAP; KHA; OFF); *Dhanyika* (Sansk.; DEP); *Dhennika* (Sansk.; KAB); *Dhoney* (Bengali; POR); *Dimbilal* (Ethiopia; POR); *Dyovunco* (Ocaina; EGG); *Falscher anis* (Ger.; KAB); *Gad* (Hebrew, KAB); *Gakaka* (Piro; EGG); *Gartenkoriander* (Ger.; TEU); *Gemeiner Coriander* (Ger.; Sweden; KAB; NAD); *Gemeiner Coriender* (Ger.; KAP); *Geshnes* (Iran; POR); *Goid* (Punic; ZOH); *Gosangn* (Newari; NPM); *Gouzbir* (Berber; BOU); *Grain(e) du Coriandre* (Fr.; *Havija* (Kan.; DEP; NAD);

Haraa Dhania (Hindi; POR); *Havija* (Kan.; POR); *Hiang T'sai* (China; KAB); *Hom phak* (Ic.; KAB); *Hom pom* (Ic.; KAB); *Ho tuy* (Ic.; KAB); *Hridyagandha* (Sansk.; KAB); *Hsiang hsui* (China; EFS); *Huang thai tu* (Ic.; KAB); Hu Sui (Pinyin; China; AH2; DAA; POR); *Indische Petersilie* (Ger,; POR); *Iuen siu* (China; KAB); *Janapriya* (Sansk.; KAB); *Kabzara* (Arab.; GHA); *Kajbira* (Arab.; KAB); *Kambari* (Kan.; POR); *Karbijar* (Arab.; KAB); *Kashmirkhuska* (Iran; KAB); *Kashniz* (Iran; KAP); *Kasriza* (Iran; KAB); *Katumba* (Sumatra; IHB); *Katumber* (Java; IHB); *Katunchar* (Sunda; IHB); *Kazbarah* (Arab.; KAP); *Kerti koriander* (Turkey; EFS); *Kesbour* (Arab.; BOU); *Ketumbah* (Malaya; KAP); *Ketumbar* (Malaya; IHB; POR); *Khabzara* (Arab.; GHA); *Khotbir* (Mar.; DEP; KAB); *Khotmir* (Mar.; DEP; KAB); *Kishnetz* (Russia; KAB); *Kisnis* (Turkey; EB49:406); *Kisnish* (Turkey; POR); *Kishniz* (Iran; DEP; EFS); *Kizniz* (Turkey; EFS); *Koendoro* (Japan; POR; X11776997); *Kolendra* (Poland; POR); *Kolendra Siewna* (Poland; POR); *Koliander* (Ger.; Teu); *Koljandra* (Russia; POR); *Konphir* (Guj.; ADP; KAB; POR); *Korander* (Dutch; KAB); *Koriadnon* (Greek; AGG); *Koriander* (Den.; Dutch; Ger.; Hung.; Norway; Russia; Sweden; EFS; KAB; POR; TEU); *Korianderfrucht* (Ger.; POR), *Koriandr* (Czech.;Russia; POR); *Koriandr Posevnoi* (Russia; POR); *Koriandrze* (Poland; KAB); *Koriannon* (Greek; POR); *Korijander* (Croatia; POR); *Korion* (Greek; POR); *Koriyun* (Greece; DEP); *Koryander* (Poland; KAB); *Ko Soo* (Korea; POR); *Ko Su* (Korea; POR); *Kotamalli* (Tam.; KAB); *Kotambari* (Kan.; DEP; KAB); *Kotamrbi-beeja* (Kan.; DEP; EFS); *Kot bor* (Kon.; KAB); *Kot bori* (Kon.; KAB); *Kothamali* (Tam.; POR); *Kothamalli* (Tam.; ADP; KAP; POR); *Kothambala* (Kashmir; POR); *Kothambalari Kothambri* (Kan.; POR); *Kothamira* (Bombay; DEP; KAB); *Kothambri* (Kan.; WOI); *Kothimber* (Mar.; POR; WOI); *Kothmir* (Mar.; DEP); *Kothmiri* (Guj.; POR); *Kothmiri Bija* (Kan.; POR); *Kotimiri* (Tel.; DEP; KAB; NAD; POR); *Kothumpalari,* (Mal.; ADP; POR); *Kothumpalati* (Mal.; KAB); *Kothumpkalari Bija* (Mal.; POR); *Kottamali* (Mal.; Sinh.; Tam.; DEP; EFS; KAP; POR); *Kottamalli Virae* (Tam.; POR); *Kottambari, Kothambari* (Kan.; POR); *Kottampalari* (Tel.;NAD); *Kotthamalie* (Sinh; KAB; POR); *Kottmir* (India; EFS); *Kottumburi* (Kon; NAD); *Koyendoro* (Japan; POR); *Kunati* (Sansk.; KAB); *Kurbusar* (Arab.; DEP; KAB); *Kusbara* (Arab.; Hebrew; BOU; DEP; EFS; POR); *Kusbarah* (Arab.; DEP); *Kushniz* (Iran; EFS; KAB); *Kusthumbari Kustumburi* (Sansk.; EFS; KAB; POR); *Kuzbarah* (Arab.; KAB; POR); *Kuzbura* (Arab.; Arab.; POR); *Libdhane* (Guj.; POR); *Mexican Parsley* (Eng.;

AGG); *Nan Nan Bin* (Burma; POR); *Nan Nan Zee* (Burma; POR); *Nau-nau* (Burma; DEP; KAP; NAD); *Ngo* (Vn.; EB42:413); *Ngo tham* (Ic.; KAB); *Nisara* (Sansk.; KAB); *Ongsay* (Pi; KAB); *Pak chi* (Siam; IHB); *Penjilang* (Java; Malaya; IHB; POR); *Persil Arabe* (Fr.; POR; TEU); *Petite coriandre* (Fr.; KAB); *PhBBk Kaawm* (Laos; POR); *Phak Hom* (Laos; POR); *Pucioagna* (Romania; KAB); *Rau mjji* (Vn.; KAB; POR); *Rüügeliküümmi* (Swiss; POR); *Saquil* (Ma.; JFM); *Schwindelkorn* (Ger.; Teu); *Schwindelkornerr* (Ger.; EFS); *Shakayogya* (Sansk.; KAB); *Silantro* (Peru; EGG); *Stinkdill* (Ger.; KAB); *Sukshmapatra* (Sansk.; KAB); *Sugandhi* (Sansk.; KAB); *Tabel* (Arab.; BOU); *Tansanaqua* (Ma.; JFM); *Tumbaru* (Sansk.; KAB); *Tunchar* (Sunda; IHB); *Uchung* (Lepcha; NPM); *Ushu* (Ladakh; MKK); *Ussu* (Bhoti; KAB); *U-su* (Tibet; NPM); *Vedhaka* (Sansk.; KAB); *Veshana* (Sansk.; KAB); *Vitunakka* (Sansk.; KAB); *Wanzendill* (Ger.; POR; TEU); *Wanzenkraut* (Ger.; TEU); *Wanzenküümmel* (Ger.; POR; TEU); *Wan Swee* (China; POR); *Xiang Sui* (China; POR); *Yan Sui* (China; POR; USN); *Yuan Sui* (China; Pinyin; AH2; EFS); *Yuan Sui Zi* (Pinyin; AH2); *Yuen Sai* (China; AGG); *Zaub Thwb Qaib* (Hmong; EB57:365); *Zaub Txib Gab* (Hmong; EB57:365).

Reported Activities for Coriander

(key: f = folklore; 1 = with animal, chemical, or epidemiological evidence)

Alexeteric (f; BIB); Allergenic (1; TEU; X16881566); Analgesic (f1; AGG; B; VAD); Anaphrodisiac (f; HHB; JFM; LIL); Anaphylactic (AGG; Anthelminthic (1; AGG; X17113738); Antiaggregant (1; PMCID: PMC3083808); Antiaging (f; LIL); Anti-Alzheimers (1; X20848667); Antiamnesic (1; X20848667); Antiarachidonate (1; AGG); Antiatherosclerotic (1; X21718774); Antibilious (f; KAP); Antibiofilm (1; X21660258); Anticholinesterase (1; X20848667); Antidementic (1; X20848667); Antidermatitic (1; X21815228); Antidiabetic (f1; AGG; DIA; TEU; X19003941; X21365993; X21718774 ; Infarct (1; XX22750725); Antidote (Lead) (1; AGG; X19902160); Antidote (Mercury) (1; X15721537); Antiedemic (f1; APA); Antigenotoxic (1; X20858524); AntiHIV (1; AGG); Antihyperglycemic (1; KHA; X21365993); Antihyperlipidemic (1; TEU); Antihypertensive (1; AGG); Anti-implantation (1; APA; TEU); Anti-infarct (1; X22750725); Anti-inflammatory (f1; PNC; VAD; X20549653); Antileishmanic (1; X 21320755); Antileukemic (1; AGG); Antimalarial (f; LIL); AntiMRSA (1; X21815228; X21862758); Antimutagenic (1; AGG; APA; X15451560); Antinitrosaminic (1; X15451560); Antiobesity (1; AGG; X15462185; X18831331;X21718774); Antioxidant (1; JAF51:6961; X22671941X21988208 X21523411; X21365993; ' X19168417; X19146910; X18924419; X15364640); Antiperoxidant (1; TEU; X15364640; 21523411); Antiproliferant (1; AGG); Antiradicular (1; JAF51:6961; X21365993; X21523411; X21988208); AntiROS (1; X22750725); Antiseptic (f1; AGG; LIL; PH2; TEU; X18831345; X20057155 X21788125 X21815228 X21862758; X22276482); Antispasmodic (f1; AGG; BGB; HHB; LIL; PHR; PH2); Antistaphylococcal (1; X21815228); Antiviral (1; AGG); Anti-yeast (1; X 21788125); Anxiolytic (f1; AGG; X15619553; X22022003; X22276482); Aphrodisiac (f; AGG; APA; BOU; DEP; LIL; SUW); Apoptotic (1; X20492211); Bactericide (1; APA; PHR; PH2; TEU; X15612768; X21815228; X21862758); Calcium-Antagonist (f; X19146935); Candidicide (1; X21660258; X 21788125); Cardioprotective (f1; BIB; GHA; LIL; X18831331; X21718774; X22750725); Cardiotonic (f; GHA); Carminative (f1; AGG; APA; DEP; GHA; HHB; JTR; LIL; PHR; PH2); Catalase-Genic (1; X22671941); Cerebrotonic (f; KAB); Chelator (Lead); (1; AGG); Choleretic (1; TEU); Cholinergic (f; X19146935); Contraceptive (f; APA); COX-2-Inhibitor (1; X20549653); Dermatitigenic (1; VAD); Diaphoretic (f1; AGG); Digestive (f1; AGG; BGB; BIB; GHA; IHB; TEU); Diuretic (f1; APA; BIB; DEP; X17961943; X19146935); Emmenagogue (f; BIB; EFS; LIL); Estrogenic (1; VAD); Febrifuge (f; DEP); Fungicide (1; APA; PHR; PH2; TEU; X 21660258; 21788125); Gastrogogue (1; PH2); Glutathiogenic (1; X22671941); Gram(+)-icide (1; AGG; X21815228; X21862758); Gram(-)-icide (1; X21862758); HDL-Genic (1; TEU; X18831331; X22671941); Hepatoprotective (1; X19146910; X21988208); Hepatotonic (f; KAB); Herbistatic (1; TEU; X18831331; X22671941); HMG-CoA-Reductase-Inhibitor (1; PMCID:PMC3083808); Hypnotic (f; KAB); Hypocholesterolemic (1; TEU; X15462185; X18831331;X20848667; X21718774; X22671941); Hypoglycemic (1; AGG; APA; DIA; KHA; LIL; PNC; X21718774; X22671941); Hypolipidemic (1; AGG; X15462185; X18831331; X21718774; X22671941); Hypoprogesteronic (1; TEU); Hypotensive (f1; APA; X19146935); Hypotriglyceridemic (1; X15462185; X22671941); Immunomodulator (1; AGG; X22446868); Insecticide (1; AGG; X21692682); Insulinogenic (1; X19003941);

Iron-Chelator (1; X21988208); Lactogogue (f; NMH); Larvicide (f1; AGG; APA; PNC; X15623234; X21692682; X22208224); LDL-Lytic (1; X22671941); Lipolytic (f1; BGB; LAF); Lipoxygenase-Inhibitor (1; X21988208); Memorigenic (f1; ATT; X20848667; X22114531); Mercury Chelator (1; X15721537); Mosquitocide (1; AGG; X21692682; X22208224); Myocardioprotective (1; X22750725); Myorelaxant (1; AGG; APA; X15619553); Narcotic (f; LIL); Nematicide (1; AGG; X18605734); NF-Kappa-B-Inhibitor (1; X20549653); NO-Inhibitor (1; X20549653); Orexigenic (f12; EFS; LIL; PH2; TEU; VAD); Ovicide (1; X17113738); Pectoral (f; BIB; DEP); PG-E2-Inhibitor (1; X20549653); Phototoxic (1; AGG); Pro-oxidant (1; X20608729); Saluretic (1; X17961943); Sedative (f1; AGG; BIB; DEP; X15619553; X21988208); Sialogogue (1; TEU); SOD-Genic (1; X22671941); Spasmogenic (1; AGG; TEU; X19146935); Spasmolytic (1; AGG; TEU; X19146935); Stimulant (f1; AGG; BGB; BIB; DEP); Stomachic (f1; BGB; BIB; HHB; JTR; LIL); Thripicide (1; X17066806); TNF-alpha-Inhibitor (1; X22446868); Tonic (f; BIB; DEP; GHA); Vermifuge (f1; JFM; LIL; X17113738).

Reported Indications for Coriander

(key: f = folklore; l = with animal, chemical, or epidemiological evidence)

Adenopathy (f; KAB); Allergy (f; AGG); Alzheimers (1; X20848667); Ameba (f; AGG; PH2); Amenorrhea (f; JFM); Amnesia (1; X20848667); Anorexia (f12; AGG; APA; EFS; KOM; PH2; TEU; VAD); Anxiety (f1; AGG; X15619553; X22022003); Arthrosis (f1; AGG; BIB; HHB; VAD; X22446868); Asthenia (f; BOU); Atherosclerosis (1; X21718774); Bacillus (1; HH2; X21462837); Bacteria (1; PH2; TEU; VAD; X20057155); Biliousness (f; BIB; DEP; KAP; SUW); Bleeding (f; ADP; DEP; EGG; PH2); BO (f; APA); Bronchosis (f; KAB); Burn (f; AGG; BOU); Campylobacter (1; X20057155); Cancer (f; JLH); Cancer, abdomen (f; JLH); Cancer, colon (f; JLH); Cancer, sinew (f; JLH); Cancer, spleen (f; JLH); Cancer, uterus (f; JLH); Candida (1; X21660258X 21788125);Carbuncle (f; ADP; BOU; DEP); Cardiopathy (f1; BIB; GHA; LIL; X18831331; X21718774; (1; X22750725); Catarrh (f; BIB; KAP; LIL); Chickenpox (f; PH2; SKJ); Childbirth (f; IHB: PH2); Cholecocystosis (f; PHR); Cholera (f; BOU); Cold (f;

LIL); Colic (f1; DEP; GHA; HHB; LIL; X19146935); Condyloma (f; JLH); Conjunctivosis (f; ADP; DEP; GHA); Coryza (f; KAB); Cough (f; AGG; IHB; LIL; PHR; PH2); Cramp (f1; BGB; BIB; LIL PH2); Cystosis (f; AGG; PH2; VA); Dementia (1; X20848667); Dermatosis (f1; AGG; PHR; PH2; X21815228); Diabetes (f1; AGG; DIA; JFM; KHA; LIL; TEU; X17852503; X19003941; X21718774); Diarrhea (f; APA; EGG; HHB); Dizziness (f; AGG); Dysentery (f1; APA; PHR; PH2); Dyslactea (f; LIL); Dyspepsia (f12; AGG; APA; DEP; GHA; HHB; JTR; KOM; LIL; PH2; TEU); Dysuria (f; PH2); Edema (f1; PH2; X22446868); Enterosis (f12; AGG; BGB; JLH; JTR; KAP; PHR; PH2; X16868824; X19146935); Epistaxis (f; AGG; EGG; PH2); Erotomania (f; BIB; LIL); Erysipelas (f; BIB; LIL); Erythema (f; DEP); Escherichia (1; HH2; X21462837; X21862758); Fever (f; AGG; JTR; PHR; PH2); Flu (f; AGG); Food Poisoning (1; X21462837; X21862758); Fungus (f1; PH2; TEU; X 21788125); Gas (f1; AGG; APA; BGB; DEP; EGG); Gastrosis (f1; AGG; BGB; HHB; JTR; LIL; PHR); Gingirrhagia (f; KAB); Gleet (f; ADP; KAB); Halitosis (f; ADP; AGG; APA; DEP; LIL; PHR; PH2); Hay Fever (f; AGG); Headache (f; AGG; BIB; DEP; EGG; JTR; PHR; PH2); Hemorrhoid (f; ADP; APA; DEP; PH2); Hepatosis (f1; JTR; X19146910; X21988208; X21988208); Hernia (f; BIB; LIL); Hiccup (f; KAB); High Blood Pressure (1; X19146935); HIV (1; AGG); Hysteria (f; BIB; BOU; JFM; JTR; LIL); IBS (1; AGG; X16868824); Impotence (f; AGG; BIB; BOU); Induration (f; JLH); Infarct (1; X22750725); Infection (f1; AGG; HH2; LIL; PH2; TEU; X21815228); Inflammation (f; KAB; VAD); Influenza (f; AGG); Insomnia (f1; AGG; X21988208); Intoxication (f; BIB; DEP); Itch (f; AGG); Jaundice (f1; JTR; KAB; X21988208); Kernel (f; JLH); Leishmania (1; X 21320755); Leprosy (f; AGG; PHR; PH2); Leukemia (1; AGG); Listeria (1; AGG; X11929164; X21462837); Malaria (f; LIL); Measles (f; APA; HAD; LIL; PH2); Metabolic Syndrome (1; X21718774); MRSA (1; X21815228; X21862758); Mycosis (f1; DEP; HH2; VAD; X21788125); Myocardiopathy (1; X22750725); Nausea (f; BIB; GHA; IHB; LIL); Nephrosis (f; AGG); Nervousness (f; BIB); Neuralgia (f; APA; BIB; EGG; KAP; LIL; NAD); Neurosis (f; BOU); Obesity (1; AGG; X15462185; X18831331; X21718774); Oliguria (f1; AGG; X17961943; X19146935); Ophthalmia (f; BOU; DEP; GHA); Orchosis (f; BOU); Otosis (f; BOU); Pain (f; KAB; PH2); Parasite (f; BOU); Pharyngosis (f; AGG; KAP; PHR; PH2); Ptomaine (f; BIB); Puerperium (f; AGG; PHR); Rash (f; PHR; PH2); Respirosis (f;

AGG); Rheumatism (f1; AGG; BOU; HHB; LIL; NAD; X22446868); Rhinosis (f; AGG); Salmonella (1; HH2; X15161192; X21462837; X 21862758); Scabies (f; KAB); Sclerosis (f; BIB); Scrofula (f; LIL; PH2); Smallpox (f; DEP; LIL); Snakebite (f; BIB); Sore (f; AGG; DEP); Sore Throat (f; AGG; KAP); Soroche (f; EGG); Spasm (1; VAD); Splenosis (f; BIB; LIL); Staphylococcus (1; X21815228; X21862758); Stomachache (f1; BIB; EGG; 16868824EB49:406); Stomatosis (f; ADP; AGG; KAB; PHR; PH2); Streptococcus (1; X21815228); Stress (1; X22022003); Swelling (f1; ADP; DEP; GHA; X22446868); Syphilis (f; BIB; KAB); Thirst (f; NAD); Thrush (f; DEP); Toothache (f; APA; LIL);); Tuberculosis (f1; KAP); Tumor (f; JLH); Ulcer (f; BIB; TEU); Urethritis (f; AGG; VAD); Urticaria (f; AGG); Uterosis (f; JLH); VD (f; BIB; KAB); Vertigo (f; AGG; HHB; NAD; PH2); Virus (1; AGG); Vomiting (f; AGG); Wart (f; JLH); Wen (f; JLH); Worm (f1; AGG; APA; BOU; JFM; LIL X17113738); Wound (f; HH2); Yeast (f1; DEP; X 21788125).

Dosages for Coriander

Seeds, the size of a peppercorn, have a sharp but pleasant aroma, pleasing to many ethnic groups, e.g., Arabs, Egyptians, some Europeans, Asian Indians, sometimes flavoring breadstuffs, cakes, and confections therewith. Used as early as 1550 B.C., the dried fruits, called coriander seed, combining the taste of lemon peel and sage, have been used in pastries, cookies, buns, processed meats (such as sausage, bologna and frankfurters), pickling spice, and curry powder. Coriander has also used to flavor liqueurs, such as gin and vermouth, as well as in the cocoa, chocolate and cordial industries.

Young plants are in salads as a vegetable and in chutneys, sauces, soups, and curries (BIB; FAC; JTR; TAN). 1-2 teaspoons crushed fr/cup water up to 3 x a/day (APA); 0.1 g essential oil, 2-3 x/day (HH2); 3 g fr (KOM; PHR); 0.3-1 g powdered fr (PNC); 0.5-2 ml liquid fruit extract (PNC); 0.05-2 (they said 2, I'd d have said 0.2; cf. celery seed (close kin) ml essential oil (PNC). One cup tea (30g/l) after meals (VAD); 30-50 drops tincture (1:5) after meals (VAD); 1-3 drop EO in sugar cube; 3-5 g pulverized and mixed with honey (VAD).

- Asian Indians paste powdered seed on carbuncles, headache, sores, and gargle for thrush (DEP)

- Asian Indians report pulverized roots and leaves in alcohol for measles eruptions (KAB)

- Asian Indians suggest seed infusion or tincture for biliousness, catarrh, dyspepsia, enterosis, gas, sore throat (NAD)

- Asian Indians suggest equal parts coriander, cardamom, and caraway 1:1:1 as digestive (NAD)

- Asian Indians suggest powdered seed consumed for colic, dyspepsia, halitosis (DEP)

- Asian Indians suggest equal parts coriander, cottonseed, poppy seed, and 2 parts sugar to take with rose water for vertigo (NAD)

- Ayurvedics recommend for biliousness, bronchitis, dysentery, fever, nausea, and thirst, viewing it as aphrodisiac, apertif, anthelmintic, antipyretic, diuretic, laxative, refrigerant, stimulant, and stomachic

- Cubans suggest the seed decoction for diabetes and neuralgia (Cuba; JFM)

- Ethiopians chew the leaves for colic and stomachache (BIB)

- Iranians use for anxiety, gas, headache, inappetence, and pain (BIB; X22114531)

- Jordanians use for diabetes (X17182483)

- Latinos say tea 2 x a day is a female anaphrodisiac (JFM)

- Latinos boil 1 teaspoon fruits in 0.25 liter wine as emmenagogue and vermifuge (JFM)

- Middle Easterners steep seed in vinegar a day and drink with sugar as cardiotonic, general tonic (GHA)

- Lebanese use seed decoction as a stimulant, or as a narcotic anodyne (HJP)

- Moroccans use folklorically as a diuretic (X17961943)

- Iranians use their carmint (total extracts of coriander, lemon balm and spearmint) as clinically proven antispasmodic, carminative, and sedative, useful in IBS (irritable bowel syndrome) (X16868824)

- Moroccans recently proved the antidiabetic folklore (X21718774)

- Muhammadans use carminative, pectoral, sedative seeds, in a collyrium to prevent smallpox from destroying the eyes, as well as for chronic conjunctivosis (DEP)

- Peruvians paste the crushed leaves on the forehead for altitude sickness (EGG)

- Peruvians suggest the leaf tea for gas, headache, neuralgia, pain, stomachache (EGG)

- Saudis suggest seed decoction for failing vision (GHA)

- Yunani use the leaves, considered analgesic and hypnotic, for bleeding gums, eye pains, gleet, hiccup, inflammation, jaundice, piles, scabies, stomatitis, toothache, and tubercular glands. They use the seed to prevent bronchitis and coryza, for biliousness, dyspepsia, headache, syphilis, and ulcers on the penis, viewing the seed as aphrodisiac, cardiotonic, cerebtotonic, hepatotonic

- Seed ground with raisins for tumors (JLH); with honey or raisins for burns, carbuncles, orchosis, sores, and sore ears (BOU)

Downsides for Coriander

Class 1 (AHPA,1997). None known (KOM). "Health hazards or side effects following the proper administration of designated therapeutic dosages are not recorded" (PH2). Leaves may harbor Listeria, especially in hot moist situations. Although the plant contains several antioxidant phytochemicals, under some conditions the oil can be pro-oxidant (X20608729). Mexican scientists recently published some downsides for high doses of coriander extracts, e.g., apoptotic, mutagenic (X20492211). Burdock's earlier safety assessment says that, based on the history of consumption of coriander oil without reported adverse effects, lack of its toxicity in limited studies and lack of toxicity of its major constituent, linalool, the use of coriander oil as an added food ingredient is considered safe at present levels of use (X19032971).

Extracts of Coriander

Indian researchers concluded that extracts 100 and 200 mg/kg dose produced anti-anxiety effects almost comparable to diazepam. At 50 mg/kg, there were no anxiolytic effects (X22022003). Of 8 herbs commonly consumed in Ireland, basil and coriander were richest in beta-carotene, beta-cryptoxanthin, and lutein + zeaxanthin (X20443063). Of 12 essential oils, Thai scientists identified coriander oil as a natural antimicrobial compound against *Campylobacter jejuni* in food (X20057155). Essential oil is particularly effective against *Listeria monocytogenes* (X11929164); LD50 (EO)=4,130 mg/kg orl rat HH2). Coriander is reportedly hypoglycemic (X16361181).

CORIANDRUM SATIVUM L.
"CORIANDER"
CONVERSION FACTOR LF ZMB
    to APB = divide by 3.7
ACETIC-ACID 1 FR BML
ACETIC-ACID-ESTER FR AGG
    WOI
ALIPHATIC-ALDEHYDES -8,300
    LF TEU
ALKYLPTHALIDES LF TEU

TRANS-ANETHOLE 1-2 FR BML
ANGELICIN FR AYL
ANTHOCYANINS SH X21523411
    APIGENIN FR 411/
APIGENIN -10,200 LF AGG
ARBUTIN -36,100 LF AGG
ASCORBIC-ACID 780-6,290 LF
    CRC KAP WO2
ASCORBIC-ACID SH X21523411
ASH 19,000-153,000 LF CRC

ASH 6,000-49,800 FR AGG CRC

BORNEOL 2-54 FR BML PH2

BORNYL-ACETATE FR CCO

BORON 9-29 FR BOB

GAMMA-CADINENE PL
  X17511354

CAFFEIC-ACID FR LF AYL HHB
  TEU

CAFFEIC-ACID -16,500 LF AGG
  X21988208

4-CAFFEOYLQUINIC-ACID FR
  TEU

5-CAFFEOYLQUINIC-ACID FR
  TEU

CALCIUM 6,465-14,469 FR CRC
  USA

CALCIUM 1,330-13,441 LF CRC

CAMPESTEROL 30 FR GAS

CAMPHENE 2-208 FR AGG BML
  JAF50:2870

CAMPHOR 0-2,600 FR BML PH2
  TEU JAF50:2870

CARBOHYDRATES 549,900-
  603,240 FR USA

CAPRINALDEHYDE FR CCO

CARBOHYDRATES 73,000-589,000
  LF CRC

BETA-CAROTENE 29-228 SH CRC
  X20443063

BETA-CAROTENE 0 FR CRC USA

CAROTENOIDS SH X20443063
  X21523411

CARVONE 21-26 FR BML

CARYOPHYLLENE 1-8 FR BML

CARYOPHYLLENE-OXIDE FR
  LAF

CHLOROGENIC-ACID 200 FR
  HH2 TEU

CHLOROGENIC-ACID 305-320
  PL ABS

CHLOROPHYLLS SH X21523411

CHROMIUM 28.8 FR ABS 5/

1,8-CINEOLE FR BML HH3

CINNAMIC-ACID 40 PL ABS

CITRONELLOL 0-8 FR BML

CITRONELLYL-ACETATE (1.77%
  EO) SD X22208224

COBALT 0.9 FR ABS 5/

COPPER 10-13 FR ABS USA

COPPER 18 LF USA

CORIANDRIN 20-45 LF HH2 TEU

CORIANDRINOL FR LAF

CORIANDRINONDIOL FR LAF

CORIANDROL 400-10,250 FR BML
  PH2 WOI

CORIANDRONE-A LF TEU

CORIANDRONE-B LF TEU

CORIANDRONE-C LF TEU

CORIANDRONE-D LF TEU

CORIANDRONE-E LF TEU

CIS-P-COUMARIC-ACID 273 PL
  ABS

CIS-P-COUMARIC-ACID 1,440 FR
  BAS

TRANS-P-COUMARIC-ACID 173
  PL ABS

TRANS-P-COUMARIC-ACID 1,120
  FR ABS

COUMARINS FR AGG

P-COUMAROYLQUINIC-ACID
  FR TEU

BETA-CRYPTOXANTHIN SH
  X20443063

CYCLODECANE EO X21660258

CYCLODODECANOL (23.11%
  OIL) LF X21692682

3-CYCLOHEXENE-1-METHANOL, ALPHA, ALPHA4-TRIMETHYL-ACETATE (4.72% EO) SD X22208224

P-CYMENE 0-728 FR BML PH2 TEU JAF50:2870

P-CYMOL FR AGG HH2

DECANAL 400-1,800 LF BML FNF TAD TEU

DECANAL (2.33% OIL) LF X21692682

DECANAL 6-80 FR BML

1-DECANOL (7.24% OIL) LF X21692682

TRANS-2-DECANAL 1-18 FR BML

(E)2,2-DECENAL 2-100 FR JAF50:2870

(E)2-DECENAL 1,200-4,600 LF FNF TAD TEU

5-DECENAL 101 LF BML

DEC-2-ENOL-900 LF TEU

DECYLALDEHYDE 2-27 FR AGG BML WOI

DECYLIC-ACID-ESTER FR WOI

(7,7)-DIHYDROCORIANDRIN LF HH2 TEU

DIHYDROQUERCETIN -39,000 LF AGG

DIOSMIN -18,400 LF AGG

DIPENTENE FR AGG BML WOI

DODECANAL 1,627 LF BML

DODECANAL (5.16% OIL) LF X21692682

DODECANAL (3.18% OIL) ST X21692682

DODECANOL FR BML

1-DODECANOL (6.54% OIL) LF X21692682

2-DODECANAL FR LF CCO

1-DODECANOL (2.47% OIL) ST X21692682

2-DODECENAL (9.93% OIL) LF X21692682

(E)-2-DODECENAL LF

7-DODECENAL 2,131 LF BML X17511354

ELEMOL FR AYL

EO 10,000 LF BML

EO 1,000-26,000 FR AGG BML HHB HH2 PH2 TEU

EPICATECHIN -26,200 LF AGG

EPIGALLOCATECHIN LF AGG

ESCULETIN -19,600 LF AGG

ESCULIN -19,400 LF AGG

ETHYL-LINOLATE 13-166 FR BML

ETHYL-MYRISTATE 12-153 FR BML

ETHYL-PALMITATE 46-598 FR BML

ETHYL-PENTEDECANOATE 0-5 FR BML

ETHYL-STEARATE 42-546 FR BML

EUGENOL PL X17511354

FAT 110,000-210,000 FR ABS AGG HH2 PH2 TEU WOI

FAT 6,000-50,000 LF CRC

FERULIC-ACID 200 FR HH2

FERULIC-ACID -42,800 LF AGG

CIS-FERULIC-ACID 467 PL ABS

CIS-FERULIC-ACID 1,360 FR ABS

FERULOYOLQUINIC-ACID FR TEU

FIBER 16,000-129,000 LF CRC

FIBER 284,000-319,000 FR AGG CRC

FLAVONOIDS LF AGG TEU X19168417 X21988208

FLAVONOIDS SD X21365993

FLAVONOLS SH X21523411
FOLATE -16 LF X22492274
FOLATE -32 TC X22492274
FRUCTOSE FR HHB
FURFUROL 60,000 FR HHB
GALLIC-ACID -20,400 LF AGG
GERANIAL FR BML
GERANIOL 0-1,820 FR AGG BML
    PH2 TEU JAF50:2870
GERANIOL (4.83% EO) SD
    X22208224
GERANYL-ACETATE 10-5,200 FR
    AGG BML TEU JAF50:2870
GLUCOSE FR HHB
GLYCITIN PL X21988208
HEPTADECANE FR BML
HESPERIDIN -28,300 LF AGG
HEXADECANOIC-ACID (2.65%
    EO) SD X22208224
2-HEXEN-1-OL EO X21660258
3-HEXEN-1-OL EO X21660258
HOMOERIODICTYOL FR 411/
P-HYDROXYBENZOIC-ACID 252-
    333 PL ABS
P-HYDROXYBENZOIC-ACID 960
    FR ABS
HYDROXYCINNAMIC-ACID FR
    TEU
HYDROXYCOUMARINS FR TEU
4-HYDROXYCOUMARIN -20,300
    LF AGG
HYPEROSIDE -5,600 LF AGG
IRON 30-528 LF CRC USA
IRON 112-227 FR USA ABS 5/
ISOCOUMARINS LF TEU
ISOQUERCETIN PL X21988208
ISOQUERCITRIN FR AYL HH2
ISOQUERCITRIN LF HH2 TEU
KAEMPFEROL 3 FR HH2

KAEMPFEROL 9 LF HH2
KAEMPFEROL-3-O-GLYCOSIDE
    LF HH2 TEU
LIMONENE 0-1,238 FR AGG BML
    PH2 TEU JAF50:2870
LINALOOL 400-22,360 FR
    BML PH2 TAD TEU WOI
    JAF50:2870
LINALOOL 0-3,800 LF FNF TAD
LINALOOL (55.09% EO) SD
    X22208224
LINALOOL-OXIDE 2-21 FR BML
LINOLEIC-ACID 13,030-18,260 FR
    BML USA
LINOLENIC-ACID 15,400-29,400
    FR HH2
LUTEIN 270-993 LF X17602649
LUTEIN SH X20443063
LUTEOLIN -69,300 LF AGG
MAGNESIUM 6,940-7,488 LF USA
MAGNESIUM 2,939-4,016 FR USA
MANGANESE 18-19 FR ABS USA
MANGANESE 64 LF USA
D-MANNITOL FR HHB
3-O-METHYLKAEMPFEROL FR
    411/
15-METHYLTRICY
    CLO[6.5.2(13,14),0(7,15)]-
    PENTADECA-1,3,5,7,9,11,13-
    HEPTENE (7.01% OIL) ST
    X21692682
8-METHYNON-5-ENAL 96 LF BML
MYRCENE 6-235 FR AGG BML
    JAF50:2870
MYRISTIC-ACID 200-219 FR AGG
    USA
MYRISTICIN FR BML

(Z)-MYROXIDE PL X17511354
TRANS-2-DODECANAL 9-114
FR BML
NEOCNIDILIDE FR 411/
NEROLIDOL 14-17 FR BML
NEROL FR BML
NERYL ACETATE PL X17511354
NIACIN 13-136 LF CRC USA
NIACIN 21-23 FR USA
NICKEL 2.4 FR ABS 5/
NONANAL 1-18 FR BML
NONYL-ALDEHYDE LF LAF
OCIMENE FR HHB
CIS-OCIMENE FR BML
TRANS-OCIMENE FR BML
OCTADECANE FR BML
DELTA-5,6-OCTADECENOIC-
ACID FR HHB
2,6-OCTADIEN-1-OL,3,7-
DIMETHYL-ACETATE(5.70%
EO) SD X22208224
OCTANOL 504 LF BML
3-OCTENAL 97 LF NML
OLEIC-ACID 39,930-167,819 FR
ABS USA WOI
ORIENTIN -16,700 LF AGG
OXALIC-ACID 50 LF WBB
PALMITIC-ACID 2,160-16,800 FR
USA WOI
PALMITOLEIC-ACID 1,000-1,097
FR USA
PECTIN FR HHB
PENTADECANAL LF BML
PENTOSANS 100,000-103,000 FR
AGG HHB
PETROSELINIC-ACID 40,700-
111,300 FR PH2 TEU WOI
ALPHA-PHELLANDRENE FR BML

BETA-PHELLANDRENE 1-13 FR
HHB
PHENOL-CARBOXYLIC-ACIDS
FR AGG
PHENOLICS SH X21523411
X21988208
N-PHENYLPROPENOYL-L-
AMINO-ACID- AMIDES PL
X17295182
PHOSPHORUS 720-6,452 LF CRC
PHOSPHORUS 3,907-4,687 FR USA
PHYTOL (61.86% OIL) ST
X21692682
PHYTOSTEROLS 460 FR GAS
ALPHA-PINENE 30-13,780 FR BML
HHB PH2 TEU JAF50:2870
ALPHA-PINENE (7.49% EO) SD
X22208224
2-ALPHA-PINENE (2.39% EO) SD
X22208224
BETA-PINENE 4-130 FR AGG BML
JAF50:2870
POLYPHENOLICS SD X21365993
POTASSIUM 5,600-48,177 LF CRC
POTASSIUM 11,866-14,781 FR USA
PROTEIN 110,000-170,000 FR AGG
HHB
PROTEIN 26,000-236,000 LF CRC
PROTOCATECHUIC-ACID 167-
179 PL ABS
PROTOCATECHUIC-ACID 760
FR ABS
PSORALEN FR AYL
PYROGALLOL PL X21988208
QUERCETIN 55 FR HH2 PNC
QUERCETIN 360 LF HH2
QUERCETIN PL X21988208
QUERCETIN-3-GLUCURONIDE
FR AYL

QUERCETIN-3-O-GLUCURONIDE LF TEU
QUERCETIN-3-O-GLYCOSIDE LF HH2
RHAMNETIN FR 411/
RIBOFLAVIN 1-21 LF CRC
RIBOFLAVIN 3-4 FR BML
RUTIN FT AYL
RUTIN LF HH2 AGG TEU
SABINENE 1-83 FR AGG BML JAF50:2870
SACCHAROSE FR HHB
SALICYLATES 1-27 FR X16608205
SALICYLIC-ACID TR-8 FR X16608205
SALICYLIC-ACID -21,900 LF AGG
SCOPOLETIN 1.5-3 FR HHB HH2 PH2 TEU
SCOPOLETIN -17,900 LF AGG
BETA-SITOSTEROL 220 FR GAS HHB
BETA-SITOSTEROL-D-GLYCOSIDE FR AYL
DELTA-SITOSTEROL FR AYL
SODIUM 940-7,581 LF CRC
SODIUM 308-430 FR USA
STARCH 100,000-105,000 FR AGG HHB
STEARIC-ACID 1,100-1,207 FR AGG USA
STIGMASTEROL 180 FR GAS
SUGARS 192,000-200,000 FR AGG AYL
SUGARS SH X21523411
TANNIN FR AYL
TERPINEN-4-OL 0.4-130 FR BML JAF50:2870
ALPHA-TERPINENE 1-15 FR BML

GAMMA-TERPINENE TR-33,900 FR BML JAF50:2870
ALPHA-TERPINEOL 4-130 FR BML JAF50:2870
TERPINOLENE 4-340 FR AGG BML JAF50:2870
TETRADECANAL 132 LF BML
TETRADECANOIC-ACID (2.49% EO) SD X22208224
9-TETRADECENAL 924 LF BML
(E)2-TETRADECENAL 100-1,300 LF FNF TAD TEU
TETRADECANAL (23.11% OIL) LF X21692682
13-TETRADECENAL (6.85% OIL) LF X21692682
THIAMIN 1-16 LF CRC USA
THIAMIN 2-3 FR BML
ALPHA-THUJENE FR BML
THYMOL FR HH2
ALPHA-TOCOPHEROL SH X21523411
GAMMA-TOCOPHEROL SH X21523411
TOCOPHEROLS SH X21523411
TOLUENE 117 LF BML
TRIACONTANE FR AYL
TRIACONTANOL FR AYL
TRICOSANOL FR AYL
TRIDECANAL 168 LF BML
(E)-2-TRIDECENAL PL X17511354
5,8-TRIDECADIENAL 561 LF BML
TRANS-TRIDEC-2-EN-1-AL FR BIS PH2
TRITERPENES FR TEU
UMBELLIFERONE 1.5-3 FR HHB HH2 PH2 TEU
UMBELLIFERONE -14,000 LF AGG

UNDECANAL 304 LF BML
1-UNDECANOL (2.28% OIL) LF
   X21692682
(E,E)-2,4-UNDECADIENAL LF
   X20923150
3,6-UNDECADIENAL 342 LF BML
6-UNDECENAL 130 LF BML
UNDECANAL 1-8 FR BML
UNDECANAL (1.29% EO) SD
   X22208224
VACCENIC-ACID FR AGG

VANILLIC-ACID 221-347 PL ABS
VANILLIC-ACID 960 FR ABS HH2
VICENIN -35,400 LF AGG
WATER 73,000 LF USA
WATER 86,000-114,000 FR AGG
   USA WO2
ZEAXANTHIN. SH X20443063
ZINC 34-52 FR USA ABS 5/
(5/ Abs= Pak. J. Sci.Ind. Res. 28:
   234.1985)

WARNING: He/she who self-diagnoses and self-medicates intelligently may be depriving synthetic pharmaceutical vendors and synthetic physicians of their higher standard of living.

Dr. James A. Duke is a PhD economic botanist and ethnobotanist. He holds an AB (1952), MA (1955), and PhD (1961), all from the University of North Carolina, Chapel Hill. Jim worked with the Missouri Botanical Garden until 1963, joining the USDA until 1965, then joining the Battelle Columbia Laboratories for ecological and ethnobotanical studies in the Sea Level Canal Survey in Panama and Columbia. In 1971 he returned to USDA, Beltsville, working on an alternative crops program. From 1977-1982, he directed the USDA program, collecting plants from China, Ecuador, Panama, and Syria, in collaboration with the NCI Cancer-Screening Program. That is when he started compiling his phytochemical database, still online and growing at the USDA. Retiring in 1995, he wrote *The Green Pharmacy*, one of the the 30 books he has published. Jim started an ethnobotanical database in collaboration with the NCI, available online at ars-grin.gov/duke.

Cilantro's # 1 Mimic: Culantro

(*Eryngium foetidum*)

James A. Duke, Ph.D

MOST GRINGO PEOPLE think I'm making a Freudian slip when I say *culantro* instead of *cilantro*. But in lowland Panama and adjacent countries, culantro is a weedy thistle-looking herb, *Eryngium foetidum*, whose leaves have roughly the same chemistry, smell, and culinary aspects as the upland herb *cilantro*, *Coriandrum sativum*, rarely known to sedentary lowlanders, as is the tropical *Eryngium* little known to the sedentary uplanders.

To further complicate matters, some gringoes and Latinos in Florida think of a leafy coriander variety (*Coriandrum*) as cilantro, and the more usual seeded variety of *Coriandrum* as coriander, the classical McCormick coriander. In upland Colombia Costa Rica and Panama, they usually mean *Coriandrum* when they say *cilantro*, and in lowland, they usually mean *Eryngium*.

Cubans call this tropical species *Culantro cimarron*, calling the temperate coriander *culantro*. It is common, almost a weed in low open. AH2 gives two standardized common names for *Coriandrum sativum*, which is what most North Americans know by those common names, *cilantro* for the leaves, *coriander* for the seed. This again will be confusing in places like Peru where *Coriandrum* is the species used in the Andes, whereas *Eryngium foetidum*, of the same family, bears the name *cilantro* in the lowlands. AH2 gives *culantro* as the standardized common name for *Eryngium foetidum*.

Since the chemistry and taste of the leaves of both *Coriandrum* and *Eryngium* are so similar, they may be used—says non-cook Jim Duke—interchangeably in recipes. How well I remember this plant as a vital constituent of the chicken caldos called *sancocho* in Panama. Sancocho, the national dish of Panama, would not be sancocho without culantro. When you leave Panama, your baggage smells of culantro. After my first beloved career-changing week in Panama, I smelled like culantro—and liked it.

But elsewhere it's almost as much a medicine as a spice. It contains 0.02-0.04% of a volatile oil. The Spanish name "recao de monte" indicates that it is a wild spice. It is a weed. But the leaves constitute a powerful spice, a love it or hate it spice. Roots are also used, almost as spice vegetables, in meat dishes and soups. One spice mixture called *sofrito* (chiles, cilantro, and culantro) is sold in the West Indian markets of New York and other large cities. Leaves are used in tropical America and elsewhere as condiment in stews, pastries, soups, and meat dishes to impart an agreeable flavor, though some say it smells like bedbugs. The leaves of culantro (*Eryngium*) retain their aroma and flavor better than leaves of cilantro (*Coriandrum*) on drying. Javanese add the tenderest leaves to rice as a lalab.

Ochse says the plant multiplies only by its many seeds, produced in great numbers. Seed lose their viability quickly, so must be sown as soon as they are ripe. It is easily grown in moist United States garden soils if started indoors and outplanted after the last frost. After the spring plant *Coriandrum* has quit producing leaves due to the heat, *Eryngium* continues to produce, rewarding the gardener for his/her efforts. Slugs and mealy bugs tend to like culantro. Storage at 50º F (10º C) can extend shelf life of the leaves (ambient shelf life four days) up to two weeks. Blanching at 205ºF (96 º C) before drying preserves the green color.

Common Names for Culantro

Acapate (Ma.; Sal.; JFM; SEM); Achicoria (Ma.; JFM); Acopate (Sal.;Ven.; AVP); Alcapate (Sal.; Sp. KAT; POR); Akakasin (Galibi; GMJ); Ashe (Shipibo/Conibo; Peru; EGG); Auslafer (Ger.; AVP); Awarussan (Palikur; GMJ); Azier la Fièvre (Fr.; Fr. Guin.; AVP; POR; USN); Azier la Fivre (Fr. Guian.; POR), Balang Katunchar (Sunda; IHB; POR); Bandanya (Trin.; WIK); Bandhana (Nepal; NPM); Bhandhania (Hindi; KAT); Bhandhanya (Hindi; Trin.; KAT; WIK); Black

Benny (Eng.; KAT); Brahmdhaniya (Nepal; NPM); Cardo (Sa.; EGG; SOU); Cardo Santo (Ma.; Trin.; JFM; JTR); Cây Ngò Tàu (Vn.; POR); Chadron Benee (Dom.; KAT); Charderon (Ma.; JFM); Chardon Bene (Fwi.; Guy.; AHL; GMJ; WIK); Chardon Étoilé (Fr.; USN); Chardon Étoile Fétide (Fwi.; Fr. ;AHL; KAT); Chardon Etoile Puant (Haiti; AHL); Chardon Roland (Fg.; AVP); Chardron (Fwi.; AVP); Chi Banla (Khmer; KAT); Chi Baraing (Khmer; KAT); Chicoria (Ma.; JFM); Chicória-de-caboclo (Por.; KAT); Chi Pa-la (Khmer; KAT; POR); Chi Parang (Khmer; KAT; POR); Chi Sangkaech (Khmer; KAT); Cilantro (Bel.; Col.; Cuba; Eng.; BNA; CR2; SEM); Cilantro Ancho (Dr.; SEM); Cilantro Cimarron (Ma.; Mex.; Sp.; JFM; POR); Cilantro de la Habana (Mex.; POR); Cilantro Extranjero (Méx. Sp.; KAT); Cilantro Habanero (Sp.; KAT; POR); Cilantro Sabanero (Dr.; AHL); Cimaron (Bel.; BNA); Ci Qin (China; POR); Ci Yan Sui (China; POR); Coantro da Caboclo (Brazil; AVP); Coentro Bravo (Por.; AVP; KAT; MPB; USN); Coentro-de-Caboclo (Por.; KAT); Coentro da Colonia (Brazil; Por.; AVP; MPB); Coentro da Columbia (Por.; AVP); Coentro da India (Por.; AVP); Coentro de Caboclo (Brazil; Por.; AVP; RAR); Coentro do Sertao (Por.; JFM); Coriander (Belize; SEM); Coriandre Chinoise (Fr.; POR); Coriandre de Java (Fr.; POR); Coriandre du Mexique (Fr.; POR); Coriandre Mexicain (Fr.; KAT); Coulant (Creole; Haiti; VOD); Coulante (Haiti; AHL; AVP; KAT; POR)); Coulante Chardon (Fwi.; AVP); Coulantre (Fr.; AHL); Culantre de Monte (Sp.; AVP); Culantrico (Dr.; AHL); Culantrillo (Ecu.; SEM); Culantro (Bel.; Cr.; Cuba; Eng.; Haiti; Pan.; Scn.; Sp.; AH2; BNA; CR2; IED; JTR: NPM; POR; RyM; SEM; USN); Culantro Burrero (Ven.; WIK); Culantro Cimarrón (Cuba; Sp. AVP; JTR); Culantro Coyote (Cr.; Sp.; AVP; SEM); Culantro Chuncho (Peru; Sa.; EGG; SEM; SOU); Culantro de Burro (Brazil; Por.; AVP; MPB); Culantro de Coyote (Cr; POR; SEM); Culantro de la Tierra (Cuba; Ma.; JFM; JTR); Culantro de la Tierra (Cuba.; JTR); Culantro del Monte (Hon.; Ma.; Pr; Ven.; JFM; JTR); Culantro de Pata (Hon.; SEM); Culantro de Perro (Ma.; JFM); Culantro de Pozo (Hon.; SEM); Culantro Extranjero (Ma.; JFM); Culantro Hediondo (Brazil; AVP); Culantro Real (Ma.; JFM); Culantro Silvestre (Sal.; SEM); Donnia (Sin.; WIK); Duck-Tongue Herb (Eng.; WIK); Escorzonero (Ma.; JFM); False Coriander (Eng.; Ocn.; AH2; FAC; POR; USN); Feuille Coulante (Haiti; AVP); Fit Bush (Ma.; JFM); Fitweed (Eng.; JTR; KAT; NPM; WIK); Gakaka (Piro; Peru; EGG); Herbe a Fer (Ma.; JFM); Herbe Puante (Fr.; Fwi.; AHL; KAT; POR); Hom-pomkula (Thai;

KAT); Hosszú Koriander (Hun.; KAT; POR); Iringó (Hun.; POR); Jeraju Gunung (Malaya; POR); Jia Yuan Qian (Pin.; DAA); Jintenan (Java; IHB); Juruju Gunong (Malaya; IHB); Kankong Kerbau (Malaya; IHB; POR); Katumbar Londa (Java; IHB); Katumbar Mungsi (Java; IHB); Katuncar Walanda (Sunda; POR); Katuncar Walang (Sunda; POR); Katunchar Walanda (Sunda; IHB); Katuncha Walang (Sunda; IHB); Kawawat (Ma.; JFM); Ketumbar Jawa (Malaya; IHB; KAT; POR); Ketumbar Jawa (Indonesia; POR); Ketumbar Landa (Malaya; POR); Kisauri (Ulwa; ULW); Kolentro (Bel.; BNA); Koriander Dlhý (Slovak.; KAT); Koulan (Creole; Haiti; VOD); Kvapioji Zunda (Lit.; KAT); Langer Koriander (Ger.; POR); Long Coriander (Eng.; KAT; WIK); Mae-lae-doe (Thai; KAT); Mei Guo Ci Yan Sui (Taiwan; POR); Meksikanski Koriandr (Rus.; KAT); Mexican Coriander (Eng.; KAT; POR; WIK); Mexicanischer Koriander (Ger.; POR); Mexikansk Koriander (Swe.; KAT; POR); Mexikói Koriander (Hun.; KAT); Mùi Tàu (Vn.; KAT; POR); Ngò Gai (Vn.; KAT; POR; EB42:413); Ngo Tau (Vn.; KAT; WIK); Ngò tây (Vn.; KAT; POR); Nokogiri-korianda (Jap.; KAT); Pak Chi Farang (Thai; IHB; KAT; WIK); Panicaut Fétide (Fr.; Fwi.; AVP; JFM; JTR; KAT; POR); Pereniaru-korianda (Jap.; KAT; POR); Phakchi Farang (Thai; KAT) Phak Hom Thet (Laos; KAT; POR)); Puerto Rican Coriander (Eng.; KAT; POR); Puerto Ricó-i Koriander (Hun.; KAT; POR); Racao (Pr.; Sp.; KAT); Radie la Fievre (Creole; Guy.; GMJ); Rau Ngò Gai (Vn.; POR); Rau Ngò Tây (Vn.; POR); Recao (Pr.; Sp.; KAT; WIK); Recao de Monte (Sp.; FAC); Roland Fetide (Fwi.; AVP); Sabanero (Sp.; AHL); Sacha Culantro (Ma.; Que.; JFM; RAR; SEM); Samat (Ma.; JFM); Saw Leaf Herb (Eng.; KAT; WIK); Saw Tooth Coriander (Eng.; KAT; POR); Saw Tooth Herb (Eng.; WIK); Shado Beni (Trin.; WIK); Shadon (Wi.; WIK); Shado Seni (Sp.; Trin.; KAT); Shadow-Beni (Eng.; USN; WIK); Sinegolovnik Vonyuchi (Rus.; KAT); Singa Depa (Sunda; IHB; POR); Sirkha Culandro (Que.; DLZ); Siuca (Sa.; EGG; SOU); Siuca Culantro (Ma.; Sa.; EGG; JFM; SOU); Snekie Wiwirie (Ma.; JFM); Spiny Coriander (Eng.; KAT); Spiritweed (Ma.; Ocn.; AH2; JFM; WIK); Stinkdistel (Ger.; POR; USN); Stinking Weed (Eng.; AHL); Stinkweed (Eng.; Ocn.; AH2; POR; USN); Tumbaran (Java; IHB); Tumbar Mungsi (Java; IHB); Txuj Lom Muas Loob los yog Nplooj Hniav Kaw (Hmong; WIK); Vetnamski Koriandr (Rus.; KAT); Walangan (Indonesia; KAT; POR); Walang Anjing (Sunda; IHB; POR); Walang China (Sunda; IHB; POR); Walang Duri (Sunda; IHB; POR); Walang Geni (Sunda; IHB; POR); Walang Katunchar (Sunda;

IHB; POR); Long-leaved coriander (Eng.; POR); Wild Coriander (Eng.; POR; SEM; WIK); Xamat (Ma.; JFM); Yang Yan Sui (China; POR); Yerba del Sapo (Cuba; Ma.; JFM; JTR). The name *cilantro* is also applied to leaves of *Coriandrum*.

Reported Activities of Culantro

(key: f = folklore; l = with animal, chemical, or epidemiological evidence)

Abortifacient (f; EGG; FAG; JFM; JTR; MPB); Analgesic (1; TRA; WIK); Androgenic (1; HOS); Anesthetic (1; HOS); Antemetic (f; RAR); Anthelmintic (1; X21062639); Antiandrogenic (1; HOS); Anticancer (1; HOS); Anticonvulsant (1; TAD; WIK; X21062639); Antidyspeptic (1; HOS); Antiedemic (f1; HOS; PR13:75; X10189959); Antiepileptic (f; WIK); Antiestrogenic (1; HOS); Antifeedant (1; HOS); Antifertility (1; HOS); Antigonadotropic (1; HOS); Antihepatoxic (1; HOS); Anti-inflammatory (f1; HOS; SEM; WIK; PR13:75; X10189959 X21062639); Antileukemic (1; HOS); Antilymphomic (1; HOS); Antimalarial (1; HOS); Antimutagenic (1; HOS); Antiophidic (1; HOS); Antioxidant (1; HOS); Antiprogestational (1; HOS); Antiprostaglandin (1; HOS); Antiprostatadenomic (1; HOS); Antiprostatotic (1; HOS); Antipyretic (f1; TRA); Antiseptic (f1; TRA; X21062639); Antispasmodic (f1; HOS; TAD; TRA); Antitumor (1; HOS); Antitussive (f; FAG); Antiviral (1; HOS; TRA); Aperitif (f; FAG; JTR); Aphrodisiac (f; FAG; JFM; JTR); Artemicide (1; HOS); Bactericide (1; HOS; TRA; X21062639); Candidicide (1; HOS); Carminative (f1; DAV; FNF; HOS; JTR: SEM); Diaphoretic (f; AHL; JFM); Digestive (f; BOW; WIK); Diuretic (f; MPB; SEM); Ecbolic (f; HOS); Emmenagogue (f; AHL; EGG; FAG; HHB; HOS; JFM; JTR;SEM; VOD); Estrogenic (1; HOS); Expectorant (1; TRA); Febrifuge (f; AHL; FAG; HOS; JFM; JTR; TRA; X17362507); Fungicide (1; TRA); Gonadotropic (1; HOS); Hemostat (f; FAG; JFM); Hepatoprotective (1; HOS); Herbicide (f; RAR); Hypocholesterolemic (1; HOS; SEM); Hypoglycemic (1; HOS; JAC7:405); Hypolipidemic (1; HOS); Hypolipoproteinaemic (1; HOS); Hypotensive (1; HOS; JFM; TRA); Laxative (f;JFM); Nervine (f; SEM); Orexigenic (f;JFM; WIK); Pectoral (f; DAV; HOS); Plasmodicide (1; TRA); Sedative (1; HOS); Spermicide (1; HOS); Stimulant (f; HHB; HOS; JFM); Stomachic (f;

HOS; NPM); Sudorific (f; EGG; JTR); Tranquilizer (f; EGG; HOS); Ulcerogenic (1; HOS); Vermifuge (f; JFM; SEM); Vulnerary (f; VOD).

Reported Indications for Culantro

(key: f = folklore; l = with animal, chemical, or epidemiological evidence)

Abscess (f; EGG); Amenorrhea (f; JTR); Anemia (f; HOS; MPG; SEM); Anorexia (f; HOS; JFM); Arthrosis (f; DAV; HOS; MPG); Asthma (f; IED; HOS; MPG; X21062639); Biliousness (f; HOS; JFM); Bronchosis (f; DAV; EGG; HOS); Burn (f; X21062639); Cancer (1; HOS); Cancer, breast (1; HOS); Cancer, cervix (1; HOS); Cancer, lung (1; HOS); Cardialgia (f; IED); Cardiopathy (f; HOS; MPG; SEM); Catarrh (f; HOS; IED); Childbirth (f; EGG); Chill (f; BOW); Cicatrizant (f; VOD); Cold (f; DAV; EGG; HOS; JFM; VOD); Colic (f; AHL; DAV; FAG; HOS; JTR; MD2; WIK); Constipation (f; HOS; JFM); Convulsion (f1; HOS; JFM; TAD; X21062639); Cough (f; AHL; DAV; FAG; HOS; JTR; JFM); Cramp (f; EGG; HOS; MPB); Debility (f; HOS; MPG); Dermatosis (f; SEM); Diabetes (f1; HOS; JFM; MPG; JAC7:405; Infertility (f; X21062639); Diarrhea (f; DAV; EGG; HOS; MD2; RAR; SEM; ULW); Dropsy (f; MPB); Dysmenor-rhea (f; SEM); Dyspepsia (f1; BOW; DAV; HOS; SEM; ULW; VOD; WIK); Earache (f; HOS; MPG; SEM; TRA; X21062639); Edema (f1; HOS; PR13:75); Enterosis (f; SEM; VOD); Epilepsy (f; BOW; HOS); Erwinia (1; X21062639); Fatigue (f; SEM); Fever (f1; AHL; DAV; EGG; HOS; JFM; SEM; TRA; VOD; X17362507); Fit (f; BOW; EGG; HOS; JFM; X21062639); Flu (f; DAV; EGG; GMJ; HOS; JFM; SEM); Gas (f1; DAV;EGG; HOS; JFM; JTR: MD2; SEM;WIK); Gastrosis (f; SEM; VOD); Headache (f; VOD); Hemorrhage (f; JTR); Hepatosis (f; EGG); High Blood Pressure (f; DAV; IED; HOS; MPG; X21062639); High Cholesterol (f; HOS; MPG; SEM); Hysteria (f; VOD); Impotence (f; JTR: MPB); Infection (1; X21062639); Infertility (f; X21062639); Inflammation (f1; HOS; SEM; WIK; PR13:75; X21062639); Insom-nia (f; DAV; EGG; HOS; TRA); Leukemia (1; HOS); Lymphoma (1; HOS); Malaria (f; DAV; HOS; X21062639); Metrorrhagia (f; FAG; JTR); Nausea (f; DAV; EGG; HOS; MD2; RAR; TRA); Nematode (f; X21062639); Neuralgia (f; DLZ); Obesity (f; HOS; MPG; SEM); Oliguria (1; HOS); Pain (f1; HOS; SEM; WIK); Palpitation (f; SEM);

Parasite (f; HOS; IED; SEM; ULW; X21062639); Pneumonia (f; DAV; HOS); Pulmonosis (f; VOD); Respirosis (f; ULW); Rheumatism (f; AHL; DAV; HOS; JFM; VOD); Salmonella (1; X21062639); Snakebite (f; HHB; HOS; JFM; X21062639); Spasm (1; HOS); Stomachache (f; DAV; EGG; HOS; MPG; SEM; WIK; X21062639); Strongyloidiasis (f; WIK); Swelling (f1; HOS; PR13:75); Syncope (f; HOS; JFM); Trypanosome (f; X21062639); Tumor (f; DAV; HOS; JLH); Vomiting (f; SEM); Water Retention (f; HHB); Worm (f; IED; HOS; JFM; X21062639); Wound (f; VOD); Yellow Fever (f; HOS; JFM).

Reported Dosages for Culantro

Leaves are used as a veggie with rice, or as condiment or pickled; fruits also used as spice. Roots are often used in meat dishes and soups. I consider it THE culinary herb of Panama (IHB; NPM; EB42:413); Facciola mentions a spice combo often found in West Indian markets, e.g. in New York City. Sofrito is a mixture of true coriander, eryngium, and small ajicitos, usually mild bonnet peppers (FAC).

- Belizeans use leaf tea for dyspepsia, for diarrhea and other pediatric ailments (SEM)

- Caribbean Islanders use leaf decoction for chest pain, palpitations, and tiredness, the whole plant for fever, the leaf tea for gas and influenza (SEM)

- Costa Ricans regard the plant as aphrodisiac (JFM)

- Cubans consider the plant abortifacient, aperitif, aphrodisiac, emmenagogue, febrifuge, and sudorific, use leaf decoction for colic and cough, and root decoction for uterine hemorrhage (JTR)

- Francophone West Indians boil the plant, with or without castor oil added, for biliousness, constipation, fits, and yellow fever (JFM)

- Guatemalans respect the plant as a potent emmenagogue and abortifacient (JFM)

- Haitians drink or massage with the decoction as a febrifuge or sudorific (EGG)

- Hondurans use crushed leaves as earplug for earache, using boiled root for obesity, root decoction for stomachache, and topical leaf poultice for headache (SEM)

- Jamaicans take the plant decoction, internally or topically, for convulsions and fits (JFM)

- Panamanians claim the decoction lowers blood pressure (JFM)

- Peruvians recommend a decoction of 7 leaves when the pains of childbirth begin (EGG)

- Peruvians suggest the leaf decoction, or tincture, with or without lemon, for bronchitis, diarrhea, childbirth, cold, fever, flu, gas, nausea, stomachache (RAR; SEM)

- Salvadorans use boiled leaves for eruptive fevers (SEM)

- Surinamese take the leaf decoction for colds and fevers (JFM)

- Trinidadans take for menstrual pain, inflammation, and fever, the leaf tea for colds, diarrhea and flu, the root decoction for cold, constipation and cough (JFM; X17362507)

- Trinidadans take the root infusion (or rum or wine tincture) for worms (JFM)

- Venezuelans use the root as carminative, diuretic, emmenagogue and vermifuge (SEM)

Downsides for Culantro

Not covered (AHPA). The abortifacient and emmenagogue folklore might suggest cautious use, if at all, by pregnant women. Many samples in Mexico City are loaded with salmonella and fecal coliforms, partially reduced with colloidal silver treatment (X17061512).

Extracts of Culantro

LD50 (Leaf) 11,500 mg/kg; LD50 extracts 1,000 mg/kg orl rat; >50 mg/kg ivn rat. (SEM). The most abundant aroma compound in *E. foetidum* was E-2-dodecenal (63.5% with either eugenol or a trimethylbenzaldehyde isomer, beta-ionone, Z-4-dodecenal, dodecanal, and E-2-tetradecenal. (X16013833)

ERYNGIUM FOETIDUM L.
"CULANTRO"
DELTA-5-AVENASTEROL LF
    PR13:7 X10189959
DELTA-7-AVENASTEROL LF
    PR13:75 X10189959
BRASSICASTEROL LF PR13:75
    X10189959
CAMPESTEROL LF PR13:75
    X10189959
CAROTOL (10% EO) LF TAD
CAROTOL (19% EO) SD TAD
ALPHA-CHOLESTEROL LF
    PR13:75 X10189959
CLEOSTEROL LF PR13:75
    X10189959
DODECANAL PL X16013833
2-DODECEN-1-AL (46%-60% EO)
    PL TAD WOI
E-2-DODECENAL (63.5% HS) PL
    X16013833
Z-4-DODECENAL PL X16013833
2-DODECENOIC-ACID (16% EO)
    PL TAD WOI
5-DODECANONE 50-100 PL TAD
EO 200-400 PL WOI
ERYNGIAL LF X21062639

EUGENOL PL X16013833
BETA-FARNESENE (10% EO) SD
    TAD
FLAVONOIDS LF X21062639
HEXADECANOIC-ACID (12% EO)
    LF TAD
4-HYDROXY-3,5-DIMETHYLACE-
    TOPHENONE 50-100 PL TAD
BETA-IONONE PL X16013833
PHYTOSTEROLS LF X21062639
Alpha-PINENE PL MPG
SAPONIN LF X21062639
SAPONIN RT HHB
SAPONOSIDES PL MPG 2,4,5-TRI-
    METHYLBENZALDEHYDE
    (21% EO) LF TAD
BETA-SITOSTEROL LF PR13:75
    X10189959
DELTA(5)24-STIGMASTADIENOL
    LF PR13:75 X10189959
STIGMASTEROL LF PR13:75
    X10189959
TANNINS LF X21062639
E-2-TETRADECENAL PL
    X16013833
TRITERPENOIDS LF X21062639

TRIMETHYLBENZALDEHYDE LF
X21062639

2,4,5-TRIMETHYLBENZAL-
DEHYDE 50-100 PL TAD
X16013833

Medicinal Uses

Roots contain saponin, have an offensive odor, and are used as a stomachic. A decoction of root is valued in Venezuela as a stimulant, febrifuge, a powerful abortive and sedative; in Cuba it is a valuable emmenagogue; and it is used throughout Tropical America as a remedy for
seizures and high blood pressure. Its infusion with salt is taken for colic.
Leaf infusion used for stomachaches. Around Pucallpa, Peru, culantro
with meat broth, is taken for bronchitis and fever. Chamis Indians braise
the dried fruits and have the children inhale smoke to treat diarrhea.
Green fruits are crushed and mixed with food to treat insomnia Créoles
drink the decoction for colds and flu; they rub crushed leaves over the
body to reduce high fever. Elsewhere it is used for arthritis, colds, colic,
cough, diabetes, diarrhea, fever, fits, flu, herbicide, hypertension, malaria,
nausea, pneumonia, rheumatism, and tumors (DAV; DAW; RAR).
Antimalarial, antispasmodic, carminative, and pectoral activities are also
reported (DAW).

Bios for Illustrators
and Photographers

Susan Belsinger—see bio on page 116.

Susan Betz—see bio on page 56.

Peter Coleman grows herbs, vegetables, and at-risk plants on 106 acres in Middlefield, New York. He photographs woods, trees, streams, plants, and the world with social, political, and historical perspectives.

Pat Crocker—see bio page 123.

Pat Kenny who began drawing and painting flowers with watercolors at the age of ten continued studies in art and biology through college and the masters program in Medical and Biological Illustration at Johns Hopkins University. In her 30 years at the National Institute of Health (NIH) and work with The Herb Society of America, Pat has contributed illustrations to a variety of publications.

Shawn Linehan photographs small farms and farmers mostly around the Portland, Oregon, area. With a journalist's sense of narrative and an artist's eye, she creates intimate, authentic images that celebrate the lives of our environmental stewards. Her photos first appeared in *The Culinary Herbal* (Timber Press, 2016).

Alicia Mann—see bio on page 134.

Gail Wood Miller is an amateur watercolorist, and a professional health coach and educational consultant, who twice-daily checks her window-boxed herbs on a fire escape in Manhattan. She's a member of the Musconetcong Watercolor Group, New Jersey, and studied painting at the Herzfeld School of Art, Wiesbaden, Germany.

Karen O'Brien—see bio on page 134.

Stephanie Parello—Stephanie's illustrations grace the section introductions. See bio on page 98.

Yvonne Sisko, a retired Assistant Professor of English at Middlesex County College, loves to read, draw, and grow flowers in her garden. Author of over 15 reading and literature textbooks, Yvonne splits her time between New Jersey and Florida.

Skye Suter has contributed drawings to eight Herb of the Year™ books. See bio on page 178.

Jane Taylor—see bio on page 138.

Color Insert credits

Page 1
Cilantro seedlings, Pat Kenny; Cilantro leaves, Susan Belsinger; Cilantro in Madeline Hill's garden, Susan Betz; Cilantro blooms, Pat Kenny

Page 2
Pollinator on cilantro flower, Susan Betz; Cilantro flowers, upstate NY, Peter Coleman; Cilantro flowers, Susan Belsinger; Green coriander seeds, Karen O'Brien

Page 3
Coriander seeds ready to grind in suribachi, Susan Belsinger; Coriander seeds on stalk, Susan Belsinger; Ferny cilantro and parsley ready for salsa, Susan Belsinger; Cilantro leaves with wooden pestle, Pat Kenny

Page 4
Black bean soup with cilantro, Susan Belsinger; Coriander roots, Pat Crocker; Mango habanero salsa with cilantro, Susan Belsinger; Tomatoes with cilantro salsa verde, Susan Belsinger

Cover Credits

Front Cover:
Background image: Cilantro leaves—Susan Belsinger
Right overprint: Green coriander seed—Karen O'Brien
Middle overprint: Coriander Seeds—Susan Belsinger
Left overprint: Flowers—Susan Belsinger

Back Cover:
Left: Seeds—Susan Belsinger
Middle: Salsa—Susan Belsinger
Right: Pollinator with bloom—Susan Betz

Herb of the Year™ Selection

How the Herb of the Year™ is Selected

Every year since 1995, the International Herb Association has chosen an Herb of the Year™ to highlight. The Horticultural Committee evaluates possible choices based on their being outstanding in at least two of the three major categories: medicinal, culinary, or decorative. Many other herb organizations support the herb of the year selection and we work together to educate the public about these herbs during the year.

Herbs of the Year™: Past, Present and Future:

1995	Fennel	2008	Calendula
1996	Monarda	2009	Bay Laurel
1997	Thyme	2010	Dill
1998	Mint	2011	Horseradish
1999	Lavender	2012	Rose
2000	Rosemary	2013	Elderberry
2001	Sage	2014	Artemisia
2002	Echinacea	2015	Savory
2003	Basil	2016	Capsicum
2004	Garlic	2017	Cilantro & Coriander
2005	Oregano & Marjoram	2018	Humulus
2006	Scented Geraniums	2019	Agastache
2007	Lemon Balm	2020	Rubus

Notes:

_____

_____

_____

_____

_____

_____

_____

_____

_____

_____

_____

_____

_____

_____

_____

_____

_____

_____

_____

_____

_____

_____

_____

_____

_____

_____

_____

Notes:

_____
_____
_____
_____
_____
_____
_____
_____
_____
_____
_____
_____
_____
_____
_____
_____
_____
_____
_____
_____
_____
_____
_____
_____
_____
_____
_____
_____